Cloud Without Compromise
Hybrid Cloud for the Enterprise

Paul Zikopoulos and Christopher Bienko
with Chris Backer, Chris Konarski, and Sai Vennam

Beijing · Boston · Farnham · Sebastopol · Tokyo

Cloud Without Compromise

by Paul Zikopoulos and Christopher Bienko, with Chris Backer, Chris Konarski, and Sai Vennam

Published by O'Reilly Media, Inc., 1005 Gravenstein Highway North, Sebastopol, CA 95472.

O'Reilly books may be purchased for educational, business, or sales promotional use. Online editions are also available for most titles (*http://oreilly.com*). For more information, contact our corporate/institutional sales department: 800-998-9938 or *corporate@oreilly.com*.

Acquisitions Editor: Rachel Roumeliotis	**Indexer:** Sue Klefstad
Development Editor: Michele Cronin	**Interior Designer:** David Futato
Production Editor: Kristen Brown	**Cover Designer:** Karen Montgomery
Copyeditor: Charles Roumeliotis	**Illustrator:** Kate Dullea
Proofreader: Kim Cofer	

August 2021: First Edition

Revision History for the First Edition

2021-07-29: First Release

See *http://oreilly.com/catalog/errata.csp?isbn=9781098103736* for release details.

978-1-098-10373-6

[LSI]

Table of Contents

Preface: Who This Book Is For

The five of us got together and wrote a book that might (at times) be too technical for business leaders, but "too business-y" for technical people. If this is a complaint you've got after reading this book…perfect! While we definitely put some technical stuff in here, if you're looking for a book on how to use `kubectl`—the CLI interface for Kubernetes—or use `generator` to create a `ConfigMap`, this is not the book for you.

Our experience has shown us—more than any one of us wants to admit—that too many business people don't truly understand the technology they're signing the bills for (or for that matter, that technology's potential). Nothing good comes of this: late projects, missed expectations, excessive costs, and worse yet—lost opportunities. If business teams lack the "chops" to challenge IT or understand technology discussions within their organizations, it's akin to using a decades-old word translation algorithm. For example, one famous algorithm took a US phrase, "The spirit is willing but the flesh is weak," and translated it into Russian as, "The vodka is good but the meat is rotten." We think you get our point. Business people—if your spirit is willing, we can't promise you good vodka; but we can promise you a good (in fact, a great) foundation to a cloud strategy that lets you lead from the front and helps you be the leader you want to be.

At the same time, this book is for all those propeller heads (we know you well, we are you) who get enthralled with the underpinnings but fail to realize that technology for technology's sake doesn't help a business succeed. If you fit that profile, this book is going to really help drive your career because there are not a lot of people that have your technical backgrounds. Beyond helping the organizations you work for succeed, this book will give you options to "pond jump" into myriad leadership roles across your company and accelerate your career. For whatever pothole or mountain of accomplishments our authoring team has, we can tell you that it all came from a deep technology start with layers of business experience and acumen added over the years. We're not saying be like us (that may or may not be a good thing), but we are telling you this: technology people who understand business outperform technology people who don't understand business.

So just whom is this book for? We think anyone. You might be informed on all aspects of cloud, or you might just be getting started and have little understanding of how it works, why it works, or how to implement and *scale* a successful cloud strategy. While we targeted this book for all business leaders, no matter who you are, we think this book is going to help you. Naturally it'll help those leaders who are not sure where to start, but we also think our personal experiences will greatly benefit those who have started and are unsure of where to go next. With all that said, we're confident there is a cohort of business and technical individuals that this book is really going to resonate with. These folks typically work in large organizations that have been around for a while. These organizations have a mix of generational technology. They have monolithic apps they don't want to touch because those rock-solid apps literally keep "the lights on," but they've also built some cool mobile stuff using service-oriented architecture (SOA) or microservices (don't worry if you don't know what those are, we get into them in Chapter 4). If you work big-box retail, oil and gas, banking, airlines, government, insurance, consumer packaged goods (the list goes on and on), we can pretty much *guarantee* you that you fit into this group. This book is for you because you've definitely got some cloud going on, but you may not be making the progress you'd hoped for or (quite commonly) you're not getting the returns you thought you'd be getting and wondering if you're doing it right.

This book requires no previous knowledge of cloud. The topics we introduce will be helpful for a vast audience, ranging from business leaders to technical folks across all industries. If you're a business leader, you'll know just the questions to ask, the corners to look around, and the ideas to challenge as you tactfully plan your forward-thinking cloud strategy. If you're a technical person, you'll understand how your expertise can drive forward the organizations you work for with a solid understanding of how cloud challenges (especially for large-sized companies) are much different than a startup's "Swipe your credit card and let's get going" approach.

Whomever you are, we think the concepts you need to know to successfully scale a cloud strategy and get all the value out of cloud can be found in the pages that follow.

Conventions Used in This Book

The following typographical conventions are used in this book:

Italic
: Indicates new terms, URLs, email addresses, filenames, and file extensions.

`Constant width`
: Used for program listings, as well as within paragraphs to refer to program elements such as variable or function names, databases, data types, environment variables, statements, and keywords.

`Constant width bold`
: Shows commands or other text that should be typed literally by the user.

`Constant width italic`
: Shows text that should be replaced with user-supplied values or by values determined by context.

 This element signifies a tip or suggestion.

 This element signifies a general note.

 This element indicates a warning or caution.

O'Reilly Online Learning

 For more than 40 years, *O'Reilly Media* has provided technology and business training, knowledge, and insight to help companies succeed.

Our unique network of experts and innovators share their knowledge and expertise through books, articles, and our online learning platform. O'Reilly's online learning platform gives you on-demand access to live training courses, in-depth learning paths, interactive coding environments, and a vast collection of text and video from O'Reilly and 200+ other publishers. For more information, visit *http://oreilly.com*.

How to Contact Us

Please address comments and questions concerning this book to the publisher:

O'Reilly Media, Inc.
1005 Gravenstein Highway North
Sebastopol, CA 95472
800-998-9938 (in the United States or Canada)
707-829-0515 (international or local)
707-829-0104 (fax)

We have a web page for this book, where we list errata, examples, and any additional information. You can access this page at *https://oreil.ly/cloudWithoutCompromise*.

Email *bookquestions@oreilly.com* to comment or ask technical questions about this book.

For news and information about our books and courses, visit *http://oreilly.com*.

Find us on Facebook: *http://facebook.com/oreilly*

Follow us on Twitter: *http://twitter.com/oreillymedia*

Watch us on YouTube: *http://youtube.com/oreillymedia*

Our Collective Thank Yous and Acknowledgments

This book would not have been possible without the insights and efforts from some really fine people we know. Terry Bird and Meg Murphy jumped in on the idea and never let go of it from the get go, across divisional line changes and reorganizations; they are always so forward thinking and we thank them for that. Thank yous are also in order for Shelia Bereszniewicz (who handled all the contracts and lawyers), Paul Amrbaz and Pamela Chace (our web presence peeps), Bill "Mr. Quantum" Minor (helped review some sections), and Filipe Miranda (for his insights on SELinux and access controls—a true technologist with a deep understanding of everything cloud). Of course, a collective thank you to Linda "Eagle Eye" Snow (and not because she's from Philly) for always being willing to read a chapter and use her sharp eyes to catch almost anything wrong.

Finally, we want to heartfully thank (although at times we cursed their deadlines) the O'Reilly crew's personal efforts that went into getting this book from an idea we had while Slacking each other wondering how long on average it takes for people to realize they are double-muted on a WebEx call to what's in your hands today. Some people show up at their job every day to earn a paycheck, but we're glad these folks go to work to build something: Michele Cronin, Mike Loukides, Sharon Cordesse, Kristen Brown, and Rachel Roumeliotis...thanks!

Our Personal Dedications and Reflections

Paul Zikopoulos

If you've read any dedication for any book I've written in the last five years, you've concluded I'm a liar. Seriously, you can't keep telling people you're writing your last book and keep writing, so I won't make any promises not to put pen to paper again. That said, I know one thing I will never do again: write a book with three people named Chris, especially when two of them share the same first letter of their surname! No offense, these are some of the most talented guys I know—but it sure is confusing and makes calls difficult because you can't even say, "Chris B..." (add to this Chris Backer is pronounced like Baker). On a serious note—to a fantastic group of professionals and friends, some new to me, some not, and one like a brother.

Let me tell you, it's a lot of work to write a book. Lots of cursing (at times, my kid thought I was watching an HBO show in my office) aimed at the people that were there from the get go (Terry Bird, one of the finest people I know, was an f-bomb victim) across weekends and long weeknights wondering if you're making a difference. After all, it's not like I'm writing *50 Shades of Hybrid Cloud*, so these works don't bring me early retirement. Every book I write, I learn. And with that I write to tell stories (truthful ones), to wrap technology in a manner that you can understand and with hopes that you might find a smile here and there as you read through it. So why do I write? Honestly, my parents instilled me with a never-ending thirst for learning; I'm all too well aware that one of the biggest blessings in my life right now is a Caller ID that says, "Mom or Dad."

To Brad Arnott. The most talented guy that refuses to see it. I mean who else decides to golf and breaks 80 in 3 years, decides to be a fisherman and goes pro, decides to be a marksman and wins awards, decides to do anything and becomes great. Take a moment Brad, look in the mirror, and know the awe you inspire.

To my wife (Kelly) and kid (Chloë)—forever by my side—nothing more needs to be said.

Professionally, to the group of people that inspire me on the daily to try to be a better person and use my brains for something bigger. Stephanie Trunzo, Deb Jenson, Deb Bubb, and Kelly Lyndgaard—you're the kind of ladies any father wants their daughter to follow—you've become sisters, and I stand in awe of you on the daily. To Chris Hugill and Bob Picciano, who continue to inspire me and leave me in awe of their knowledge—I wonder if these guys even use Google. Within IBM, there are so many people to mention, so I'll just random sample the list. I took over a new division in 2021—lots of new team members that I asked to buy into a new team ethos, a mission (with a steep climb) and to all of them that followed, thank you. To Drew Valentine and John Teltsch who have always been a text message away. And to a new boss, Sebastian Krause, who has just the right amount of everything to be tremendous—there's a quality of leadership that drives you where you need to be driven (even if I don't like it at times) and gives you the autonomy to create…that's his recipe. A shout-out to Steve Astorino (an incredible leader) and to the transformation he has done with culture—your ideas are even bigger than the engine in that supercar you drive, and the Toronto lab adores you for it. Finally, it seems I can't write a book without thanking, consulting, or coauthoring with Rob Thomas. For 10 years, you've been 20% pushing me (in a way I don't like) into personal growth zones with your challenges and 80% inspiring me to never take my foot off the knowledge gas pedal. What you're doing at IBM is something beyond special.

Remember everyone, health is wealth—so stay positive and *forever* test negative!

Paul Zikopoulos

Christopher Bienko

To those friends and family that inspire me to live authentically, thank you. It would be an understatement to call 2020 merely a challenging year—I think, for all of us to an extent, it has been a rare opportunity to evaluate what's important to our lives and make an honest measure of how we are spending the precious time we have. And most remarkably of all, it was (and continues to be) a strangely universal experience shared by every person across each corner of the globe. Those events are few and far between.

It's my fervent hope that collectively we hold on to the silver linings of a taxing year: the remarkable quiet and calm of those first weeks of lockdown, the added time at home with family or friends in lieu of globe-trotting or commuting, the recognition of the selfless work carried out day after day by others to make our lives safe and secure. I've been an avid outdoorsman for the whole of my life, and it's been wonderful to see how COVID-19 has rekindled in the public mind a renewed draw towards natural spaces, public lands, and healthy ecosystems. With greater public interest comes additional pressure on these delicate environments, but likewise a mutual interest in their stewardship and conservation. My belief is that the more stakeholders we have in protecting public lands and natural systems, the more likely we are to succeed in preserving these treasures for the future. Let's keep that momentum going.

In hindsight, it seems halfway absurd to have started writing a book amidst all the uncertainty and personal reckonings of the last year. None of this, frankly, would have been possible without the unwavering commitment and talent of my coauthor and contributors. Paul, Chris B., Chris K., Sai, and our incredible publisher—you have my sincere thanks and gratitude.

Chris Backer

As an early professional, I spent countless hours reading O'Reilly technology books, learning and growing my skills. With every new project that I embarked on, I often sought out an O'Reilly book on the topic. I am truly grateful to have had this opportunity as a coauthor for a topic that has become one of the most transformational technology shifts of my time. To my coauthors, it has been an absolute pleasure working with and learning from each of you. A special thank you to Paul Z for the invitation to contribute to this book. You are an inspiration to many!

To Anna Shugol, Elton de Souza, Filipe Miranda, Patrick Fruth, Roberto Calderon, and Vic Cross (aka The Z Acceleration Team). You've led our brand into a new era of Hybrid Cloud—and in the midst of the most challenging event our society has faced in modern times. You all are the "best of the best." I am truly grateful for your dedication and entrepreneurial mindset. #TogetherWeWin

To my wife (Anna), thank you for your support and encouragement over the years. You push me to be a better person every day. And to my incredible boys (Ty, Colton, and Caden): each of you make me so proud! Set your goals high and never stop learning.

Chris Konarski

When I look back at all my professional and personal accomplishments, it all started with an inner hunger and work ethic that was instilled in me by my parents John and Grace. The lessons I learned about hard work, competition, setting high goals, and how to treat people have served as my recipe for success. I dedicate this book to you and thank you for always pushing me outside my comfort zone to be "even better."

To my boys, Ryan and Noah, set high goals and go after your dreams. If it is hard then you are growing; learn to be comfortable with being uncomfortable because that is where the magic happens. Feed your inner curiosity and fire with goals you never thought possible. I will always be there to love, support, and push you to greatness wherever your passions take you.

Sai Vennam

A voice, written or spoken, is the single most important thing a person has—it enables one to communicate their thoughts, expand others' beliefs, and influence the world. I'd like to thank my colleagues and mentors that helped me create my own voice—Adam Gunther, Jason Gartner, Andrew Hoyt, Jason Goode, and Nathan Smith.

Personally, I'd like to thank my older brother, Ram Vennam, who always served as a role model to me from a young age all the way through blazing the trail for me as a developer and leader at IBM. Finally, I'd like to thank my wife Reena, my sister-in-law Belinda, and my parents for always being there to support me—the only reason I've made it this far in my career is the love and care from those dear to me.

Introduction

There are three things that dominate 90% of technology conversations today: AI, cybersecurity, and cloud—we're guessing you figured out what this book is about by the cover. (And we know you're wondering: the animal is a black swan—quite fitting when you think about the state of the world when we started writing the book.)

Collectively our authoring team has well over a century of IT expertise and that means we've seen a lot of stuff (we had a different word in here, but it looks like the editor changed that). If you've ever stumbled across the Gartner Hype Cycle (*https:// oreil.ly/YKqPS*), you'll know that just because a technology is the "talk of the town," it doesn't guarantee success in the grand scheme of things. We've found that even for those technologies that find their way out of Gartner's "Peak of Inflated Expectations" and into the "Plateau of Productivity" part of their Hype Cycle curve, the calculus can still become a damp squib (a wet firework that fails to go off). Time and time again, we see an upstart technology that becomes all the rage, but just doesn't quite manage to stick the landing the first time: Knowledge Graphs (we still think something will happen here), Learning Gamification (at least the way most people implement it), governance (most organizations have a least effort to comply approach), and Hadoop…just to name a few.

Let's be clear on something: *Cloud is not in a hype cycle!* In fact, it's one of the most significant platform inflection points of our time (especially when you start thinking about cloud in the way we describe it in this book). It's true, sometimes we look at each other and say, "I can't even keep a cell phone connection, how is the world going to totally run on cloud?" Make no mistake about it, cloud is here and it's here to stay —you need to pivot the way you think about cloud if you want to get all you can out of it.

However, we've found that most businesses aren't getting the value out of the cloud that they were expecting (the mental model around cloud was too narrowed by the hype). Some might feel that there's more value yet to be uncovered, other organizations are guilty of not even knowing what to expect (just like AI, many jumped on the notion that the gains will be instant—like magic), and some are even repatriating public cloud workloads back to their traditional runtimes. Why? Too many compromises.

How do you get to cloud without compromise? It's not a vendor thing. We're not here to tell you the only way to get cloud without compromise is to migrate everything to a particular vendor's public cloud. For example, while we think there are nuances for specific types of applications that make the IBM Public Cloud a standout (highly regulated industries like finance), other public cloud providers have their own characteristics that are differentiated too (take a look at the catalog and configuration options on AWS).

There are two things to really grasp before you can get to a cloud without compromise. First, internalize what will become a mantra of this book: *cloud is a capability, not a destination.* Cloud without compromise means you're shifting your mindset from a place to an *operational model.* Second, cloud without compromise means you're embracing a unified distributed hybrid cloud strategy. A *hybrid cloud* unifies public cloud, private cloud, and on-premises infrastructure with consistent management and orchestration to create a single, flexible, cost-optimal IT infrastructure (the distributed part means it doesn't matter what vendor you select for your public cloud resources. Let the gravitational pull to a cloud vendor be the strengths—its cloud capabilities—that uniquely serve your business. This is why we'll advocate again and again for looking at cloud as a capability (instead of a destination), so that your business and the things it needs to be successful can run (and interoperate) anywhere to everywhere. The outcome? Companies with a no compromise cloud strategy are empowered businesses that can:

- Combine best-of-breed cloud services and functionality from multiple cloud computing vendors
- Choose the optimal cloud computing environment for each workload
- Move workloads freely between public and private cloud as circumstances change

When no compromises are made, companies are free to pursue their technical and business objectives more effectively and cost-efficiently than they would otherwise be able to through any single public or private cloud vendor alone. In fact, according to one recent study (*https://oreil.ly/WydS3*), companies derive up to 2.5x more value from a hybrid cloud strategy than from following a single-cloud, single-vendor approach.

Initially, hybrid cloud architectures focused on the mechanics of transforming portions of a company's on-premises datacenter into private cloud infrastructure, and then connecting that infrastructure to public cloud environments hosted off-premises by a public cloud provider. Today's hybrid cloud architecture needs to be focused less on physical connectivity, and more toward supporting workload portability across all cloud environments (the location or vendor doesn't matter) and on automating the deployment of those workloads to cloud environments (again, agnostic to vendor or location) with the most gravitational pull for your application's needs.

Several trends are driving this shift. As part of the next critical step in their digital transformations, organizations are building new applications (and modernizing legacy applications) to leverage cloud native technologies—technologies that enable consistent and reliable development, deployment, management, and performance across cloud environments and across cloud vendors, including on-premises infrastructure. Specifically, they're building and transforming applications to use microservices architectures, which deconstruct unwieldy monolithic applications into smaller, loosely coupled, reusable components focused on specific business functions. And they're deploying these applications in containers—lightweight executable units that contain only the application code and just enough of the virtualized operating system dependencies required to run it. These technologies serve as a foundation for enabling businesses to drive a new-age culture of productivity, such as development cycles that last days or weeks (instead of quarters or years) and the inclusion of highly effective methodologies like test-driven development, continuous integration and continuous delivery (CI/CD), A/B testing, and more.

At a higher level, public and private clouds are no longer physical "locations" to connect together. For example, many cloud vendors now offer public cloud services that run in their customers' on-premises datacenters. Private clouds, once run exclusively on-premises, are now often hosted in off-premises datacenters, on virtual private networks (VPNs) or virtual private clouds (VPCs), or on dedicated infrastructure rented from third-party providers (who may happen to be public cloud providers).

What's more, infrastructure virtualization with the aid of automation (infrastructure as code) allows these environments to be created, on demand, using any resources located behind (or beyond) a firewall. This takes on added importance with the advent of edge computing, which offers opportunities to improve global application performance by moving workloads closer to where data is created and consumed.

Cloud native development makes it possible for developers to transform monolithic applications into units of business-focused functionality that can be run anywhere and reused within a variety of applications. A standard operating system (like Linux) lets developers build any hardware dependency into a container. And Kubernetes orchestration and automation delivers granular, set-it-and-forget-it control over container configuration and deployment—including security, load balancing, scalability, and more—across multiple cloud environments. (Don't worry if you don't know anything about what we just wrote; this book is going to teach you about all of this.)

We talk a lot in this book about the untapped cloud value that remains for those downtrodden on their cloud journeys. To the uninitiated, they might think, "Yes, that means if I move everything to a public cloud vendor, I will get all this value." That's not what it means—remember, cloud is a capability, not a destination. But the right cloud strategy (which you'll learn how to craft in this book) will certainly deliver:

Improved developer productivity
> This helps expand the adoption of Agile and DevOps (*https://oreil.ly/M0YRU*) methodologies, and enables dev(elopment) teams to build once and deploy anywhere.

Greater infrastructure efficiency
> With on-demand granular control over rapidly provisioned compute and storage resources, development, and IT operations, teams can optimize their spend across public cloud services, private clouds, and cloud vendors. Hybrid cloud also helps companies modernize applications faster and connect cloud services to data on cloud or on-premises infrastructure in ways that deliver new value.

Larger breadth and depth
> Access to a larger number of services spanning AI (which includes machine learning and deep learning) capabilities, storage, data processing, analytics, automation, and more. These are services that cloud vendors have tailored for your business's needs with the expertise and depth to run them at enterprise scale.

Improved regulatory compliance and security
> A unified platform lets organizations draw on best-of-breed cloud security and regulatory compliance technologies, implementing Zero Trust security and compliance across all environments in a consistent way.

Overall business acceleration
> This includes shorter product development cycles; accelerated innovation and time-to-market; faster response to customer feedback; faster delivery of applications closer to the client (like edge ecommerce); and faster integration with partners or third parties to deliver new products and services.

If you want cloud without compromise, without a doubt in our minds, almost every medium to large organization requires a hybrid cloud strategy that starts with capabilities and not destinations (let that fall into place afterward) and folks...that's what this book is all about.

CHAPTER 1

Cloudy Skies Are the Best Forecast Ever

A cherished bottle of Rémy Martin Louis XIII Cognac is blended from 1,200 different cognacs aged up to 100 years, with each bottle representing the career achievements of generational cellar masters. Parmigiano-Reggiano Stravecchione's (the Italians refer to it as the "King of Cheese") complex flavor and texture are a result of no less than four years of aging. Bruce Springsteen spent an unbelievable six months editing the lyrics of his famous song "Born to Run."

Oh, the sung praises of slow mastery—great things take time. But while cognac, cheese, and songs can be *slowly* aged into masterpieces, technology years are like dog years: things change, and change happens quickly. While the romanticism of slow change is valuable for some things, today's businesses and institutions need more speed to market, more flexibility, and nimbleness to respond to changes in the economy, buyer behavior, supply chains, geopolitical realities, climate change, and more. If you had to prioritize a list of all the things you could do to deliver a better product or service in the most optimized fashion, infusing technology into all parts of your business should be at the top of the list.

The changes we've seen in the past few years are rewriting the basic behaviors and assumptions we've had about IT. Technology has the very real effect of redefinition. Businesses must rethink how they create and deliver value, how they compete, how they transact, and ultimately how the business itself works. Technology provides a strong basis for business and institutional innovation by creating a lingua franca for data, applications, and workflows where an ecosystem of ideas from customers, suppliers, and partners can be brought together.

In the US, the Black Friday shopping bonanza[1] is a great example of how technology changes IT practices. Many retailers still impose a blackout period against pushing any technology changes during those dates because they don't want to risk anything that could impact profitability in the final days of the year. Then microservices came along, which allowed a few retailers on the leading edge to change those behaviors. For example, Amazon's website isn't a monolithic page of logic; it's an eloquently orchestrated set of microservices that come together and work harmoniously to form a real application. Jeff Bezos, former Amazon CEO, once famously said, "Build services or look for a job somewhere else." This is exactly why we tell clients their goal isn't to build applications, but rather to compose them! Amazon's web pages are hundreds (if not thousands) of small services that have single jobs. Building software this way completely redefined how that organization creates and delivers value, how it works, how it competes, and how it transacts.

With technology, almost everything about a business—its logic, purpose, and differentiation—can be rendered in code, making digital innovation the most powerful way to drive transformation and change (or to pivot during a crisis). The emergence of public clouds has, until recently, led the debate on one of the fastest ways to prepare a business for the future; however, a closer examination suggests that most workloads (about 80%) have yet to move. Most companies have only taken on lifting and shifting what they could "as is" to the cloud, or building "greenfield" (net new or born on the cloud) apps on public clouds.

As it turns out, the mission-critical workloads that run large businesses and institutions often span extensive IT estates that include traditional on-premises investments and multiple clouds—private, public, and even on edge devices. Another inhibitor to the realization of cloud value is that almost every client we've ever talked to has invested with multiple cloud vendors and technologies. Add to this business operations that span geographic locations, each with unique government and regulatory requirements, and you've got a jumble of experiential and implemented cloud solutions without interoperability. The end result? The inadvertent creation of a hybrid cloud without a strategic approach, leading to messy, high-friction barriers to innovation and realization of your cloud aspirations. Our recommendation? Embrace the diversity by building a purposeful hybrid cloud strategy (we'll tell you how throughout this book). If you're familiar with Hadoop, its fate was sealed because too many business leaders thought they could build a single analytics strategy around it. The cloud is the same: a single cloud strategy just isn't realistic thinking.

---

1 The nickname for the Friday following US Thanksgiving Day where stores offer deep discounts for the Christmas shopping rush; many refer to this event and the days from it up until Christmas as "make or break" in terms of sales for the current year.

Thrivers, Divers, and New Arrivers

Without question, the events of 2020 were an awakening for many. In 2021, the effects of the COVID-19 fallout continue to impact nations the world over, changing commerce and lifestyles in ways that would have seemed unthinkable just a short while ago. The only certain fact in these uncertain times is that "things" will never be the same, even with a vaccine. Whatever the future will be dubbed—"back to normal," "the new normal," or our preference "the new abnormal"—leaders must reckon with a new set of challenges that span the gamut from societal reform, to global health, to new ways of conducting business and education. One area of upheaval that has often been treated as an afterthought but has been profoundly changed by the events of these last few years: the way business is (and will be) done.

The COVID-19 pandemic has been an eye opener on many fronts. From a business point of view, most companies have come to realize (COVID aside) they are simply not modernized (prepared) for a digital economy. Each of us has had experiences that could fuel stories to be told. We've heard early anecdotes of people attempting to order toilet paper online from a big-box store, then walking by a toilet paper endcap in a brick-and-mortar store because they didn't want to panic buy, only to find out that their online order could not be fulfilled and was cancelled!

Another big-box store had an outage and could not process transactions; yet another familiar household name left customers in a web chat queue for hours, waiting for answers to basic questions such as order status or finding open locations. Some people waited for hours on both the phone and in chat queues to see which would resolve the problem (or get a response) faster, and discovered that these two channels made the business seem like different companies—so much for your omnichannel support (insert your experience here...). There's no coincidence that all of these big-name stores weren't born online. They (and us as customers) figured out quickly that their transformation journeys weren't nearly on the well-trodden path that they thought they were. The truth is that they realized that their hard-won "digital transformation" wasn't anywhere near as effective as they thought.

One thing is certain: large or small, those companies that didn't have a true pulse on their digital transformation before most certainly do now. They've seen customer satisfaction drop to nonexistent levels because of a lack of digitized self-service resolution and overall order fulfillment frustrations (can you say, "negative Net Promoter Score"—don't snicker, it's a real possible score). For many, it took months to set up curbside pickup; many vendors' online SKU catalogs *still* don't match what's in-store; search engines "found" merchandise that was out-of-stock, but didn't tell the customer until checkout (just when you thought you finally found what you needed); and many recommendation engines surfaced highly sought-after items in stock-out positions to go along with your in-stock purchases...frustrating.

These are all examples of a value chain that ignored user centricity and collapsed upon itself—supply chain disruption that was carelessly surfaced to clients in need at the most inopportune time. These companies were all guilty of not knowing what they already could have known—an enterprise amnesia if you will. It's perfectly fine to be sold out of a hot item; it's quite another to take a user right through to checkout, and then surface an out-of-stock position or direct customers to a brick-and-mortar store based on inventory data that's more stale than the "Last Day for Sale" rack at the seediest donut shop you've even been in. But was this avoidable? Yes!

These actions (or perhaps better said, inactions) cost sales, eroded customer loyalty, diluted trust, and opened the front doors with a "Welcome to our Home—Take What you Want" mat for modernized businesses to steal market share—and so some of them did. COVID-19 has caused many businesses large and small to fail; you just need to read the headlines to see what happened. While it's nearly impossible to understate the devastating impact of COVID-19 on global commerce and people's well-being, there is something few are speaking about: the harsh toll inflicted on businesses who've been talking (for a long time) about things like resilience and agility but didn't make them true priorities (some might call it "walk the talk"). Contrast this with those who prioritized these values and were well prepared to seize unexpected opportunities for growth. These companies became digitally touchless and fully (and consistent) omni-channel; it didn't matter if you were on a mobile app or website, phone or chatbot: your interactions had the same capabilities in either medium. That isn't to say there wasn't a downside or pain for even the most prepared companies; however, it's fair to note that if most companies had a six-month warning of what was coming, they would have done a lot of things differently and prepared in different ways. That's the point.

During the unprecedented challenges of COVID-19, many companies were divers, while some were thrivers. Consider two famous branded US-based craft and bulk food stores. Both enabled their omni-channel presence with backend business operations to support a seamless curbside pickup experience within days of closing their retail stores (the thrivers). In contrast, because of outdated monolithic ordering systems and static infrastructure, a number of large grocery stores and retailers took weeks or months to get their order fulfillment processes in line with the current reality—despite having far more IT resources and budget. Others found their way as new providers as they rose to the occasion: the new arrivers. For example, think about the growth of internet-connected fitness class apps like DownDog (provides a studio-like yoga experience in the comfort of your home) or fitness equipment companies like Ergatta (rowing) or Tonal (pulley weight training with a large screen assistant), and so on. These new arrivers differentiate from those that thrived (like Peloton). As you can see, across all industry, some thrived, some arrived, but many dived.

In another instance, a sporting goods store couldn't process orders (or they took minutes to process) leading to a record number of abandoned online shopping baskets. Desperate customers ran to what were once virtually unknown vendors who could swiftly answer questions or tell them their order was processed in a timely manner (and where an order confirmed meant you were actually getting the item, which wasn't a guarantee with the divers)—a warm welcome to the new arrivers!

There are far more bad stories than good—many more divers than thrivers or arrivers—and the consequences of shaken consumer confidence continues to outlive the pandemic. The one undeniable advantage shared by arrivers and thrivers alike was a well-thought-out renovation and innovation framework. As we move into emerging-from-pandemic discussions with clients, it's clear that their digital modernization plans just got accelerated by five years as digital-first becomes even more critical to their future.

Business Vaccination: The Arriver's Guide

As the world deploys COVID-19 relief in the form of vaccination, a business "vaccination" has long already existed—it's the activation of a well-proven innovation and renovation strategy (we'll give you a framework for understanding renovation and innovation at the end of Chapter 2). That's a bold statement, and the point isn't to make light of the seriousness of COVID-19 from a personal health perspective, but to seriously consider the components of an agenda that has the net effect of moving the mindset (and the business for that matter) away from "survive" and into "thrive and arrive."

Figure 1-1 shows a well-trodden and proven path to renovate and innovate your IT estates. We'll discuss each of the steps in the sections that follow.

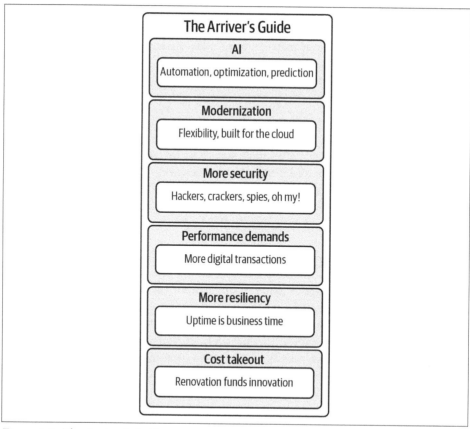

Figure 1-1. The Arriver's Guide

Cost Takeout

Undoubtedly, COVID-19 has hit many bottom lines and that will surely mean (to many) reduced budgets and sensitivities to investments that don't have direct impact on profit. One cost-savings strategy is cloud computing. As it turns out, many who think they'll just flip their apps to a public cloud often come up short on cost savings (some spend more—read "The Cost of Cloud, a Trillion Dollar Paradox" (*https:// oreil.ly/kHnRf*)) or never fully realize the cloud's benefits; this is why experts agree that about 80% of applications haven't become "cloud-ified" (we'll talk about this later in the book). Folks that come up short are often tying the word cloud to a destination and not a capability.

An additional cost-takeout winner will be consolidation, which can impact hardware and software costs (never underestimate the ability for good hardware to reduce software core licenses). The use of cloud native technologies like containers and Kubernetes are huge, as consolidation and virtualization play into the hands of any cost-savings strategy. This all enables business in an economically savvy and concentrated fashion. This also frees resources (computational and financial) that can be funneled toward other critical areas that make up an infrastructure agenda—such as resiliency, security, and performance. Bottom line: cost-savings opportunities will come with other considerations that need to be well understood and planned, and those that think the cost savings opportunity is strategically but a simple click away will be as successful as those business leaders who think AI is magic.

Resiliency

This matters more than ever before: in the new "abnormal," consumer behaviors of buying, selling, and socializing have been drastically altered. Even after populations have been vaccinated en masse, long-term buying habits, underwriting car insurance in a hybrid workplace environment (this hybrid is a destination), banking (and more) will be permanently changed. Consider the effects of a potential future COVID-19 flare up: the storefront you offer clients for transactions has to keep on running; your contactless payment method must work (in some places you weren't even allowed to take cash for purchases). These solutions need to be in place before the next potential challenge arises. In other words, getting caught on your heels again will not be an option. You should ensure you're familiar with key performance indicators (KPIs), such as mean time to repair (MTTR) and mean time between failure (MTBF), recovery point objectives (RPOs), and recovery time objectives (RTOs), among others. In plain speak, these KPIs provide answers to questions like: "How long can you typically go without an outage?", "How often will an outage be expected as a function of time?", "How much data can you stand losing?", and "How fast do you need to get back up and running?" You'll need to know the answers to these questions like the back of your hand.

Performance

The shift to more online procurement and contracting means more performance demands on the infrastructure. Think about panic buying. While much fun can be made of toilet paper hoarders amidst lockdowns and supply chain breakdowns, think about critical drug therapies and interventions. For many, medical prescriptions became a legitimate panic and so began a race to pharmacies to fill them. Pharmaceutical systems had to keep running, even under the unprecedented transaction levels they experienced in the first weeks of the COVID-19 pandemic (not just from individuals buying their medicine, but from pharmacists needing to pull medical records, allergy information, cross-drug interactions, warnings, and more). There were pharmacies during this challenge that didn't miss a beat, and those that sadly got beat up. It's also worth a moment of thought to consider how the accelerated movement to contactless payment methods helped to mitigate the spread of disease. Those payment systems not only needed to work (resiliency) but they needed to respond quickly (performance)—before the COVID-19 crisis began, if point-of-sale systems went down, accepting cash only was merely a frustration. As COVID-19 infections became more and more prevalent, these systems going down literally meant "no sale."

Security

As more and more businesses harden their online presence in response to growing customer demands, security is paramount. Evidence suggests that hackers used the COVID pandemic as an opportunity to up their attack frequencies—Forbes (*https://oreil.ly/dkBiT*) noted a 238% rise in attacks on banks and a 600% increase on cloud servers between January 2020 and April 2020! We expect to see concepts such as Zero Trust, Security Information and Event Management (SIEM), and Trusted Execution Environments (TEEs) move from "great to talk about" to real plans to do it. The more and more people transact online, the more risk we face with fraud and identity theft. The more data that's in-flight or at-rest, the more it needs to be protected (hint: today, the world isn't doing the job well enough). In fact, contactless pay providers like Apple Pay, PayPal, or Android Pay (among others) should see a surge because credit card information doesn't have to land or flow through the vendor, thereby lowering the risk of credit card details falling into the wrong hands. What about the protection of data at rest? We're betting (because we were shocked at how much we didn't know until we knew) most don't fully appreciate how much of a role even storage considerations play in a truly hardened cyber-resilient strategy.

Now consider the fact that the amount of data breaches and data heists for crypto ransoms has never been more plentiful (2021 is proving this in monthly intervals) and dangerous (a disproportionate number of data ransom schemes are mounting up against healthcare facilities—and now think about COVID).

Fact: corporate boards everywhere are asking all kinds of security questions and the job market is thriving (last we checked, we saw well over 200,000 Information Security jobs). This means that if your answer to the question "Where did the hacker go with our data?" begins cheekily with "He ransomware," that won't be cute or funny to anyone. This suggests that companies (now more than ever) need to align, protect, and manage threats to their ecosystem (both on-premises and off-premises)—and COVID-19 has made it readily apparent just who is (and who isn't) ready to offer those assurances to their customers.

Modernization

Modernization is a must-have mindset for both thrivers and arrivers. Flexibility will be a difference maker—and flexibility leads you to the cloud. The term *hybrid multi-cloud* (a mix of multiple cloud vendors and cloud technologies on-premises and in public cloud providers) is a hot topic these days because its very name embodies flexibility, and this is a space you've got to know and focus on. The emerging space of distributed cloud (the same cloud technology across multiple cloud destinations, delivered by technologies like IBM Cloud Satellite, Amazon Output, and Google Anthos) is becoming a hot topic as companies examine the management and skills costs associated with multiple cloud vendors. Whatever the hybrid cloud genre (multicloud, distributed, mix of on-prem and public, or all of them), dynamic (metered) pricing models for consumption of resources is today's marketplace trend. That's a cloud capability. Infrastructure that's flexible in capacity to scale up (or down) in a utility-like fashion at the most granular levels—down to the minute. That's a cloud capability. A service catalog to self-provision modern development environments or applications to accelerate workflow. That's a cloud capability. We could go on (and we will).

But there are right and wrong ways to go about building a cloud strategy. To do it right, we've developed a mantra for this book: "Cloud is a capability, not a destination." What does that mean? If you think of the cloud as a destination, you'll be thinking about AWS, or Azure, or Google, or IBM. And you'll be tempted to unify behind one of them. That's not how the cloud era is playing out for individuals or companies. Think about your personal computing infrastructure. If you have an Apple phone, tablet, or laptop, you're probably using iCloud for something (like backing up your contacts). If you watch movies on Netflix, you're using Netflix's cloud providers (yes, they run on two different clouds that must work together seamlessly to deliver you new episodes of *Grey's Anatomy*). Same for Spotify. And if you use Gmail, you're in Google's cloud.

Businesses are no different. A company's cloud journey usually starts with a few pilot projects in different departments, often because no one wants to wait for IT to approve new hardware: perhaps it's easier to train your "playing around" AI model using Google Collab's free GPU resources versus going to the "Department of No!" (Finance) to get some GPUs. By the time the C-suite starts thinking about a "cloud strategy," the company is already on multiple clouds. It's already multicloud. (This is classic "Shadow IT": you see it in choice of databases, cloud platforms, and the lot.)

But multicloud itself is a dead end if there's no effort to provide a uniform programming and operational interface to those clouds. You shouldn't have to care about where your data is located or where your software runs. That's why the "cloud" isn't a destination. If it is, you'll end up with a fight between marketing doing BI on AWS, finance doing business planning on IBM, and R&D doing AI on GCP. These efforts all need to collaborate. Hybrid clouds are all about integrating multiple cloud providers and in some cases, creating a single unified interface to them (distributed cloud) —and, for that matter, to your own on-premises data and applications. That's where the value of the cloud lies: in the flexibility of not having to worry about where your data is, or where your code is running. That's what it means to say, "Cloud is a capability."

According to McKinsey (and many others) 80% of enterprises are choosing to work in a hybrid multicloud environment, now and in the future. Tying these value statements to a destination does nothing but cheat the enterprise.

 Most cloud strategies have been focused on building new applications on the cloud (they are called *greenfield* apps) or a lift-and-shift of existing applications to the public cloud. We refer to this cloud strategy as "Cloud Chapter 1" (an epoch in the journey to cloud, not an actual chapter in this book). We think the hybrid cloud—and its ability to capture the true value of its capabilities—will be the next chapter in the cloud storyline and thus we often refer to it as "Cloud Chapter 2" (the next epoch of the cloud journey). Think of it as getting deeper into the cloud story, where the characters, the plot, and immersion thickens and provides more value.

If you're having a conversation about modernization, bringing the right apps and services up to par with containers, orchestration, and microservices-based architectures should be among your highest priorities. You should definitely be investigating Kubernetes (K8s). K8s platforms such as Red Hat OpenShift Container Platform (OCP) are becoming the new "operating system." Open Container Initiative (OCI)–compliant storage containers, enterprise-ready Kubernetes orchestration of those containers, and automation via Ansible and Terraform are the essential pillars for creating an agile IT foundation. (Don't worry if those words don't mean anything to you yet; we'll dig into them throughout this book, but understand them as the technologies that make "Chapter 2" of the cloud possible.) If you build containerized applications to the open standard OCI governance structure, those containerized applications can be provisioned anywhere (on-premises or in the public cloud), regardless of the cloud vendor. Modernizing applications and services on containers deployed with K8s orchestration is one of the best strategies that you can invest in. It doesn't matter whether your applications are solely apps born on the cloud (people refer to these as cloud native; they were built with modern approaches like microservices and containerized from the start), legacy apps that run your business, or a mishmash of them all (which is more likely the case). This is a winning strategy.

It's been said that basketball is a game where a single player can take a team to a title; however, in soccer, it's your weakest link that can keep you from winning anything. With that in mind, remember that the orchestration platform (K8s) always emulates the ethos of the infrastructure. Was the infrastructure built for resiliency and fast recovery? Was it built to scale? Was it built securely right down to the virtualization level and for Confidential Computing? This all matters; these are all good questions to ask. The modernization journey is a soccer game, not a basketball game.

AI

Can there be a tech-minded book written without the word AI these days? We think not. Yes, it's hyped, and the world tends to overhype what's possible in the next two years. But we can promise you that it often underestimates the profound changes brought about by the technologies that stick around for the next five to ten years. We think that in the future "AI" won't stand for Artificial Intelligence, but rather Ambient Intelligence. Why the word "ambient"? Think of ambient lighting; when done correctly, you don't really notice that it's there, but it's doing its job. AI will serve a similar role in our day-to-day lives and jobs: it will be everywhere, and become just a natural part of our environment. We will stop thinking of it as strange and different.

To us, the opportunities of AI can be summed up as: automation, optimization, and prediction. AI will drive costs down and client engagement up. Without question, successful businesses will unlock the power of data with AI—according to Forbes (*https://oreil.ly/AaEKg*), up to 73% of data goes unused in most organizations—that's why your AI needs an IA (information architecture). What's more, automation will be unavoidable; some reports suggest that enterprises can use automation to reclaim 120+ billion hours per year spent on low-value work. As companies move from defining their AI progress via algorithm counts in the dozens (at best) to the thousands, discussions will move well beyond how fast and accurate you can train your AI. We will be talking about inferencing speeds (scoring), lifecycle management (the moment you publish your AI algorithm is the moment it's out of date), sourcing data, explainability, bias, and more. Despite being a cloud book, we're going to give you a skills hotlist that any successful enterprise adopting AI needs to master: language, automation, and trust. Cloud is going to be the conduit for great AI...so these themes go hand in hand.

So Why Are Cloudy Skies the Best Forecast Ever?

From golf birdies to bankers, free drops to rain drops, highways to back roads, cloud technology affects them all (and all parts in between). Hybrid cloud is the next major shift in the evolution of IT...think about it, when any new IT architecture emerges and spreads, it has the potential to change the world and the concept of hybrid cloud (which will eventually just be called "cloud") will completely change the way renovators renovate and innovators innovate.

We believe we're at a key inflection point on the continuum of human history and innovation. Our world is set to pivot from a world of automation where humans are supported by technology to a data-rich ambient intelligent world where the technology is supported by humans. To us, this pending shift means that the largest wave of business transformation architecture is just ahead, and it'll be driven by three major shifts:

1. The modernization of critical workloads to build scalable applications at speed.

2. The adoption of Kubernetes to orchestrate those applications across any environment, no matter the vendor or location of the compute runtime.

3. This will all compound to serve as a springboard for the growing use of operational AI and edge applications to create data-driven insights that shape business outcomes.

As you go through this book, we think it'll be obvious that only a hybrid cloud architecture can provide a consistent, standards-based approach to development, security, and the operational hygiene that'll be required. It is a smarter open architecture that allows for workload portability, orchestration, and management across multiple environments. We won't be able to stress it enough in this book: get into the cloud as capability mindset (as opposed to destination) and you'll be a leader of an organization that simply does better.

CHAPTER 2

Evolution of Cloud

In the first chapter, we introduced you to the thrivers, divers, and new arrivers; we boldly declared the mantra of this book ("Cloud is a capability, not a destination."), and gave you a guide to digital transformation. In this chapter, we'll discuss the evolution of cloud, where it's going, and some things to keep in mind as you begin (or continue) your capability journey.

Are You on the Intranet, Internet, or Extranet? Nah—Just Internet

To get a feeling for what we're talking about, consider the ubiquitous phrase: the internet. At one time, many would subdivide internet technologies into an access control list of sorts. There was talk of the EXTRAnet: a controlled private network limited to vendors, partners, suppliers, or other authorized groups. Today, most would say an extranet provides access from outside the firewall to resources inside the firewall for a value chain based on membership. For example, when you return equipment to a store that sends your broken item back to the manufacturer who deals with the warranty claim, the store is likely to log in to the manufacturer's site and open a ticket, but that's about it. Even so, bringing your items to the store is a necessary step because the store has access that the customer doesn't.

At work we used the intRAnet: an internet that was behind a firewall and dedicated to providing information and services within an organization, usually to the exclusion of access to outsiders. In other words, if you didn't work at the company, you had no access to it. This intranet would have department operational manuals, performance reviews, sensitive documents, code repos: all the stuff used to run your business that is nobody else's business.

Then it started. A rallying cry around a set number of standards by groups like the Internet Engineering Task Force (IETF) or the World Wide Web Consortium (W3C). Communities ratified all kinds of standards, from documents (HTML), to fetching those documents (HTTP), to the concept of time, and all parts in between; soon enough, things just became referred to as the INTERnet. Think about it, when was the last time you used a word other than internet to describe these kinds of networks? When was the last time you heard someone at work say, "I found it on our intranet?" Answer: you were probably dancing the Macarena and weren't embarrassed doing it. (Sure, there will be some roles where this differentiation matters, but this isn't how business talks and it isn't how most people think.) The bottom line: intranet, extranet, and internet just became internet.

Are You on a Private Cloud, Public Cloud, or Community Cloud? Nah—Just Cloud

History has a way of repeating itself. Think "cloud." Cloud-talk today centers around terms like public clouds, community clouds, and private clouds; but work has started on a bunch of standards that have started to evolve and unify the patterns.

We think cloud will follow the same naming path as the internet and will settle on hybrid cloud (again, cloud as a capability not a destination), or just cloud for short. We're already seeing technologies that support cloud computing in general (just like those that supported internet technologies). Think of the standardized open source technologies (many of which we cover in this book) such as Jenkins, Terraform, Ansible, Docker, and Kubernetes (K8s), all supported by major vendors for the orchestration and management of cloud native applications. These are the technologies that are creating integrated hybrid clouds.

With this in mind, we want to officially anoint our book's mantra (you'll hear it time and time again through the book); say it with us: *"Cloud is a capability, not a destination!"* If we can agree that cloud is a capability, then it's perfectly aligned to where IT wants (and needs) to go: decentralized, flexible, performant, open, and secure.

Just like the "prevent defense" (an American football defense that's happy to let the offense move downfield but holds defenders further back to try to prevent a major score) we think prevents a win, a "one location and vendor cloud fits all" approach won't work either. Believe us, we've seen it fail, we've even seen some overzealous competitor sales (and IBM) reps try to push it. It often doesn't work and it's not the right tone for your business. Companies need the flexibility to run their workloads across any platform without having to rewrite everything as they go.

History Repeats Itself: From Granularity of Terms to General Terms

This is why our book's mantra, *"Cloud is a capability, not a destination,"* encompasses a mindset shift you (and the organizations you work for) have to make to fully exploit the opportunities that those servers in the cloud offer. We've seen success in the cloud —mostly companies producing greenfield apps; that's great if you're a startup or building net new in a roll your own (RYO) fashion. But what about established investments? Many of these companies looked at the cloud as a pure cost-saving opportunity, and while some had success (most in limited fashions that didn't nearly match the promises), others were left unpleasantly surprised. While the cloud can offer you some cost savings (cloud toe dippers typically start with archive or test), it all depends on the running workloads, data gravity, and your business. But cloud can't just be about cost savings—in fact, over time it'll prove to be more about agility than cost savings. Sure, that capability has potential to reduce the obvious costs, but it's about putting your business in the best position possible to deliver.

But here is the cold hard truth: we estimate that a mere 20% of the potential value (*https://oreil.ly/4YNUK*) from cloud computing is being realized today by mature enterprises via the public cloud. As you will learn about in this book, cloud is more than cost savings; it's a renovation opportunity that delivers flexibility. When you think about it the right way, you'll start to think beyond "lifting and shifting" as-is applications to the cloud. For example, releasing software frequently to users is usually a time-consuming and painful process. Continuous integration and continuous delivery (CI/CD) can help organizations become more agile by automating and streamlining the steps involved in going from an idea, a change in the market, a challenge (like COVID-19), or a business requirement to ever-increasing value delivered to the customer.

Adoption of cloud being a capability and not a destination opens up your world to rethinking how applications are built, delivering continuous streams of improvement to engage your user base (think about how often apps get updated on your iPhone), and so much more. We believe this mantra will have you look at the technologies that support the cloud (Kubernetes, Docker, Jenkins, Terraform, and oh so many more) and appreciate how they make for agile organizations and encompass the entire end-to-end lifecycle of an idea, pivot, or change of course you need for your business.

So how do you access the 80% of value that's yet to be unlocked? You embrace a hybrid strategy and all its components (on-premises, public cloud, multicloud, distributed cloud). In fact, don't just embrace it—demand it. When vendors come knocking, talk about capability. Discuss the ability to dynamically access and move capacity that your business needs regardless of location. Not just on-premises or in a public cloud—but taking an app from one cloud provider and seamlessly running it on another; remember, we want the ultimate flexibility here. Start to think about breaking down the monoliths and containerizing those apps with a fundamental change to the operating model.

Building a hybrid cloud strategy and playbook is essential if you want to unleash the full potential of your cloud; in fact, studies (*https://www.ibm.com/cloud/hybrid*) suggest such a strategy can deliver 2.5x more value than a public-only strategy (the 20% of current captured cloud value we alluded to earlier).

Cloud is cloud—it's an operational model and this shift from a place to an operational model will deliver superpowers to the organizations you serve; it's about opening doors to more sources of value, including:

- Infrastructure cost efficiencies
- Business continuity and acceleration
- Increased developer (and IT) productivity
- Security and regulatory compliance
- Flexibility to seize opportunities and drive value

Our definition of cloud (hybrid meaning multiple places and vendors) means there is lots of choice in the marketplace.

As practitioners in the field and running businesses, we've made some mistakes along the way, have the scar tissue to prove it, and offer you this list of characteristics that any vendor should demonstrate:

- Industry expertise
- Proven security
- Confidential Computing and Zero Trust architectures
- Build once and run anywhere with consistency
- Capture the world's innovation

Hybrid Cloud's "Chapter 2": Distributed Cloud

Cloud service providers (CSPs) are forever innovating, learning from their own (or other people's) past mistakes, identifying new challenges, and pushing the boundaries of what is possible. With the rampant growth of hybrid cloud, several pesky challenges have surfaced like weeds, threatening to choke out the potential held by this new computing paradigm. How can customers tap into the capabilities of public cloud, without needing to actually be deployed *on* public cloud? How can one public cloud vendor's capabilities be introduced on-premises, brought to the edge (especially with the onset of 5G), or even made available on other public clouds—running in a manner that is not only consistent, but also not overwhelming from a management perspective?

Enter another term for your repertoire: *distributed cloud*. A distributed cloud is a public cloud computing approach that replicates the power of your favorite CSP on infrastructure *outside* of that CSP's datacenters. Essentially, you're extending the public cloud to on-premises, private cloud, and edge environments. Distributed cloud is offered as a service by major cloud providers, and includes IBM Cloud Satellite, AWS Outposts, Google Anthos, and Azure Stack; each of these is unique in their own way, but all are focused on the idea of extending public cloud capabilities to customer environments. Throughout this book, we stress our mantra multiple times: cloud is a capability, not a destination! With a distributed cloud (a subset of hybrid cloud), companies can bring the capabilities of cloud that they need to an environment of their choosing. When done correctly, distributed cloud removes the challenges of running in different locations and occludes the needless details from you. Essentially, it makes running cloud services within your on-premises datacenter just as easy and seamless as running those same services in a public cloud datacenter.

Figure 2-1 gives you a rough idea of how a distributed cloud works. You start with an underlying foundation of providers—be they rooted on public clouds, on-premises environments, or edge locations. Building on that, you have a standard layer of distributed cloud hosts (simply referred to as hosts); this layer is essentially compute power. Upon a standardized layer of hosts, organizations can leverage services from the public cloud, or even build their own custom applications; quite simply, distributed cloud brings the power of a CSP right to your doorstep and gives you all the placement control you could ask for.

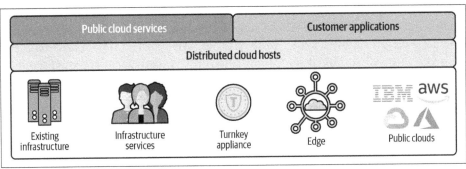

Figure 2-1. Distributed cloud

Distributed Cloud On-Premises

Unification of your technology stack is table stakes for any successful hybrid cloud strategy. For example, imagine using VMware workloads on-premises, but container-based Kubernetes in the cloud. In preparation for a potential spike in traffic, your team would be unable to rapidly utilize the elasticity of Kubernetes in the cloud. Translating from VMs to containers is simply inefficient and difficult! Instead, one ideal solution is to begin implementing Kubernetes on-premises and modernize the VMware workloads to run as containers on K8s instead. Here's where things start to get tricky. In the public cloud, customers are able to readily utilize *managed* services to easily create and run Kubernetes clusters. They can use tools like Terraform with provider plug-ins that integrate with a CSP to automate the creation of one or many clusters with minimal effort.

 Let's clarify what we mean by the term *managed* service, as it has become overloaded with a lot of assumptions (and potential baggage). In this context, we're referring to services that CSPs manage for you, while still providing you administrative access and control. For example, managed Kubernetes services automate the process of upgrading clusters (done by the CSPs) *but* allow you to choose when and which version for the actual operation.

You can probably guess where we're going with this: the on-premises and private cloud experience is nowhere near as streamlined as a managed Kubernetes service. Organizations will need to train an operations team to handle the deployment and management of Kubernetes clusters. In addition, they'll need to hire and train a site reliability engineering (SRE) team to ensure high availability and—in the worst-case scenario—respond to late-night critical situations (crit-sits).

Here's where a distributed cloud offering shines. These organizations can continue to leverage the power of their CSP while running on-premises. We think IBM has done something quite special with its cloud strategy that truly puts the hybrid into hybrid cloud. First, the Red Hat OpenShift Container Platform is truly write once, run anywhere. (Remember how Java was "write once, test everywhere"? It's not like that.) Second, a product called *IBM Cloud Satellite* runs inside a customer's datacenter or out at the edge; each Cloud Satellite location is connected using IBM Cloud Satellite Link to provide connectivity to a consistent and centralized control plane (this is important) hosted on the IBM Cloud. For example, let's say your business enabled the use of IBM Cloud Satellite for all of your environments, including on-premises. As an operations engineer, when it comes time to create a new OpenShift cluster on-premises, you'd first start by logging in to the control plane. When it comes time to choose which datacenter to deploy the cluster into, you select an on-premises "Satellite location." (This Satellite location could be on any CSP too!)

By extending the power of cloud to on-premises environments, your hybrid cloud operations are optimized. Your operations teams no longer need to worry about learning how to deploy a cluster on-premises, as they can just use the managed public cloud approach. This demonstrates the true power of distributed cloud—the cloud is used as a capability, not a destination; what's more, the capabilities all have a consistent management interface which is essential to flatten time to adoption curves and keep things simple.

Living on the Edge: Distributed Cloud

Data is everywhere around us. Many times, we get so caught up with focusing on data being processed in our datacenters that we forget where a heck of a lot of data is actually created—by humans like us. Every time we open our phone, walk into a supermarket, buy a movie ticket, or pour a drink at a fountain station, we're generating data. Generally, this data is captured, sent off to some datacenter for processing, stored in some database, and more data is sent back. However, it's not always reasonable to wait for the data to go all the way back to a datacenter. Imagine you're in a self-driving car and that car is processing thousands of photos per second (video is nothing more than a bunch of still-frame pictures stitched together). Meanwhile the car is applying computer vision algorithms, along with data analysis from the advanced driver assistance system (ADAS) sensors, radar, and lidar. How safe would you feel if that car was sending data to a datacenter for processing (think back to your last dropped call)? For the driver, the latency (and risk) would simply be too high.

Edge computing provides a number of advantages—and it's not just speed. It also allows businesses to scale more effectively by placing data collection and processing closer to the edge, rather than having to scale out expensive centralized datacenters. In addition, security is a major advantage as data never has to leave the edge—this can be critical for compliance with regulations like GDPR. Furthermore, some industries have regulations that state if you "land" that data (store it in the datacenter) it becomes subject to all kinds of data-retention rules.

One of the key challenges with edge computing is rapid growth, as each edge location will have its own set of workloads, microservices, and databases. Customers need a unified strategy to manage the multiple locations consistently. Distributed cloud shines again for edge use cases, where you can register your edge locations and manage them as if they were any other cloud datacenter. This means utilizing the power of the cloud, including DevOps toolchains, security policies, and advanced machine learning services all within your edge locations.

Imagine a furniture company with distribution centers across the world. Chances are that similar workloads are required to run in every distribution center, such as inventory management, employee clock-ins, IoT sensors for temperature and humidity, and outgoing shipment tracking. Instead of having an operations team handle each distribution center as a unique (but connected) environment—which can quickly get very expensive—why not use a distributed cloud approach to manage all these edge locations centrally? With a distributed cloud offering, you can create abstractions that enable you to simplify the management of grouped locations. This allows you to roll out application services, compliance policies, and security rules across multiple environments at once.

Distributed Cloud for Multicloud

The primary advantage of distributed cloud is that you can *extend the benefits of a public cloud anywhere*. Naturally, if you want to run all of your workloads on a specific vendor's cloud, so be it. But the reality (in our experience of having worked thousands of customer engagements over the years) is that no medium-to-large enterprise is running on a single cloud.

 Flexera's "Cloud Computing Trends: 2021 State of the Cloud Report" (*https://oreil.ly/yXgbr*) noted that organizations are using (on average) 2.6 public and 2.7 private clouds *and* they're experimenting with an additional 1.1 public clouds and 2.2 private clouds.

Organizations everywhere want to retain the ability to choose the right cloud provider for their workloads (some public clouds are purpose built for finance and insurance), but this can be a real conundrum for many: at a minimum, maintaining multiple cloud environments will be taxing on administration resources. Ops teams will need to firmly understand the differences between each CSP, including methods for automation, deployments, pricing, auto-scaling, and more. Deploying a simple Kubernetes cluster on AWS forces you to learn their specific approach with Amazon Elastic Kubernetes Service (EKS)—unique datacenters, user interface (UI) flows, automation paths, and more. The same approach on IBM Cloud requires you to use IBM Cloud Kubernetes Service (IKS), with a different set of steps that essentially results in the same challenges we just surfaced for AWS; and on it goes. In the end, you have Kubernetes in both clouds that operates the same, but the process to get there is very different, which in turn is a recipe for higher costs, more status meetings, and an overall tax on an organization's agility.

Distributed cloud enables you to simplify these differences with *one consistent experience*. You start by choosing one CSP as your home base, and then leverage the infrastructure as a service (IaaS) offerings of other CSPs to run your workloads. *This means regardless of which cloud provider you're using, you can deploy consistently across all of them.*

Let's give an example of how this works. Start by picking one distributed cloud offering as your central management environment (like IBM Cloud Satellite). Next you set out to run some workloads on AWS but they are consistently managed from the control plane that sits on the IBM Cloud. You spin up AWS IaaS resources like some EC2 instances (these are essentially VMs). Finally, you register these instances as a "Satellite location," which enables you to extend IBM Cloud to datacenters in AWS! You can now provision Red Hat OpenShift on IBM Cloud, a managed OpenShift offering, directly on AWS datacenters. You might be wondering, "What's the point?" Let's assume you happened to have databases or other services running directly on AWS; you can now network them with your OpenShift cluster with ease. In addition, you gain consistency with a standard way of deploying OpenShift, whether it's on IBM Cloud or AWS.

A Caveat to Distributed Cloud

Moving forward with any one particular cloud requires buy-in. Distributed cloud offerings come with the assumption that you will use one cloud to drive all of your workloads. To be fair, all CSPs require some extent of buy-in—each cloud has its own quirks and features, whether it's datacenters, capabilities, or cost. With distributed cloud you gain freedom in the choice of infrastructure provider but are limited to choosing one primary cloud provider to manage your services. For some, this distinction is acceptable, because they would prefer to build skills with one cloud provider rather than many; but think back to the Flexera report. In addition, extending public cloud to on-premises is a no-brainer. Of course, you don't have to manage every workload with a distributed cloud, but now the more capabilities that are left outside, the more liability there is for managing one-off environments.

Distributed Cloud: The Ultimate Unification Layer

Hybrid cloud emerged as a necessity, not because it's the ideal approach. Customers may have data residency requirements forcing them to run on-premises, subscribed-to software as a service (SaaS) properties requiring them to run in a vendor-specific environment, legacy applications that are too difficult to move to the cloud, or data gravity considerations. Amidst these challenges, the benefits of utilizing the cloud are impossible to deny (cloud the capability), and are exactly why customers will thrive in hybrid cloud environments for years to come. When the challenges of hybrid cloud result from division, distributed cloud aims to solve them with unity.

Although we are strong proponents of technologies like Kubernetes and containers that support a hybrid cloud strategy, even a well-architected hybrid cloud can feel broken at times. For developers, a hybrid cloud environment means multiple environments with differing technology stacks to code and test against. For operations teams, a hybrid cloud leads to more environments that are prone to failure, more late-night pager duties, and more challenging approaches to integration. For security teams, hybrid cloud means a larger surface area for attack and complex security policies that are unique to the environment. Distributed cloud starts to fix these DevSecOps problems by offering the ultimate unification layer—one public cloud control point to rule them all.

Hybrid Cloud

In this section we introduced you to the concept of a *distributed cloud*—a child of hybrid cloud, if you will. Throughout this book we're just going to use the term *hybrid cloud* to reference any combination of cloud capabilities and deployment of them, too. Like we talked about with the internet, we expect that the final resting place will be a single word—but for now, we'll use hybrid cloud to get us all on the same "page" in our cloud discussions. Is the cloud capability on-premises or public? That means hybrid cloud. Are you using multiple public cloud vendors? That's a hybrid cloud. Are you stitching together all kinds of SaaS services hosted on various clouds—yup, hybrid cloud.

Industry Expertise in Mission-Critical Business Processes

Downtime means no time…for you to serve your clients. We're certain this isn't new to you, so we're not going to hit you with the cost per hour of downtime. That said, the number of times a call dropped or a VOIP call was garbled during the planning of this book on a web conference really hits home our point: your business is solely going to depend on a well-ingrained culture of mission-critical thinking and planning.

But there are other considerations we want you to think about in this area:

You are unique
> Every client we've ever talked to, on any project (cloud, AI, you name it), is starting from a different place. You need to be able to start from your place, wherever you are; there are no one-size-fits-all recommendations here. We suggest you tier your projects into value drivers and requirements, such as Platinum, Gold, Silver, and so on, but also differentiate between projects that are "low-hanging fruit," projects that require thoughtful execution to modernize, and projects that don't need to be modernized at all but could greatly benefit from the capability offered by cloud.

Demand experience
> Never underestimate the difference that industry and business domain expertise can make. Look for proven reference architectures and scalable assets—your partners should show their experience redesigning processes and workflow transformations for your industry—and yes, ask for names. This will help speed the work of business transformation and provide a scorecard that compares your organization to others that partner has worked with.

Look to the experts

When one person is teaching, two people are learning—engage with a vendor that has a rich education ecosystem (that extends beyond certification) and experts that can make your team smarter. As they do this, the vendor can learn not just about your architecture, but about your team's skill—your partner should be able to help here.

Leverage the ecosystem

An extended strong technology partner ecosystem will help deliver added value to industry-specific business process transformation. We've always been fans of true partnerships. But that partnership should extend into the open source community, and reward those that come to open source communities to feed the soil versus those that just come to grab the fruit (today's marketplace has examples of both).

Proven Security, Compliance, and Governance

Collectively, the world is doing a poor job at protecting information and preventing malware attacks. Add to this the ever-expanding set of regulations around data governance (for example, the European Union's GDPR was the starting point, California's Consumer Protection Act soon followed, and things are set to become even more dizzying with EU proposals on the usage of AI in its region). We tell our kids all the time, "You lose trust in buckets and gain it in droplets." Technology partners should be no different. Your partner and their platform have to showcase and build trust into every interaction, with a robust portfolio of data protection and security services—all embedded into a cloud run-anywhere architecture, positioned to protect your processes, applications, and cloud services, while managing compliance requirements.

But it's also very important to understand industry-specific cloud requirements to make it truly hybrid. As the cloud compute market matures, we're seeing companies asking for services that match the specific needs of an industry or workload. Consider a bank trying to leverage the public cloud with sensitive data. Such a cloud journey will require the appeasement of risk analysts who will seek (more and more) Confidential Computing environments. If you want financial information on the cloud, you need to find a vendor who will guarantee that at no time does anybody at the cloud provider have access to the hardware security module (HSM) encryption keys —that bank needs full lifecycle management over their data—including keeping its own keys.

Things to look for here include automated and auditable processes, a consistent security and controls posture across all applications or services, and capabilities for the highest levels of cloud security and monitoring (which we'll discuss next).

Confidential Computing and Zero Trust Architectures

Let's start with this sound piece of advice we freely offer to anyone that will listen: where there is data, there is potential for breaches and unauthorized access. And here's a dirty little secret no one wants to admit…very (and we mean very) few organizations know where all their security holes are, but almost all of them know there are walls they won't look around the corners of because they don't want to go to the board and tell them what needs changing.

Confidential Computing is a computing technology that isolates sensitive data in a protected CPU enclave during processing. The contents of the enclave—the data being processed, and the techniques used to process it—are accessible only to authorized programming code, and invisible and unknowable to anything or anyone else, including a cloud provider! As companies rely more and more on public and hybrid cloud services, data privacy in the cloud is imperative. The primary goal of Confidential Computing is to provide greater assurance to companies that their data in the cloud is protected and confidential. For years cloud providers have offered encryption services for protecting data at rest (in storage and databases) and data in transit (moving over a network connection). Confidential Computing eliminates the remaining data security vulnerability by protecting data in use—that is, during processing or runtimes using trusted execution environments (TEEs) that are hardware assisted for the most protection you can get.

Many people think that Zero Trust is about making a system and its users more trusted, but that's not it at all. Zero Trust is about *eliminating* trust. Its genesis comes from the notion that for all the years we've been talking about security, we assume that everyone inside an organization are actors that should be trusted; but what if those actors are imposters or there's an internal identity theft? Zero Trust involves removing trust from your data, assets, applications, and services for the most critical areas to your organization and creating a microperimeter around it. Bottom line: Zero Trust operates on the notion that trust is a vulnerability and no one should be trusted.

We think Confidential Computing and Zero Trust are set to become a brand-new bar of requirements for CSPs and will become ubiquitous to core computing concepts. These concepts are applied to the protection of all data (be it in motion or at rest, on-premises or not) within TEEs (the stuff in the cloud where your apps are running) and the surface areas where those applications run. Why the infrastructure assist? Quite simply, doing it in the software is pretty much putting your hand up and saying, "I'll put a best effort into security, but with budgets the way they are, we'll cut a corner here or there." (It hurts us more to write that than hear it.)

But even traditional protection approaches need to be challenged. Why don't we just encrypt all data and not worry about it? Seems simple enough, right? Nope. It's not that people don't care about data security, it's just really hard. It requires an appetite and resource commitments to get it right and do it right—and that's more than likely going to require application changes, unless you're using a true secure enclave technology. Application changes, performance impact, technical challenges…all reasons why many aren't adopting an "encrypt everything" strategy. It's no wonder why Ponemon noted that of all the data breaches in 2018 (*https://oreil.ly/NRunJ*), a mere 4% (on average) of them were deemed "secure" (all of the data was encrypted, which makes all of the stolen data useless.) The bottom line: consumability is the biggest issue in the security market.

 We'd be remiss to not suggest you look into true secure enclave technologies like Secure Service Containers that run hardware assisted on LinuxONE and IBM Z, which solve a lot of the friction around an encrypt everything strategy, all with the simplicity of a "light switch" to turn it on with next to zero performance impact and no changes to your applications.

There are cultural issues at play too. We say this (partially) tongue-in-cheek, but application developers really don't like security folks. Why? Because performance means different things to different people:

- Performance to a database administrator (DBA) means, "How fast does it take to run the transaction and is it within my service level agreement (SLA)?"

- Performance to an AI practitioner means, "How accurate is my AI and how are its predictions (AI nerds call this generalization) on real world data the model has never seen before?"

- Performance to an application developer means, "How fast can I build this application so I can move on to the next project in my queue?"

What does performance mean to security personnel? Nothing—unless it's how fast can I detect an intrusion or something like that. It's not on their measurement scope or in their ethos. Think about it: every single concern in the preceding list means nothing to a security professional. That's why the Chief Security Officer's division is also sometimes affectionately nicknamed "The Department of No!"

One thing is a certainty to us—in no way, shape, or form do we see any signs of the world doing a better job at protecting data. In a cloud virtualized and containerized world, you'll have lots (and we mean lots) of virtual machines running beside each other, and if in the public cloud, perhaps beside someone you don't even know. The question you have to ask is, "Are the virtual machines protected from each other?" or "What about container contents, are they protected?"

But it's more than that. If you're storing data in a public cloud provider, you must differentiate between the concepts of operational assurances and technical assurances when it comes to the protection of your data. This is a big deal and quite frankly not enough decision makers are even using this lexicon.

Let's assume you have some sort of sensitive data (be it medical, financial, intellectual property, and so on). Operational assurance is basically your cloud provider saying to you, "I promise to not access your data." They'll back that up with comments about operational protocols and procedures that ultimately add up to a giant promise that administrators will not access your data. While that's much appreciated, it may not be enough for you to pass a regulatory hurdle or have the confidence to replatform your apps. It may be OK for certain apps, but think about the ones that run the core of your business or hold the most sensitive data about your business and its clients.

What's more, the number of insider breaches is growing like crazy, and you just don't hear nearly as much about these breaches as you do external hackers. Internal breaches could be of malicious intent, but they can also be the work of inadvertent actors (folks exposing data they didn't mean to). Heck, think about bringing in an external vendor to apply maintenance to fix some disk…there is an extensive list of "trusted" actors who could access your data.

In other words, we don't think an operational model of trust is going to be enough if you're looking to capture the 80% of the remaining cloud value that's sitting there. The question you need to be asking (at least for certain apps) is "*Can* you access my data?" not "*Will* you access my data?" You don't want operational assurances—you need technical assurances. True answers will sound like, "Umm…we want to help you, but because of the technology we're using we can't." In these scenarios, even if law enforcement served a signed bench warrant, the CSP still couldn't share usable data because they can't see it and because of the way the security profile is managed. See the difference? The answer posture changes from "won't" to "can't." (It's fair to note that laws, expectations, and legal authorities have yet to catch up here and the future of data privacy will be an interesting space for years to come.)

Build Once and Run Anywhere with Consistency

This means you're not rewiring or refactoring code solely because you want to run a portion of your business on Azure and moved it from another vendor (or vice versa). You also want to vet ease of integration and a consistent application development life-cycle. Think about your experiences with Java—it was marketed as a write once and run anywhere proposition that when put into practice became write once and test everywhere. That's not what you're looking for here and you'll have to dig well beneath the veneer of websites and marketing brochures to flush this out. Open source technologies (like Linux, containers, and Kubernetes) will be key to this, but the goal is a consistent set of cloud services across any cloud or any location. If your application containerizes a certain vendor's database and wants to run it elsewhere, that's your prerogative to do so, one that must be free of friction or a "tax."

Capture the World's Innovation

Your cloud strategy should enable access to a wide range of innovations and technologies; your vendors are Sherpas to the unprecedented pace and quality of innovations in our world. Those innovations come from emerging technologies built by the vendor, but they are equally integrated or friendly to the unmatched pace and quality of innovations from the open source community.

From quantum computing (which will most certainly be a hybrid cloud platform—after all, some quantum computers operate within one of the coldest places in the universe, which is why you don't want one in your office), to leading-edge AI networks, to edge computing, and blockchain, technologies fronted with APIs and exposed for usage is what will propel your business to transform.

Perhaps one vendor captures a certain area of innovation better than another (one is exceptional at natural language processing, another at visual recognition, and so on); that's the very essence of what we're getting at and spending the time to ensure these items remain top of mind. In the end, you'll want to deploy the right systems (x86, OpenPOWER, IBM Z, LinuxONE—you choose) and cloud (AWS, Azure, Google Cloud, IBM—you choose) to specifically meet your business needs, not what the vendor is profiting from.

Cloud Solely for Savings Could Leave You with Cravings: A Trend of Repatriation

We alluded to this earlier, but we think it warrants some more musings. Today, there's a huge swath of companies who raced to the cloud while seeking cost savings–only to find themselves *still* hunting for savings. Just like when organizations went all-in on Hadoop, using cloud as a destination isn't always the right answer either. This is exactly why cloud should be thought of as a capability (and not as a destination): be it on-premises, public, or on the edge. We'll say it in a more direct way: *not all applications are suited for public cloud, but almost all applications benefit by being cloud enabled.*

Think back to that autonomous car we talked about in the book's Introduction. The term "path planning" is used by autonomous auto practitioners to describe how the self-driving car navigates (the actions it takes) on the road. Are you comfortable with high data latency to inference ratios? This refers to the time it takes to process camera, radar, and lidar data, send it up to the cloud, and receive a path planning instruction that says "Stop! There's a person in front of you." The bottom line: the cloud destination can hurt latency.

Let's illustrate this with a simple example around Manufacturing 4.0 assembly lines. Manufacturing 4.0 is named to represent what many call the fourth industrial revolution—it's the infusion of modern smart technology into traditional manufacturing and industrial practices for a better assembly line from a resiliency, quality, efficiency, and cost perspective. In automobile assembly lines, if a door assembly defect gets to the end of the line, the entire car has to be pulled off the line and reworked manually. In some cases, that means shipping the car to another facility. Fun fact: a car is manufactured every 30 to 60 seconds; this means that quality issue magnifies into huge money losses very quickly! But what about a smaller business? Material waste comes with a significant cost too (one small fabrication company we worked with loses ~$30,000 per month in ruined metals because of unrecoverable errors in production, such as a bad weld that results in a "blow through").

Let's assume you work in such a company, but your company is pretty forward thinking. You've got some snazzy on-the-line convolutional neural networks (CNNs—this is the class of AI algorithms well known for their computer vision properties), looking for defects in real time. You've been asked to cut costs and cloud (the destination kind) is how you're told to do it. Your team performs their due diligence and meets with five CSPs recommended by your favorite analyst and issues a request for proposal (RFP) to each of them to help your organization save some money and get some workloads to "the cloud."

Time passes—you look back at your accomplishments in the last year. You're on the cloud and you discover the ROI isn't quite what you expected. But heck, you're on the cloud, right? Don't worry: if this story sounds familiar to you or your business, you're not alone (you're going to hear why in a moment).

Just like Hadoop was not a one-size-fits-all answer to analytics in its heyday (which ultimately faded precisely because it was marketed as such, and that approach is why many associated projects failed to meet expectations), public cloud is not a one-size-fits-all answer either. Certain application and data gravity characteristics will help you decide where the destination goes; you focus on the application. That's why cloud the capability matters so much, and it's why a hybrid cloud strategy is so important. If you want to quickly spin up a monster GPU server to train those algorithms and converge an experimental model quickly, public cloud will very likely be a great answer (among other examples). But if you ran a small four-GPU server on the cloud for a year, nonstop, it'd cost you almost $100K, whereas you could likely buy one for $20K (or less, by the time you read this book).

One manufacturer we know implemented a computer vision solution that took tens of thousands of pictures a day, nonstop, and inferenced (this is AI fancy talk for scoring the algorithm—in this case analyzing the pictures) them to quickly identify quality escapes (defects). Public cloud? Likely not. In this scenario, it didn't matter what public cloud option we looked at (Azure, AWS, or IBM) to support this scenario, those computer vision charges were based on usage (number of pictures looked at) and this led to drastically (that's polite for crazy) more expensive public cloud solutions.

Our pro tip: always remember that public cloud pricing is utility pricing—the meter is running, just like how you're billed for electricity in your home (and that can be a good or a bad thing as illustrated earlier). Running a nonstop application, or even a developer forgetting to shut down their test instances (one of us, whose name isn't Chris, did that and cost his department $5,000), is like walking around your empty house with all the lights on and wondering aloud about all the money you could be saving. (If you have kids, this is a well-known feeling to you.)

 Enhanced data security is another example that has some rethinking a cloud destination definition versus capability. We won't delve into those details here (loss of data control, who can access your encryption keys, governance and regulations are all at play here), but suffice to say that whether you've experienced a loss of control over your data, unexpected costs, or even high latency in application response times (data gravity is at play here), you're not alone. The takeaway? Again, not all workloads are appropriate for a public cloud destination, but almost all apps are better served to be built as cloud (the capability) applications. This is why our personal experiences with clients have many asking us about hybrid clouds and the reevaluation of their decisions to blindly move all workloads with a one-strategy-fits-all approach to a CSP.

The IBM Institute for Business Value conducted an independent study with 1,100 executive interviews (across 10 countries and 18 industries) and found that nearly 51% of the respondents had plans to move at least some migrated workloads back from a public cloud service to on-premises, citing higher than expected costs and lack of data security as the primary drivers, as shown in Figure 2-2.

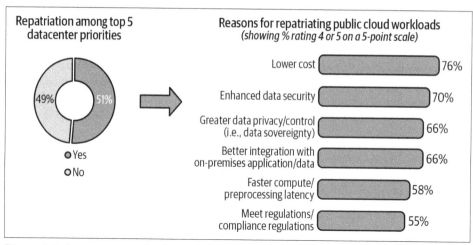

Figure 2-2. Lower costs and enhanced security are the top motivations for repatriating off-premises workloads to on-premises environments

Make sure you understand what we're saying here. We are not advocating that any client should scrap their "public cloud first" strategies. In fact, it's the opposite. Many that joined the pilgrimage to cloud are now drawing from their experiences and incorporating this knowledge into a newly defined "capability cloud first" strategy (what we call "Cloud Chapter 2"—an epoch of cloud computing, as opposed to a book chapter)—one with a broader aperture and appreciation for the capability aspects of the technology not solely focused on destination.

"Cloud Chapter 2" offers organizations a much more refined, well-rounded, and effective cloud strategy that can be used to please renovators and innovators alike! It's a blend of multicloud (vendors), hybrid cloud (location), and even has some work-loads running on the edge! This may sound like a painful and costly retreat from what seemed at first to be a well-thought-out plan and in many instances, it very well could have been; at the same time, things are changing so fast. Remember what we said earlier: the world often overhypes the impact of new technologies in the first couple of years, but the danger follows from downplaying its impact over the years to come. Cloud will change the way businesses operate in the same way that AI will— and it's why you're reading this book.

But take a moment and think about the opportunity that "Cloud Chapter 2" has to offer. Unprecedented flexibility in choice of infrastructure, agility, continuous integra-tion and continuous delivery (some call the second "d" deployment—technically they are different things, but we'll assume them to be the same to keep things simple and just refer to it as CI/CD), cost savings, and more.

Are you one of those more forward-thinking organizations that invested precious resources (time, money, and effort) into building cloud native applications as opposed to the lift-and-shift approach that often shortchanges the full realization of cloud's value? Your applications were refactored, containerized, and virtualized. Now you have to repatriate them for one reason or another (data gravity and performance, costs, governance, data control, and so on). Fear not, all is not lost. Not at all. There are opportunities here with a hybrid cloud strategy, starting with consolidation and extending all the way to more data security and control.

Before you talk to any vendor, evaluate your business and IT objectives, current and future plans, and data governance requirements. Ask: "What does the future look like for us?" Perhaps your business is just starting its AI journey? Are you trodding on an analytics path and pushing it to the edge in order to optimize your cold-chain custody transportation costs? Will you be using blockchain to evolve your food supply chain, from traceability (where the livestock came from) to transparency (where it came from, how it was transported, the record of the slaughterhouse that processed the meat, what the livestock was fed, who provided the feed, and so on). You know where you are now, but where are you trying to get to? As hard as it may be, try to anticipate how these ambitions may change over time and how cloud (the capability) can help.

By way of example: there's no denying that data privacy is increasingly front of mind for every business and consumer, and more so with each passing year. If your organization handles data that's considered to be personally identifiable information (or its subset, sensitive personally identifiable information), place your bets now that things are going to get more stringent, penalties are going to go up, and there will be less and less tolerance in the marketplace for accidental disclosures. Even if you're an organization that doesn't have any kind of sensitive information, you've got intellectual property that you want to preserve. This is just one of many considerations that need to be made when creating a winning cloud strategy—failure to do so will inevitably result in sunk costs, fines, penalties, or worse.

Be Ye a Renovator, Innovator, or Both? How You Spend Budget

There are certain ways to think about the initiatives your company is journeying on, projects you own, and even the ones you're trying to sell or gain sponsorship for. In this section we want to share with you a ubiquitous framework we've developed that simplifies even the most complex of enterprises' strategic transformation plans.

When it comes to budget planning, we recommend giving your projects one giant KISS! (Keep It Simple Silly—there's another version of this acronym floating around). Every client we talk to is doing one of two things: spending money to save money or spending money to make money. When you spend it (money) to save it, you're renovating and when you spend it to make it, you're innovating. The best strategies will do both and leverage cost savings from renovating the IT landscape (spending money to save it) to partially fund the innovation (spending money to make it).

To illustrate this model, we'll use something we call an Acumen Curve. You'll find this simple framework handy for any strategic investment decisions your company is facing across almost any domain. For example, we developed a Data Acumen Curve (Figure 2-3) and use it to help clients put their data to work (after all, data is like a gym membership; if you don't use it, you'll get nothing but a recurring bill out of it). For one client, we created different categories for their project (for both renovation and innovation) and a plotted value curve on the expected outcomes if successful projects are aligned to business needs (that's a key thing).

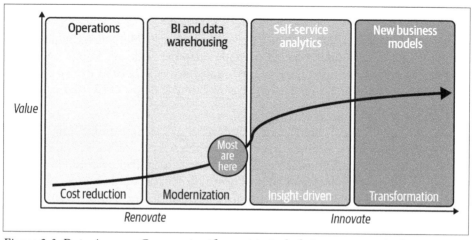

Figure 2-3. Data Acumen Curve: a terrific asset to include in any strategic planning project

You can see in Figure 2-3 the emergence of a natural border (it should be a friendly one) between renovating and innovating. This is important to understand because you should be able to derive downstream benefits of a renovation project. This will be even more profound in a Cloud Acumen Curve (which we'll introduce next). There are some key takeaways here—and the similarities across any Acumen Curve will be uncanny:

Strategies focused solely on cost reduction deliver shortchanged value
> Today's technology is about efficiency, automation, optimization, and more. If you're focused only on cutting costs, the value returned won't be enormous. Don't get us wrong, smart cost cutting is a terrific strategy and you can forward the money saved toward more renovation and compound that value into innovation, but that is not the end game (despite so many being forced to play it as if it was). Governance is a great example. Most organizations scurry to implement regulatory compliance with the *least possible work to comply approach*—mainly,

avoidance of fines (cost savings). However, this approach shortchanges the value of such a project because it misses the opportunity to create regulatory dividends from those compliance investments (data lineage, for example) to accelerate your analytics strategy. Some of us have been around analytics and AI for a long time and we can assure you, almost every governance project shortchanges its real value to the business.

Most haven't bent the curve for maximum value

When you stop and take stock of where your organization truly is on an Acumen Curve, most will wake up and think "Wow, we have a long way to go!" We doubt few of the businesses that turned into divers, or had to contend with new arrivers, had any idea how truly broken their digital strategy was until COVID and disruption hit. That's the point of these curves; you need to know ahead of time, not after the fact.

Real value comes in the innovation phase

You can't be a new arriver or thriver if all you're doing is spending money to save or make it and not also reimagining the way you work. Take, for example, an AI project on our Data Acumen Curve (which we would place on the far-right quadrant in Figure 2-3). Do you layer AI on top of existing processes or rethink them from the ground up and redesign the workflow? Whether you are on a Data Acumen Curve or a Cloud Acumen Curve, most organizations today are unwilling to do the deep rethinking of their business models and workflows that will allow them to fully embrace the opportunities presented to them by an innovation investment. Be forewarned, you'll miss out on the full gamut of potential benefits if your definition of the finish line is putting all your transformative innovations on top of existing business models and workflows. You should be thinking and planning how these models and workflows could (or should) change because of your AI and cloud innovations. We can't stress enough how important this is. As you build your Acumen Curves, reimagine your business processes from the ground up with your new capabilities—we guarantee you that the impact will be greater for having done so.

We created a Cloud Acumen Curve (Figure 2-4) to help you get started. As you read this book, build your own and populate it with projects, expected outcomes, newfound superpowers your cloud journey will bring to the organization, and more.

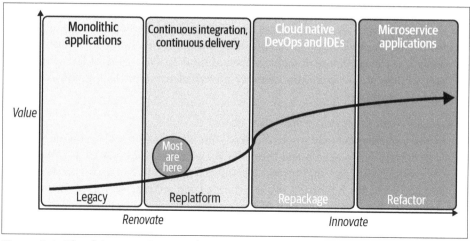

Figure 2-4. Cloud Acumen Curve: a framework for plotting value from the monoliths to microservices

You can see on this curve that the quadrants are different (don't worry if you don't fully understand the legacy, replatform, repackage, and refactor terms yet—we cover those in Chapter 5). Monolithic (legacy) apps refer to those applications where the entire application (from the interface to the inner workings) are combined into a single program that runs in one place. Uber's app, on the other hand, is the opposite of a monolithic application: it is made up of perhaps dozens if not hundreds of microservices that have very discrete jobs—one for currency conversion, another for wait time estimates, another to calculate time to distance, others to suggest local Uber Eats partners and discounts at the final destination, and more. If Uber's app wasn't on the far right of Figure 2-4, they couldn't roll out the near weekly updates we get on our mobile phones telling us about all the things they are doing to make our experience better.

 OK, we admit it. We share a guilty pleasure reading release notes from vendors whose personalities shine through in their update release notes (like Slack or Medium, among others). One of our favorites yet was Slack's "We no longer show you in your own Quick Switcher results; if you want to talk to yourself, that's fine, but you don't need us for that."

It's important to remember that some apps should stay the way they are because you have "bigger fish to fry"; your business may be looking for quick wins rather than long-haul (albeit worthwhile) projects, while some apps are too critical to the business to entertain the expense or risk of changing just yet.

This naturally brings us to the middle phases on your journey to derive the most value you can from the cloud. This is where functions (like archive, Q/A, test), or greenfield applications have been replatformed to the cloud, and that's the beginning of value drivers such as CI/CD. Of course, going back to the far-right of Figure 2-4, it's enough to say that embracing a cloud native microservices approach will allow you to capitalize on the scalability and flexibility inherent to the cloud.

Mission-critical apps can replatform to the cloud, too. For example, we've seen businesses with critical functions (running on-premises on AIX and IBM i servers) become modernized and reap public cloud benefits such as pay-as-you-go billing, self-service provisioning, and flexible management, *without having to change the code!* This approach helps you grow at your own pace and start a cloud journey without heavy up-front costs, allows your workloads to run when and where you want, and more.

The takeaway? As you move farther and farther to the right of your Acumen Curve (allowing digital properties to sit where they make sense) you gain more and more cloud acumen, which delivers more and more value to your business. In Chapter 5 we'll give you a scorecard you can apply to your Cloud Acumen Curve and see what phases unlock capabilities like agile delivery, tech debt relief, cloud operational models, and more.

There's a final consideration we want to explicitly note here: how partnerships matter. Earlier in this chapter we talked about the kinds of things you want to look for from your cloud partners (you will have more than one, we can almost guarantee that). But what we didn't articulate was the importance of a strategy. As you build out your cloud strategy, it is critical that it be open and portable: being able to build on one cloud property and move it to another either because of specific compute needs (resiliency, GPUs, quantum, and so on), vendor disagreement, or just having that option to negotiate better terms and pricing—flexibility is key! Quite simply, the assets you create should be able to be deployed anywhere across your landscape to fully realize the benefits of your hard work. We think by the time you're done reading this book you'll have great cloud acumen as a business leader and a framework to plan your journey, and also know what to look for, how to build teams, and the benefits you will come to realize from your efforts. If we've been successful in persuading you, we think you'll end up with a Cloud Acumen Curve similar to what you see in Figure 2-5.

Compare the curve in Figure 2-5 to all the other curves you've seen in this chapter. It bends drastically in the renovation phase because you have a plan. Your organization creates downstream dividends from that plan and the work done in renovation drives innovation. We can't stress enough how useful this model has been with the clients to whom we've been successful in delivering value. These acumen curves are how we get projects and conversations going, and how we hold each other accountable.

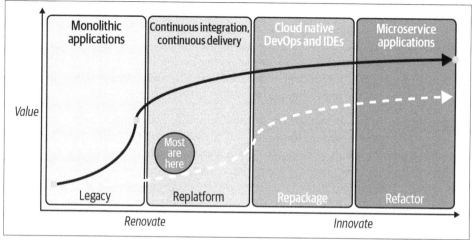

Figure 2-5. The kind of Cloud Acumen Curve you can build with the right strategy, requirements list, and partnerships

Adopting a "Learning Never Ends" Culture: A Cloud Success Secret Ingredient

What would you say if we told you that by exercising religiously for the next year, every day, you'd be fit for the rest of your life? You'd answer, "Ridiculous!" ([ri-dik-yuh-luhs]—causing or worthy or ridicule, preposterous, laughable). While the focus of this book is about redefining and expanding the aperture of the term "cloud," arming you with questions to ask as you deploy your cloud strategies, and presenting you with architectures, gotchas, ideas, and points of views you perhaps never considered before, we'd be remiss if we didn't share this secret success ingredient for organizations, their teams, and you as individuals. *Learning never ends.*

We could be writing a book about AI, cloud, or anything—those tech years like dog years we mentioned back in Chapter 1 feeds off a "learning never ends" culture. This is especially true in the cloud space because there's so much open source technology at play whose names and versions are nothing short of dizzying. As world renowned golf instructor Steve Rodriguez of GOLFTEC says, "This is a skill you will forever be learning; don't strive for perfect, just better." Practice and focus breeds success in both.

The teams you lead (and you as leaders) have to instill a culture of learning to exploit all you can from cloud computing. That isn't to say you rush in and jump on any new version or new technology, but capabilities and directional shifts are forever changing, and your goal can't be to find out about them later. Perhaps these emerging technologies aren't for your group...no problem. Or perhaps you want them pretested and "signed-off" (such as an enterprise-tested, hardened, and expanded Kubernetes platform like Red Hat OpenShift Container Platform). Keeping abreast of those compacted tech years is essential for organizations and personal careers.

As your leadership teams and employees build their cloud acumen skills, ensure they teach others along the way. Be it AI acumen, cloud acumen, blockchain acumen, or whatever—transformational shifts happen with culture changes at the top and knowledge becomes a thirst. It's a great way to get everyone in the same mindset and expand the understanding of any undertaking. Cloud will create a mindset of "We can." It will have developers thinking that continuous delivery is possible, that value can be added at almost any time to a subscription service; marketing will go into micro-campaigns focused on sprints; product designers are free to wildly create and deliver tiny features that can vastly change the client experience or reduce friction (and back out of those changes if the result misses the mark—A/B testing); and so much more.

How critical is learning for even the best employees, let alone your organization? Ever see the movie *A Star Is Born* (2018)? Music sensation Lady Gaga (the star that is born in the movie) and one of Hollywood's top box-office draws, Bradley Cooper (a rugged worn-down boozing successful singer in the movie), are headliners in a story of love, success, and sadness. We won't Siskel and Ebert the movie for you because the title kind of suggests the outcome, but we did learn something about this movie that so perfectly hits home the point we're trying to make in this section. Consider this fun fact: Bradley Cooper played and sang everything live (no auto-tuning, no lip synching)—a demand made by Lady Gaga herself. Cooper worked with a voice coach to lower his speaking voice, spent over eighteen months on vocal lessons, six months on guitar lessons, and another six months on piano lessons, all to prepare for his role in the movie. All in all, it took Bradley Cooper years to fully prepare for his part (in a remake, at that) and just 42 days to film it all.

We think this Cooper story speaks volumes. If one of Hollywood's most sought-after actors spends years building skills for 42 days of work, how important do you think preparation and learning is in the IT domain for your cloud organization?

Ready, Set, Cloud!

In this chapter we wanted to cast a different way of thinking and encourage you to challenge assumptions about your own notions of cloud, the vendors trying to sell you something, and the organizations you work for.

We talked about how 80% of cloud value is locked away (for those treating cloud as a destination) and the potential for 2.5x return on your cloud investments when you treat it as a capability (hybrid cloud). So how do you unlock the 80%? We recommend you tie business initiatives to the areas we discussed (some implicitly and some explicitly) so that you have supreme clarity over cloud capabilities and can articulate how your renovation or innovation strategies will deliver value for your business, namely:

- Business acceleration
- Developer productivity
- Infrastructure cost efficiency
- Regulatory compliance, security, and risk
- Strategic optionality (the freedom to keep options open as much as possible while achieving your goals)

Thomas Edison once remarked, "Vision without execution is hallucination." We think that sets the tone for our business practitioners' book perfectly as we journey into more of the details. We want to give you tools, knowledge, ideas, and considerations that are going to help you execute on the cloud vision we outlined in this chapter.

CHAPTER 3

"Cloud Chapter 2": The Path to Cloud Native

Throughout this book we talk about all the value that awaits organizations that put their cloud capabilities to work inside a hybrid cloud architecture, and the "cheated" value return (or disappointment) for most enterprise cloud projects today. We insinuated a new chapter of cloud computing was here (the 2.0 moniker is tiring): "Cloud Chapter 2" (notice the quotes...we're not talking about a chapter in the book). "Cloud Chapter 2" is all about cloud as a capability, and underpinning those capabilities are a bunch of Star Trek–sounding open source projects and a very large ecosystem. Kubernetes (and the enterprise hardened and tailored Red Hat OpenShift Container Platform version of it), Ansible, and Docker are the main ones. But like any great Emmy award winning movie, there is a large (and we mean very large) supporting cast of technology that can be leveraged (with just as interesting names—Fluentd, Grafana, Jenkins, Istio, Tekton, and oh so many more).

At times we struggled writing this book because we really wanted to keep its focus on the business user. Make no mistake about it, the Kubernetes ecosystem (and the software itself) can be very confusing because it's so capable—but it is both a strength and a potential weakness. Business users are sure to get lost in the never-ending layers and components that allow you to expose this service to your broader technology stack, or the multiple ways in which to manage a deployment. Not to mention that Kubernetes is very CLI (command-line interface) oriented—another hurdle for the less programmer-minded of us to overcome. What's more, there are loads of resources that detail how Kubernetes works (free and paid for) by people that can do just as good (or better) of a job than we can in describing it to you. We're big fans of what Leon Katsnelson and his team are doing at CognitiveClass.ai (*https://oreil.ly/lBKX5*) with their Kubernetes education.

In this chapter we'll talk about some concepts and technologies that we build on throughout this book. We purposely wrote this chapter so you could get a feel for the path to cloud-native where applications leverage all the capability of the cloud. We don't talk about all the technologies in this chapter—in fact, we left out quite a few. That was on purpose. However, we wrote *Appendix: Speaking Kubernetes and Other Strange-Sounding Names* to teach you how to speak Kubernetes (and some other technologies in its ecosystem) for that purpose, so feel free to jump to it at any time to get some details on many of the technologies that are part of the Cloud "Chapter 2" renaissance.

Eras of Application Development

Throughout this book we talk about application modernization hand-in-hand with cloud capabilities. As you're now aware, the reason why so many organizations can't capture the full value of the cloud is because they have significant investments in existing applications that have been the backbone of their companies for years. Typically, these applications are siloed, difficult to connect to other systems, and expensive to update and maintain, and thus they often get tagged with the word *legacy*.

A quick note here for our readers—perception and reality are not always the same. In the context of what many refer to as legacy applications or systems, we've seen many vendors (including IBM) who have done a lot over the last two decades to modernize both the software and the hardware systems, making them fully cloud native (or at least give the ability to front their legacy applications as cloud native). This means you don't have to "rip and replace" all legacy systems or processes when your point of view is cloud as a capability. You end up with opportunities to modernize that you may not have considered before. Got a COBOL copybook running on IBM Z? Grab an integration services platform (we'd like to recommend one of the containerized flavors) and wrap it up with REST API—that makes it callable like any other modern cloud native service. Developers that want to invoke that COBOL copybook (perhaps to pull from its output) simply call the API with the input parameters it expects and that returns the data to the app—they don't even know it's a COBOL copybook (what some would call legacy) piece of code. That's the whole point!

That said, the word *legacy* describes a style in which these apps were built (and used) and thus application modernization seeks to take applications through a series of transformations that make them *truly* cloud native; this allows them to accrue all the benefits of cloud (the capability), and of course you can decide where to run them (the destination). When you think about cloud as a destination, these systems can operate just like "clouds" with front-ended APIs. In fact, this is the preferred architecture for many mission-critical and data-sensitive workloads (hence the title of the book, *Cloud without Compromise*), a true hybrid cloud approach.

To keep it simple, we consider a modernized app one that is easily updated, connects seamlessly with other apps, is easy to scale, and is built for the cloud (the capability). Think back to those thrivers, divers, and new arrivers we talked about in Chapter 1—the very experiences we detailed there showcase who's running in a legacy mindset and who's running modernized (even if they have some legacy applications they depend on).

When we work with clients, we like to get a quick feel for just where they are on their cloud journey. It would be easy for us to ask to look at their cloud contracts or see what SaaS properties they are subscribed to. But that's not what we do—we go right to the app dev teams and classify their application-building approach (the Acumen Curves we talked about in Chapter 2 would serve as a tremendous harness for this conversation) as *monoliths*, *service-oriented architectures (SOAs)*, or *microservices*. These classifications don't just represent how apps are built, but how they interact and leverage the infrastructure where they run (which has everything to do with being *cloud native*—the industry term you will often hear when describing apps that are built for the cloud). Here's the promise: if you want to automate, if you want to be agile, if you want to modernize, if you want true DevSecOps, if you want to write once and deploy anywhere, if you want all the capabilities that cloud brings and the freedom to choose the destination, you need to understand how architecture, infrastructure, and the way apps are built and delivered have evolved over time—not to mention what they are (a collection of services)—and that's the primer we cover in this chapter.

In the Beginning: Monoliths and Waterfalls

Past civilizations used to mark their territories using a single enormously large block of stone (or metal) called a *monolith*. To IT people, a monolithic app (an application architecture approach) is used to describe a software app where all aspects of the app (user interface, data access code, and so on) are combined and compiled as one giant program and run in one place. If you recall, we've talked about how cloud native applications are *composed* of discrete blocks of logic (microservices)—this is the opposite.

If we think back to early in our careers in the dev labs, this is how apps were built (and many enterprise legacy apps are still built this way today). These apps ran on physical servers and used a *waterfall* development approach (each phase of a project must complete before the next phase—you'll often hear the *traditional* synonym used for this approach to development).

> ## Agile
>
> The basics of the "waterfall" software development pattern is to break down a project (developing an app) into linear sequential activities, where *each phase depends on the deliverables of the previous one*. Even by its very definition, it sounds like the antithesis of agile.
>
> We do want to point out that not everything about the waterfall development pattern is bad. We find it hard to keep up on what's going on in the agile world because the application stack is always changing. For example, when we worked on waterfall development teams, we'd have a very detailed function specification document (the new features) that showed us everything from how the code works, to how it was exposed in the CLI, and more. In agile, things often aren't as well documented and new features take us by surprise all the time. If you've ever Googled how to do something on your iOS device, you'll know what we mean: the recommended steps or screenshots are always out of date and rarely line up with the tasks you have to perform. That said, we find the agile approach to be (most of the time, but not all the time) the approach that generally yields the best results for business.

If monolithic is the application architecture, the delivery is typically waterfall and the infrastructure are typically physical servers sitting on-premises and managed by you —likely overprovisioned, underutilized, inefficient, and buried in red tape. Unless, of course, you start applying the premise of this book and turning those servers into a cloud capability! You know you're managing a monolithic project if your app project plan has distinct phases (like "Test"), and you deliver updates at well-defined and year (or multiple years) gap intervals. If you got a design wrong, you can't go back to the current release. On and on it goes.

SOA Is the SOS to Your Monolith

Despite popular belief that it stands for "Save Our Souls," SOS is actually a Morse code distress signal that isn't an abbreviation for anything. The popularized definition was simply retrofitted to suit the existing code—ironically, this is the opposite of what those that build monolithic apps have to deal with, these souls need the ability to change the base without great cost. Service-oriented architecture (SOA) was a big buzzword a number of years ago and looking back, it's evident SOA was an architectural epoch on the way to microservices (which are more cloud native).

SOA is a development style and the start of the era of application composition (versus building). It's a discrete unit of functionality that is updated independently of other services. For example, a service might pull a client record and use more pronoun-sensitive phraseology on an AI-generated summary. SOA objects are self-contained and you don't need to know how they work inside, only how to invoke them and how to handle the message that comes back (likely data in the JSON format). SOA objects might just do one thing (like in our example), or they could pipeline a number of tasks to do many things. SOA is typically deployed in distributed architectures. You might imagine an application using a number of web services, all talking to each other or resources like a database.

We feel SOAs were unsung heroes in the push to virtual machines (VMs) because they really showcased how inefficient it would be to order a new server to host a new service. Put simply, more flexibility means more utilization. SOA is also where agile takes hold, because this is where applications with coupled services are stitched together to make a full-fledged service where it's easy to iterate for feature enhancements and so on. SOA was a path to cloud native, but things had to get smaller—micro-small.

Microservices: What SOA Would Be If It Was Version 2.0

The *microservices* architecture is an iteration over SOA that more loosely couples (it's distributed in nature) services for application development. Microservices is a great name because the function unit (the service) gets more granular and more focused (it does one thing—it's micro) when compared to SOA. The protocols that support the communications and invocation of services gets more lightweight in the microservices architecture compared to SOA as well. While it's outside the scope of this book to detail SOA plumbing, it relied on heavyweight XML communications; microservices use a more lightweight API-focused architecture.

Just remember: microservices get more fine-grained in terms of function (they shrink the size of the service when compared to SOA) and their protocols (the way they operate and communicate) get more lightweight too. With microservices, you also run in a cloud native environment that delivers even more granular and dynamic infrastructure runtimes than traditional VMs.

You can see a good way to scorecard the "modernness" of your applications (Architecture, Infrastructure, and Delivery) in Figure 3-1. As you look at each epoch (each row for each modernization characteristic), you can't help but notice that as you move down each pillar, the result is ever-more agility, independence of function (which means easy to update on the fly), more elasticity and capacity control (cloud), a better DevSecOps delivery mechanism (we talk about the Sec(urity) in DevSecOps in Chapter 6), and faster time to value.

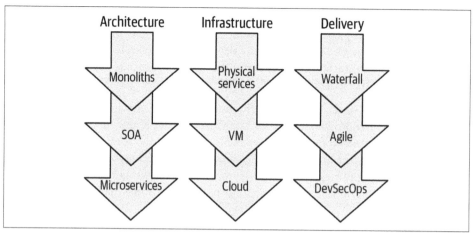

Figure 3-1. The epochs of application modernization: further down in each pillar is more modernized and cloud native

If we think about the conversations we're having with clients today, there is always someone saying they are doing a DevOps transformation; someone else is doing a cloud transformation; and yet another group is talking about microservices. If you're new to all of this and listening in, you might very well conclude that there are three separate transformations going on here—and that's "true"—*for those clients that are spinning their wheels.* If success is your navigational heading, you *need* transformation across three key areas (architecture, infrastructure, and delivery) under a single culture and mantra that permeates throughout the entire organization. If you build a new microservice, you're going to need some place to host and run that service (unless you're doing function as a service, which we talk about in Chapter 4). Your microservice's runtime must be resilient and dynamically scalable (you may need a lot of these small things, or hardly any at all)—this is all screaming for cloud the capability (which is a big change from SOA). Map these characteristics back to the monolithic architecture. How did you scale distributed or nondistributed monolithic apps on your server? You'd get a new server (scaled up) or rebuild your app to scale out.

The theme in modern application development is *speed*. Speed of scale, speed of delivery, and so on. The very nature of speed is the DevSecOps delivery nuance—bringing together the speed developers love (they think project to project), and the resiliency and assuredness that operations seek (they think about things like service level agreements, upgrades, patching, and security). By and large, the transitions outlined in Figure 3-1 are getting away from a yearly delivery project plan and moving you toward continuous delivery instead.

First "Pass" on PaaS

To truly appreciate the rise of containers (which we talk about in the next section), we wanted to ensure you had at least a brief understanding of first-generation platform as a service (PaaS) capabilities. So let's get started with the world's first foray into PaaS.

In the pursuit of speed—faster development, more agile delivery, and unimpeded elasticity—is it possible to go too far? Absolutely. That's exactly what happened during the tumultuous state of the cloud near the start of the last decade. Cloud service providers (CSPs) were shaping the cloud landscape, going beyond IaaS and iterating on the first generation of PaaS capabilities.

As businesses finally began to take advantage of the elasticity of cloud and IaaS to run their SOA-based applications on VMs, the industry began to reinvent itself yet again. This is par for the course in the world of IT—after all, change is the only thing that remains constant in this world. You either evolve or fall behind.

As your attention moves down each modernized app characteristic in Figure 3-1, you're likely to notice a pattern—the movement from physical services, to VMs, to the cloud also results in a change of responsibilities more and more away from your control. Clients eager to move from traditional IT and on-premises datacenters began to embrace IaaS. They rejoiced in the seemingly unlimited elasticity of the cloud, while adopting a flexible mode of consumption allowing them to pay for only what they use. Clients with existing applications were willing to relinquish complete control and autonomy of their infrastructure for these advantages. In addition, this paved the way for those new arrivers to run production-grade applications with a significantly reduced barrier of entry.

Naturally, CSPs continued to apply this same philosophy as consumers continued to embrace the cloud (the destination). CSPs began to offer the first generation of PaaS capabilities like Heroku, IBM Bluemix (now IBM Cloud Foundry Public), Google App Engine, and AWS Elastic Beanstalk. We (the customers) were all told to focus on what really matters—writing code—and let their cloud handle the rest. This meant moving further up the traditional IT stack and handing off control of our runtimes, middleware, and operating systems.

At first, these capabilities appeared to work like magic. You could simply write your application code in any of the many supported languages (like Node.js, Java, Swift, Python, Golang, or basically any language you could think of), then simply upload your code to the PaaS and have a running application on the web in a matter of minutes.

However, this technology came at a cost—the first generation of these PaaS solutions presented an opinionated (specific decisions and requirements made on the platform that will host your app) approach to IT. At least with IaaS, businesses were able to utilize VMs and ensure that their applications continued to run with little change required to the actual code. This was *not* the case with first generation PaaS. As much as companies may have wanted to, they couldn't simply "lift-and-shift" their apps to these new PaaS capabilities like they had done with IaaS. In retrospect, there were three major factors preventing widespread adoption of these initial PaaS capabilities:

1. It required significant refactoring (developer talk for having to rewrite portions of an app to accommodate service and configuration parameters) of existing applications to adopt. Moving from monoliths to SOA was arguably a cakewalk when compared to the eventual transition to microservices. In 2011, Adam Wiggins (cofounder of Heroku) published the Twelve-Factor App (12factor.net). This document outlined a methodology to build modern, scalable, maintainable applications on a PaaS platform—essentially, microservices. To this day, these twelve factors continue to embody the best practices for building modern applications. However, for most companies in 2011, the Twelve-Factor App may as well have been written in an alien language—it was well ahead of its time.

2. PaaS platforms were so opinionated that an application running on one PaaS couldn't be easily migrated to another. For example, consider what it was like to add a database service to Heroku versus Cloud Foundry (CF)—Heroku utilizes individual environment variables (`config vars`), whereas Cloud Foundry uses a single environment variable (`VCAP_SERVICES`) in JSON format with all variables together. This meant that in order to migrate an application from Heroku to CF, you'd have to refactor the application itself, *even when using the exact same database service in both environments*! This leads to a terrible thing in the world of cloud—*vendor lock-in*. Clients who were burned in the early ages of cloud computing were not thrilled about the prospect of yet another technology that forced them to stay with a single CSP.

3. First-generation PaaS platforms were asking for too much control and gave too many "not up for discussion" demands that made clients uncomfortable with relinquishing this much control over to the cloud. Companies were unwilling to adopt the public cloud model that PaaS required—this meant being forced to run on multitenant infrastructure on public cloud datacenters. Essentially, you had to drink the CSP-flavored Kool-Aid. In addition, clients began to find that the CSP-recommended approach (but it wasn't really recommended at all...it was required) on things like service discovery, dependency management, security, and more didn't always align with their requirements. In an opinionated PaaS, there was no room for change—you had to adopt the CSP's approach.

Across all industries, the first generation of PaaS capabilities unfortunately led organizations to view the cloud as a lofty public cloud destination instead of as a powerful capability.

Lessons Learned: The Rise of Containers

In the early half of the last decade, it became increasingly clear that businesses were not adopting PaaS in the same way that they had with IaaS. CSPs learned some key lessons from this first generation of PaaS capabilities: avoid vendor lock-in at all costs, allow businesses to maintain a reasonable level of control over their stack, and do all this while giving developers the tools to maintain world-class agile DevOps practices.

It might surprise many to know (because of all the buzz around it) that containerization is *not* a new technology; it's been around since the early 2000s but rose to greater prominence in 2013 with the release of Docker—and hasn't stopped growing since. To understand why containers are so prominent today, we'll start with the most apparent advantage—*containers introduced an era of standardization that developers tend to take for granted today.*

In 1937 the shipping container was invented by Malcom McLean—it had the effect of dropping shipping costs by 90% with this new standardized container. Just as the shipping industry was revolutionized by the use of containers, so too are the containers we're talking about changing the software industry. Containers provide a standard way of packaging software, so it runs under a standard Linux-based operating system. The container package includes just the essential libraries, data, and configuration needed to run your app (containers are the minimalists of the IT society—more on that in a bit). A container just needs to be started with a standard command; it doesn't require a complex set of commands, to say nothing of tracing back and installing a complex tree of dependencies. Containers enable automation and eliminate countless possibilities for making mistakes.

Looking back at the shipping industry, it's easy to see the analogies. Loading a ship with 1,000 bushels of wheat, 750 casks of nails, 1,200 barrels of molasses, 150 sewing machines, and so on was a recipe for trouble. In the 1800s and early 1900s, each item had to be loaded by hand, packed carefully, and if something came loose during a storm, there was big trouble. Containers solved that problem: they come in standard sizes, they can be manipulated in standard ways, and they can be moved from ships to trucks, trains, or other vehicles without problems using a consistent set of tools (as opposed to all kinds of packages stuffed in a cargo net). That's exactly what we want for software: we want standard commands to start or stop it with no complex incantations (a series of words said as a magic spell or charm—think Harry Potter); we want it to run on any kind of server without customization, and we want them all to look alike. Nobody should care whether a container contains a web server, a web application, middleware, or a database. Nobody should have to remember a paragraph-long command syntax that reads like geek haiku to get a service running—that command, with all its glorious options and parameters, should be embedded in the container. All that's important is that the container can run.

But Wait, Don't VMs Do the Same Thing!?

A discerning reader might have created parallels between the advantages of containers and using VMs. VMs can also package up all the dependencies of an application and these incantations to get them started, and standardize workloads no matter the size. But there's a catch! VMs require that you also package a "Guest Operating System (OS)," *which is redundant for containers* as they can utilize the underlying "Host OS." Therein lies the genius of containers, *allowing developers to create standardized packages of applications that are incredibly lightweight in comparison to their hefty VM counterparts.* Let's use Figure 3-2 to review this point.

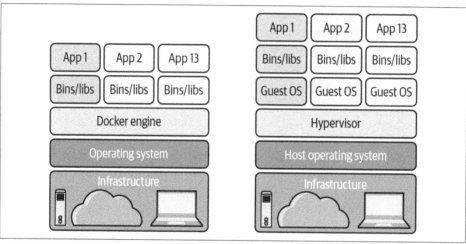

Figure 3-2. A comparison between packaging up an application using Docker (on the left) or a VM (on the right)

Imagine a team collaborating on developing a microservice where each team member develops, tests, and runs on a different operating system—Windows, macOS and Linux. Before containers, one potential approach to prevent unexpected differences from affecting the execution of the application would be to utilize VMs (the right side of Figure 3-2). This architecture has an unfortunate byproduct—it instantly kills developer productivity. Collaborating on code changes in a service when they need to be built into a VM each and every time is incredibly slow. Due to this, VMs were typically used by operations teams to run applications in production, rather than as a tool that developers used to collaborate on projects.

Containers solve this problem with lightweight, standardized packaging that allows applications to run anywhere. Developers can include the container builds as part of their local iterative development flow, eliminating the age-old problem of, "Well, it worked on my computer so it must be a you problem!" (This is the Java "write once, test everywhere" joke we joked about in Chapter 2.) In addition, sharing containers with your dev team is incredibly easy with container registries, which we'll cover shortly. Lastly, container-based environments simply run more efficiently than VMs on the exact same hardware. Whereas a bulky VM essentially "quarantines" a set amount of memory and CPU usage to run, lightweight containers free up resources when they're not being utilized. This greater efficiency translates to lower costs.

Beyond containers letting you architect your applications such that they are used in the most efficient manner possible, they change the landscape on startup times. If it took us days to get a traditional server going (once we got it in our office), then it took minutes with virtual machines and now we're talking seconds—even subseconds—with containers.

Docker Brings Containers to the Masses

Container technology has been around for ages, with FreeBSD Jails available in 2000, cgroups being introduced in 2006, and LXC implementing the Linux container manager in 2008. So why weren't people using them sooner?

In the early days, containers were a complex, commonly misunderstood, and difficult technology to utilize. No one knew how to practically use them! The rise of containers was popularized by Docker for two big reasons. First, Docker avoided vendor lock-in by supporting an open source model that runs on any environment (cloud or on premises); second, and more importantly, Docker brought containers to the masses with the Docker CLI, which instantly empowers developers to build containers with ease.

As you're well aware of by now, Docker quickly became the standard for building and running containers. Docker's Dockerfile describes how to build a container; its build command creates a container image; its run command creates (instantiate is the synonym for "create" in tech-speak) the container and runs the application packaged inside it (it actually combines two separate commands, create and run); and the stop command terminates the container. There are many more commands and subcommands (many of which have to do with managing resources and networking), but that's the essence. It really is that simple.

Another reason behind Docker's success was Docker Hub (*https://hub.docker.com*), which is a repository (cool people say repo) for container images. Docker Hub provides prebuilt containers for many commonly used applications. Docker Hub is particularly useful because containers are hierarchical: a container can reference a "parent," and only add software and configuration that's not included in the parent. For example, an application that needs a local MySQL database would be built on top of a standard MySQL container, and would only contain the application software, tools, or programs it needs, and any associated configuration files, but not another copy of MySQL. The MySQL container might, in turn, be built on top of other containers. So containers don't just help developers package software; they help developers to build software in standard ways, by taking advantage of existing container hierarchies wherever possible. The ease of publishing Docker containers made it immensely easy for developers to collaborate and paved the way for streamlined CI/CD (continuous integration and continuous delivery).

For enterprise software, one drawback of Docker Hub is that it is public. It's great that Docker Hub allows developers to share containers, but what if you provide an application or library that you only want to distribute within your company, or to a select group of business partners? Quay (*https://oreil.ly/6iroD*), a container repository designed for private use, solves this problem: it can be used to manage and distribute containers that can't be shipped outside of your organization. Quay also includes a vulnerability scanner called Clair (*https://oreil.ly/YKk16*), which helps to ensure that your software is safe. The Quay project is now sponsored by Red Hat.

A Practical Understanding of Kubernetes

Think of how you regulate climate conditions in your house. You have a control interface (like a Nest thermostat) and perhaps you set the temperature of your house to 19°C (66°F) with 30% humidity. Your house's climate systems constantly checks your declarative settings against the actual conditions using different sensors and mechanisms throughout the house. Behind that Nest thermostat is a control plane that can kick in air conditioning, the humidifier, heat, and so on—an ecosystem to bring your house to where you asked it to always remain; if anything gets out of sync from your definition of perfection, you have a system that remediates the situation.

With this analogy in mind, think of Kubernetes (say *koo-br-neh-teez*) as climate control for your operations. Why do we need a thermostat for our operational environments? Like we said earlier in this book, modern-day applications aren't built but rather *composed*, and that composition is done through piecing together discrete functional parts composed of services and containers (which have shorter life spans than traditional virtual machine approaches). Today's applications come with more capability and flexibility than ever, but with more moving parts that need to be managed (and that's where things can go wrong). More moving parts means more complexity. Quite simply, Kubernetes provides a way to run and manage an entire ecosystem of distributed functions (like microservices), including how they interact and how they scale, in a framework that is *completely standard and portable*.

Today, human error is responsible for a whopping 50% (*https://oreil.ly/eEPIa*) of downtime. Now ask yourself this question, "What adds more to human error than anything?" Answer: Complexity! Specifically, the complexity of managing applications with more objects and greater churn introduces new challenges: configuration, service discovery, load balancing, resource scaling, and the discovery and fixing of failures. Managing all of this complexity by hand is next to impossible—imagine some poor operations (ops) person tasked with looking at the logs for an application composed of two hundred services! What's more, clusters commonly run more than 1,000 containers, which makes updating these large clusters infeasible without automation.

Learning to pronounce the term Kubernetes (or *K8s* for short—the 8 is the number of letters after the *K* and before the *s*) is characteristic of learning how to actually use it —there's a learning curve. Kubernetes is Greek for "helmsman" or "pilot": the person who steers the ship. That helps: Kubernetes is the "pilot" that steers, or controls, large distributed systems. In the same way a Nest thermostat is climate orchestration for your house, Kubernetes container orchestration is a system to steer (or govern) your distributed systems so that they run correctly and safely.

Starting the Kubernetes Journey

Kelsey Hightower, the well-known Kubernetes developer advocate, has said (*https:// oreil.ly/1jYCi*), "The way it's going Kubernetes will be the Linux of distributed systems. The technology is solid with an even stronger community." While Kelsey is referring specifically to the open source community that has grown up around Kubernetes, we believe this statement could go much further. We'd be so bold as to say that *Kubernetes is the operating system for distributed systems of containers* regardless of the hardware architecture. What does an operating system like Linux, Windows, or iOS really do? It manages resources (CPU, memory, storage, communications, and so on) and that's *exactly* what K8s does: it manages the resources of a cluster of nodes— each of which is running its own operating system.

Our bold statement about Kubernetes says both more, and less, than it seems. An operating system isn't magic; it doesn't create value out of nothing. It requires an ecosystem of tools; it requires developers who build applications to run on the operating system; and it requires administrators who know how to keep it running. It can handle a lot of the day-to-day work of running your distributed systems (the Day 2 stuff we touch on later in this chapter). We won't pretend that getting Kubernetes configured correctly to manage your applications as you move to cloud native capabilities is an easy task. But it's completely worthwhile—as worthwhile as using Microsoft Office or Apple Numbers to work with spreadsheets.

We've seen already how containers have become the standard way to package applications. We've known for a long time that we want to automate as much as possible— and to automate, we need to standardize. We don't want to start each service we need with a different command; we want to be able to say, "Make this thing run, make sure it has all the resources it needs, I don't care how." That's what containers let you do.

Kubernetes takes over the job of running containers, so you no longer have to start them manually. That eliminates a lot of mumbling over the keyboard when you need to run hundreds or thousands of containers. But it's more than that. In a modern system, you might need several databases, an authentication service, a service that manages stock in the warehouse, a service that does billing, a service that queues orders to be shipped, a service that computes taxes, a service that manages currency exchange, and so on. Make your own list for your own business: it will be very extensive. And if your application is used heavily, you may need many copies of these services to handle the load. If you're a retail business, you might see a 100x peak on Black Friday. If you're a bank's investment arm, you'll see a peak on triple witching Friday (the simultaneous expiration of stock options, stock index futures, and stock index option contracts, all on the same day). If you're an accounting firm, you'll see a peak when tax forms are due. Handling those peaks is part (certainly not all, but part) of what the cloud is about. You don't want permanently allocate resources to handle those 100x peaks; you cloud-enable your application and then allocate computing power as you need it whether it is in your datacenter or someone else's datacenter. Need more compute? It's just a few clicks away.

But you also don't want some staff person trying to guess how many servers you need or writing some custom error-prone script to start new servers automatically. And that's precisely what Kubernetes allows you to avoid. Instead, your operations team may say, "We need at least 3 copies of the backend database, at least 10 copies (and as many as 1,000—depending on the load) of the frontend and authentication services," and so on. Kubernetes brings containers online to run the services you need, it watches the load and starts more copies of containers as needed, it scraps containers that are no longer needed (because the load is dropping), and it watches container health so it can scrap containers that aren't working and start new replacements. There are a lot of pieces that go into this—and we'll discuss them—but this is at the heart of what Kubernetes provides.

Kubernetes isn't magic, of course; it needs to be configured, and there are plenty of people telling us that Kubernetes is too complex. And in some ways, they're right— the complexity of K8s is a problem that the community will need to deal with in the coming years. But it's important to realize one big advantage that Kubernetes gives you. It's declarative, not procedural. A Kubernetes configuration isn't a list of commands that need to be executed to bring the system into its desired state. It's a description of that desired state (just like your Nest thermostat set at the temperature you want for your house): what services need to run, how many instances there need to be, how they're connected, and so forth. Kubernetes determines what commands need to be executed to bring the system into that desired state, and what has to continue being done to keep the ecosystem in the desired state. Kubernetes is automation that allows you to deploy complex, distributed systems with hundreds of services and thousands of servers and have them run reliably and consistently with minimum human involvement. We will never claim that administrators or IT staff are no longer needed; but K8s imbues superpowers on those teams, allowing them to manage much more infrastructure than would have been possible in the past. Is Kubernetes a "heavy lift"? Possibly. But how does that compare to managing thousands of VMs, each running its own servers, manually?

Many important ideas fall out of this discussion. Applications are composed of containers and containers implement services. The application itself provides a uniform, consistent API to the rest of the world, even though Kubernetes may be starting and stopping containers on the fly. Think about the implications: a billing service may be accessing the accounts receivable service at the address *http://ar2134.internal.aws.mycorp.com/*. What happens when this server dies? Does the system crash or hang until the accounts receivable service reboots? This might have been what happened in the past. But with Kubernetes, the billing service only needs to look up the accounts receivable service—Kubernetes takes care of finding a running instance and routing the request through to that instance. The result is bedrock solidity somehow built on top of shifting sand, in spite of the odds!

This sort of routing can work because the containers themselves are immutable and interchangeable. As we said earlier, rather than bringing up a server—with a system administrator carefully coaxing it to life by installing and starting all the software components it needs (web servers, databases, and middleware)—you build standardized containers instead. If something goes wrong, kill one, start the other, and fix up the network so that clients never need to know that anything has happened.

In the DevOps community, people often have a "pets versus cattle" debate (some of you aren't going to like the analogy they use) around the notion that how we treat pets versus cattle isn't much different than how we should think about servers versus containers. Think of your house pet—it has a name and its own unique personality. Now think of a traditional server in your company that handles warranty claims. It's not uncommon to "get to know" a server that has troubles. Just like if the family dog had issues, you'd take it to the vet for special care. What's more, you're likely to spend special time with your "IT pet"—we're not talking about the Tamagotchi you spent hours on before you had social media to make time disappear with little to show for it. You patch it, turn up the log diagnostics to try and figure out what's going on, and so on.

To DevOps, containers are cattle (remember how we said containers are "short lived") —identically produced en masse. Because containers are easily produced and immutable (you can't make configuration changes to them), you're not going to care for and nurture a sick container with the same attentiveness you might give a server. If a container instance is malfunctioning, get rid of it and replace it with another. This is only possible because containers are immutable; and because they're immutable, every instance is exactly the same. We don't even have to think about the possibility that a new instance will fail because someone installed *libSomeStrangeThing 3.9.2*, which is incompatible with *libSomeStrangeThing 3.9.1*. Administrators do need to keep containers updated and scanned for vulnerabilities—we've all seen what happens when deployed software doesn't receive security updates. But that's another set of issues (which we talked about in Chapter 6), and much of this process can be automated, too.

Because Kubernetes can start and stop containers without worrying about what's inside the containers, it can take whatever actions are needed to keep the system running. Think about just how radical an idea this truly is: Kubernetes is self-healing. Most of us can remember the era when distributed IT servers would crash and return to life an hour or so later. In many respects, that's still true: distributed IT servers may be more reliable than they were even a decade ago, but they still crash, networks still fail, and the power still goes out. Building an enterprise system without taking outages into account is wishful thinking that could easily be fatal. When commerce went online, businesses immediately realized that the cost of being offline could easily be thousands or even millions of dollars per minute—and undoubtedly the COVID-19 pandemic has made offline costs even more significant—if not fatal—to your business.

It's also important to realize that Kubernetes isn't specific to any vendor's cloud and will run on almost any hardware architecture—ranging from Raspberry Pi microcomputers, to the largest servers built on mainframes. For a few tens of dollars, you can build a Raspberry Pi cluster and keep it in the office broom closet; and once you've developed your application there, Kubernetes will (with very few changes) allow you to move that application to a cloud—to any cloud destination for that matter. Kubernetes will let you describe what zones you need, what processor capabilities you need (memory, GPU, TPU, and the like), and so on, so you don't have to hardwire your software to specific configurations. It's like we're always saying: "Cloud is a capability, not a destination!" Kubernetes is the keystone that provides organizations the ability to run software anywhere, at any scale.

Finally, Kubernetes has been designed so that it can be extended and evolved with new features. Historically, Kubernetes has been tied to Docker (as the dominant container system of the time). Recently, the Kubernetes project announced that it is "deprecating" (IT talk for no longer enhancing, still supported, but perhaps not for long) Docker. Kubernetes has standardized on the OCI (Open Container Interface) container format and runtime engine. The OCI standard allows Kubernetes to evolve beyond Docker in several important ways, including the ability to use container registries other than Docker Hub and the ability to support other kinds of containers (and possibly even applications without containers). *Read this carefully: deprecating Docker won't be a barrier to current users. Docker's container format complies with the OCI standard, too; therefore, you can still use Docker to build images that Kubernetes can run.* And you can still use Docker to run those containers for development or testing.

If you're familiar with Docker, there's no reason to stop using it—but there will now be other alternatives to explore—"let a thousand flowers bloom" goes the Apache open source slogan.

Time to Start Building

We've outlined critical cloud concepts to get you moving to cloud native—by now, we think you have a solid understanding of why we keep saying cloud is a capability not a destination. Think about it—shouldn't reducing the bloat of VMs be desirable for any destination? See the problem with thinking that this tech is only for those on a public cloud? So what's next? It's time to start thinking about your application and how you'll implement it in the cloud. Lift and shift—simply porting your application as is to a cloud provider—is probably the easiest solution, but it's also the least pro- ductive, hardest to scale in the long run, and is going to come up short on all the value you could be getting from a cloud strategy. Rethinking and reimplementing mission-critical applications as a set of services gives your company the kind of flexi- bility that couldn't be imagined a few years ago. Does your app need a new interface? Need to support a new kind of product? Are there other ways in which your software needs to evolve? Now is the time to think about reorganizing your applications so that new features and new product directions don't require an entire rewrite. That's where many IT groups fail. We want to get beyond failure.

CHAPTER 4

Cloud Computing: Patterns for The What, The How, and The Why

A couple of years ago, one of the authors was walking with a group of kids during a volunteer elementary school event. Like all kids of that age, they asked him nonstop questions about anything and everything. But one question was so intriguing ("What's in the clouds?") that he felt compelled to respond ("A bunch of Linux servers."). While the response surely left the few kids that were actually listening bewildered, it did bring a smile to the author's face. Of course, today, the answer would be well expanded to include almost any kind of server and operating system you could imagine! We're sure it doesn't need to be said (and we will explain all of this in this chapter) but being "in the cloud" doesn't mean there aren't hundreds of miles of networking cable laying around in some brick-and-mortar facility, and "serverless computing" doesn't mean there aren't servers running code—it just means they are not necessarily yours to run or worry (less) about.

Cloud has incredible momentum, and while there is so much value left to be gained as a capability from its proper use, conversations about it are well beyond the hype. The cloud—once used for one-off projects or testing workloads, has become a development hub, a place for transactions and analytics, a services procurement platform where things get done. In fact, it's whatever you decide to make it. That's the beauty of the cloud: all you need is an idea and the right mindset (cloud the capability, not the destination) and you'll be magical.

In this chapter we want to introduce you to different cloud computing *usage patterns* and the different kinds of ways to use those "servers in the sky" for your business—from an infrastructure perspective, to ready-to-build software for rolling your own apps, and even as granular as down-to-the-millisecond perspectives on a function's execution time. And of course, since we already know that cloud is a capability and not a destination, then we can apply these patterns on-premises or off in any vendor's cloud computing environments. By the end of this chapter, you'll understand acronyms like *IaaS* and *PaaS*, but you'll also know that the answer to "What is serverless computing?" won't be, "A computer that is serverless"; rather, you'll recognize it as a pattern.

 Some of the concepts covered in this chapter have been around for a while. Since the first part of this book is mostly geared toward business users, we felt it important to include these topics before we delve deeper into cloud discussions. If you know IaaS, PaaS, and Saas, you might want to consider jumping to "The Cloud Bazaar: SaaS and the API Economy" on page 76, where we get into the details of APIs, REST services, and some of the newer cloud patterns: serverless and function as a service. And if you already understand that serverless doesn't mean the absence of a physical server or that PaaS isn't a play option in American football, you could consider skipping this entire chapter.

Patterns of Cloud Computing: A Working Framework for Discussion

A journey toward the adoption of the "cloud" in many ways mimics the transition from traditional data "systems of record," to "systems of engagement," to "systems of people." Consider the emergence of social media—which has its very beginnings in the cloud. In the history of the world, society has never shared so much about so little. You simply can't deny how selfies, tweets, and TikTok dances have (for better or worse) become part of our vocabulary.

Just like how the web evolved from being a rigid set of pages to a space that's much more organic, interactive, and integrated, the last decade has borne witness to a continuing transformation in computing, from hardened silos to flexible as-a-service models that operate in a public cloud to those that operate *in a hybrid cloud*. Why? Three words: *social-mobile-cloud*.

Social-mobile-cloud has dramatically accelerated social change in unanticipated ways; in fact, it has completely changed and altered the flow of information for the entire planet. Information used to flow from a few centralized sources out to the masses. Major media outlets like the BBC, CNN, NY Times, and Der Spiegel were dominant voices in society, able to control conversations about current events. Social-mobile-cloud has obliterated the dominance of mass media voices (for better or worse, as "Fake News" is a hot topic) and changed the flow of information to a many-to-many model. In short, the spread of mobile technology and social networks, as well as unprecedented access to data, has changed humanity—disconnected individuals have become connected groups, technology has changed how we organize and how we engage, and more. We call this mode of engagement *The Why*.

Of course, all this new data has become the new basis for competitive advantage. We call this data *The What*. All that's left is *The How*. And this is where the cloud comes in. This is where you deploy infrastructure, software, services, and even monetized APIs that deliver analytics and insights in an agile way.

If you're a startup today, only in rare cases would you go to a venture capital firm with a business plan that includes the purchase of a bunch of hardware and an army of DBAs to get started. Who really does that anymore? You'd get shown the door, if you even made it that far. Instead, what you do is go to a cloud company. But what if you're not a startup? What if you're an enterprise with established assets and apps? Then you want the cloud (the capability) at your destination of choice.

The transformational effects of The How (cloud), The Why (engagement), and The What (data) can be seen across all industries and their associated IT landscapes. Consider your run-of-the-mill application developer and what life was like before the cloud era and as-a-service models became a reality. Developers spent as much time navigating roadblocks as they did writing code! The list of IT barriers is endless: contending with delays for weeks or months caused by ever-changing backend persistence (database) requirements, siloed processes, database schema change synchronization cycles, cost models heavily influenced by the number of staff that had to be kept in-house to manage the solution, and other processes longer than this sentence. And we didn't even mention the approval and wait times just to get a server in the door so that you can experience all the friction we just detailed. Make no mistake about it, this goes on in every large company—horror stories are ubiquitous. To be honest, looking back, we think it's a wonder that any code got written at all.

Development is a great example. Its shift toward agile is encapsulated by the catch phrase *continuous integration and continuous delivery*—or CI/CD for short. In the development operations (DevOps) model, development cycles get measured in days; environment stand-up times are on the order of minutes (at most hours); the data persistence layer (where the data is stored, like in a database) is likely to be a hosted (at least partially) or even a fully managed service (which means that someone else administers it for you); the platform architecture is loosely coupled and based on an API economy combined with open standards; and the cost model is variable and expensed operationally, as opposed to fixed and capital cost depreciated over time.

As is true with so many aspects of IT, the premise of this book is our assertion that this wave of change has yet to reach its apex. Indeed, there was much hype around cloud as we discussed in Chapter 1, but many practitioners are now "hitting the wall" of the hype barrier. There is *no question* that cloud delivers real value and agility today—*but it's been limited for larger enterprise*.

"As-a-service" generally means a cloud computing service that is provided for you (for a fee) so that you can focus on what's important to your business: your code, iterative improvements to custom apps, the relationships you have with your customers, and so on. Each type of cloud pattern leaves you less and less "stuff" to worry about. We broadly (and coarsely) categorize these cloud patterns (provisioning models and concepts) into what you see in Figure 4-1: infrastructure as a service (IaaS), platform as a service (PaaS), and software as a service (SaaS)—we left the serverless computing pattern out for now.

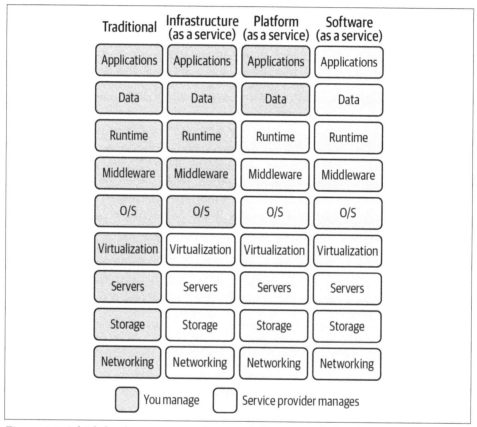

Figure 4-1. A high-level comparison of responsibilities at each cloud pattern level

These cloud patterns all stand in contrast to traditional IT, where individual groups and people had to manage the entire technology stack themselves. This is the way many of us "grew up" in our career. Cloud (the capability) has blurred the lines of where these services are hosted, which is perfect because now we can talk about these as patterns without a footnote for where they reside—as opposed to destination being the lead-with discussion. Your cloud resides where you want (or better yet need) it to reside. You no longer have to differentiate between *on-premises* and *off-premises* to get access to cloud capabilities.

The shading that changes in Figure 4-1 for the second, third, and fourth columns is intended to convey where the responsibility falls for some of the specifics around any compute solution.

This terminology gets a little blurry in a cloud (the capability) discussion because your own company could be managing and hosting the app dev frameworks (with instrumented chargeback accounting) for a good portion of your app, but you're also stitching in serverless APIs (like Twilio) for some of the workflow. When you're talking about cloud as a capability, if the environment is hosted, administrative responsibilities fall on you, and if managed, someone else has to worry about all the things you typically worry about. It's the difference between sleeping over at mom's house (where you are expected to still do a lot of work—you are hosted) or sleeping at a resort (managed—it's all done for you in a luxurious manner that you've paid for).

Order Up: Pizza as a Service

Before we delve into the descriptions associated with the cloud patterns shown in Figure 4-1, we thought it'd be a fun exercise to imagine these cloud patterns in the context of pizza—because we're confident the world over loves a good "wheel."

Note that this is a simplistic scenario: there are permutations and combinations to the story that could break it down or make it better—we're intentionally trying to keep things simple…and fun.

Let's assume you've got a child going into their sophomore year at university who's living at home for the summer. Your kid mentioned how they found a gourmet "Roast Pumpkin & Chorizo" pizza recipe (pizza traditionalists know this…we're just as aghast) from the internet and wants to use it to impress a date. You laugh and remind your offspring that you just taught them how to boil an egg last week. After some thought, your kid concludes that making a gourmet pizza is too much work (getting the ingredients, cooking, cleaning, preparation, and so on) and their core competencies are nowhere to be found in the kitchen. They announce this conclusion and share plans to take their date to a downtown gourmet pizza restaurant. You begin to ask, "How can you afford that?" but you stop because you know the answer and the question coming to you next (it has the word "borrow" in it, which really means "give"). Think of this date as *software as a service (SaaS)*. The restaurant manages everything to do with the meal: the building and kitchen appliances, the electricity, the cooking skills, the ingredients, right up to the presentation of the food itself. Your financially indebted child just had to get to the restaurant (think of that as a connection to the internet) and once the romantic duo arrive at the restaurant, all they had to do is consume the pizza and pay.

Junior year is rolling around and as you look forward to your empty nest house again, the COVID-19 pandemic assures you that the company of your loved one will remain constant for months to come. Still single (apparently chorizo pizza doesn't guarantee love), another budding romance is announced, and this time dinner location is at a little more intimate setting: your house. Convinced the perfect mate will love a pumpkin and cured sausage pizza recipe, your kid scurries off to the grocery store to get all the same ingredients but begs you for help preparing and baking the meal before you and your spouse are requested to go for a three-hour walk once the date arrives. As a dedicated parent, you want your offspring to find love (it might speed up the move out process) so you go along with the whole plan. While out of the house, your child serves up the meal, you stop and turn to your significant other with warmth in your heart and say, "Darling, we are *platform as a service (PaaS)* to our child." Your partner looks at you and says, "You're the most unromantic person I know." So how is this a PaaS cloud pattern? Think about it—you provided the cooking "platform." The house, the kitchen appliances, the cutlery and plates, the electricity, it was all there for any chef (developer) to come on in and cook (create). Your child brought in the ingredients (coding an app) and cooked the recipe. (There's a variation to this junior year PaaS story called *serverless computing*, and it sits between PaaS and SaaS. We'll get into the details later in this chapter.)

It's senior year and your part of the world has found a way past the pandemic, your beloved kid now lives on their own somewhere else (insert heavenly sounding rejoice music) and this time they're convinced they've found their pumpkin and chorizo soulmate. Your love-stricken offspring has found their own place to rent (the server), and rent includes appliances and utilities (storage and networking). Your child has invited their potential soulmate for a date, and wants the place to be as classy as possible. They take a trip to IKEA for some tasteful place settings, a kitchen table, and chairs (your 20-year-old couch wouldn't be suitable for such an important guest to sit and eat)—call it the operating system. Next stop, the grocery store for the ingredients (the runtime and middleware), and finally a cooked meal on date night. It's hard to believe your kid is finally this independent, but they essentially owned the entire process from start to finish outside of the core infrastructure rented (the server, storage, and so on). Your child has become an *infrastructure as a service (IaaS)* pizza maestro.

Your Kid Sharing an Apartment with Roommates

In the preceding scenario your child lived alone in that apartment and had sole access to all of its resources. But let's assume for a moment your child has a roommate and the apartment (infrastructure) is shared. Everything from the fridge, to the stove, to place settings, to the tables and chairs are all potentially shared; we call this a multi-tenant pattern in cloud-speak. Those roommates? They can literally be what we call "noisy neighbors" in the cloud space. In so many ways, they can get in the way of an expected planned experience. For example, perhaps they are cooking their own food when access is needed to the kitchen. In a multitenant cloud environment, you share resources; what's different from our analogy is the fact that you don't know who you're sharing the resources with. But the key concept here is that when you share resources, things *may* not always operate the way you expected or planned (obviously CSPs put a lot of measures in place to protect you from this). Of course, privacy is cornered off and such (but there are things that go wrong)—but there are nuances well beyond the scope of this book that may need some consideration. As you can imagine, sharing a space (multitenant) versus having your own space (dedicated)—be it in an apartment or in the cloud—has cost differentials.

Notice what's common in every one of these scenarios: at the end of the evening, your child eats a pumpkin and chorizo pizza (albeit with different people, but that's beside the point). In the IaaS variation of the story, your kid did all of the work. In the PaaS and SaaS scenarios, other people took varying amounts of responsibility for the meal. Today, even though your child is independent and has the luxury of their own infrastructure (the apartment), they still enjoy occasionally eating at restaurants; it's definitely easier to go out for sushi than make it. This is the beauty of the as-a-service cloud patterns—you can consume services whenever the need arises to offload the management of infrastructure, the platform, or the software itself.

It goes without saying that since cloud is a capability then the very scenarios we just articulated can be wholly contained within an enterprise on-premises. For example, Human Resources can own an app for an employee learning platform, but the CIO office is providing the IaaS platform where it runs. The CIO's office can offer up development or data science stacks that can be provisioned in minutes and charged back in a utility-like manner to different teams (perhaps one team are R aficionados, while another is Python).

As your understanding of these service models deepens, you will come to realize that the distinctions between them begin to blur. From small businesses to enterprises, organizations that want to modernize will quickly need to embrace the transition from low-agility development strategies to integrated, end-to-end DevOps. The shift toward cloud ushers in a new paradigm of "consumable IT"; the question is, what is your organization going to do? Are you going to have a conversation about how to take part in this revolutionary reinvention of IT? Are you content with only capturing 20% of its value? Are you going to risk the chance that competitors taking the leap first will find greater market share as they embrace cloud capability sooner to more quickly deliver innovation to their customers? This is an inflection point because the cloudification of IT is just about to *really* happen—because cloud will be approached as a capability, and not solely a destination.

Do (Almost All of) It Yourself: Infrastructure as a Service

In our "Roast Pumpkin and Chorizo" pizza example, when you finally got your offspring out of the house and they pretty much did all the work (found a place to live, shopped for ingredients, bought their own dishes), that was infrastructure as a service (IaaS)—what many refer to as "the original cloud." In a nutshell, IaaS is a level removed from the traditional way that computing is provisioned. It's a pay-as-you-go service where you are provided infrastructure services (storage, compute, virtualization, networking, and so on) as you need them via the cloud.

IaaS delivers the foundational computing resources shown in Figure 4-1 that you use over an internet connection on a pay-as-you-use basis. The basic building blocks needed to run apps and workloads in the cloud typically include:

Physical datacenters

IaaS utilizes large datacenters. For public IaaS providers, those datacenters are typically distributed globally around the world. The various layers of abstraction needed by a public IaaS sit on top of that physical infrastructure and are made available to end users over the internet. In most IaaS models, end users do not interact directly with the physical infrastructure (but there are some special patterns, called *bare metal*, that do), but rather "talk" to the abstraction (virtualization) layer.

Compute

IaaS is typically understood as virtualized compute resources. Providers manage the hypervisors and end users can then programmatically provision virtual "instances" with desired amounts of compute, memory, and storage. Most providers offer both CPUs and GPUs for different types of workloads. Cloud compute also typically comes paired with supporting services like auto-scaling and load balancing that provide the scale and performance characteristics that make cloud desirable in the first place.

Network

Networking in the cloud is software-defined where the traditional networking hardware (routers and switches) is made available programmatically through graphical interfaces and APIs. Although we don't cover it deeply in this book, companies with sensitive data or strict compliance requirements often require additional network security and privacy within a public cloud. A virtual private cloud (VPC) can be a way of creating additional isolation of cloud infrastructure resources without sacrificing speed, scale, or functionality. VPCs enable end users to create a private network for a single tenant in a public cloud. They give users control of subnet creation, IP address range selection, virtual firewalls, security groups, network access control lists, site-to-site virtual private networks (VPNs), application firewalls, and load balancing. (It's critical for us to note that there are a lot more things you need to be concerned about when it comes to security; this is a statement for networking.)

Storage

You need a place to store your data, right? Storage experts classify storage into three main types: *block, file,* and *object* storage. We'll delve more into storage later in this book.

If you contrast IaaS with the other cloud patterns shown back in Figure 4-1, it's safe to conclude that IaaS hands off the lowest level of resource control to the cloud. This means that you don't have to maintain or update your own on-site datacenter because the provider does it for you. Again, you access and control the infrastructure via an API or dashboard.

IaaS enables end users to scale and shrink resources on an as-needed basis, reducing the need for high, up-front expenditures or unnecessary overprovisioned infrastructure; this is especially well suited for *spiky* workloads.

Spiky workloads are those that peak at certain times (or unexpectedly) based on certain events. A great analogy would be your heart rate and exercise. When you're at work (yes, we know the jokes you're thinking to yourself right now) your heart isn't racing to deliver oxygen to your body. Now go for a run. That run is a spiky workload and jumps demands on your heart to start pumping at 130 beats per minute (bpm) when the usual demand is around 60 bpm. When you've finished your run, you don't need your heart beating at 130 bpm because your workload only demands 60 bpm. Apply this to compute. If you're livestreaming a famous movie star enjoying your product launch or you were an online toilet paper seller at the brink of COVID-19 during the panic-buy phase, you needed way more capacity at those phases (130 bpm) than you do on average or once those moments pass (60 bpm).

Quite simply, IaaS lets you simplify IT infrastructure for building your own remote datacenter on the cloud, instead of building or acquiring datacenter components yourself. While this cloud computing pattern is a staple offering from all public cloud providers, we're beginning to see many large organizations with their hybrid cloud approach offer this pattern internally (for obvious reasons)—to extract maximum value from cross-company hardware investments *and* flatten the time-to-value curve associated with delivering business constituents what they need.

Think about all the idle compute capacity sitting across your company or even in a single siloed department—Forbes once noted (*https://oreil.ly/BSPPY*) that "30 percent of servers are sitting comatose," and we think it's higher than that in practice. For example, our authoring team has our own server that we set up for this book, but the five of us aren't using it all the time. In fact, this server is so powerful we could easily share half of it with someone else. As we wrote this chapter, we did just that—we partitioned up the server and offered it to another department via a cloud pattern with a chargeback on usage. As it turned out, the first group wasn't using it much either, so we did it again, and again. By the time we finished our book, we were making money! (We're kidding…or we were told to say so.)

When organizations can quickly provision an infrastructure layer, the required time-to-anything that depends on the hardware is dramatically reduced. Talk to any team in your organization about the efforts required to order a server—we alluded to it before and it's brutal. From approvals to facilities requests, the hours and costs spent on just being able to plug the computer in is horrendous (this is why we jokingly said we made money with our server—because our "customers" are happy to avoid all the things we just mentioned). Bottom line: be it from a public cloud or an on-premises strategy within your organization, IaaS gets *raw compute* resources to those that need it quickly. Think of it this way: if you could snap your fingers and have immediate access to a four-GPU server that you could use for five hours, at less than the price of a meal at your favorite restaurant, how cool would that be? Even cooler, imagine you could then snap your fingers and have those server costs go away—like eating a fast food combo meal and not having to deal with the indigestion or calories after you savor the flavor. Think about how agile and productive you would be. Again, we want to note that if you're running a workload on a public cloud service 24x7, 365 days a year, it may not yield the cost savings you think; depending on the workload it could be more expensive, *but* agility will always reign supreme with cloud (the capability) compared to the alternatives.

Moving to the cloud gives you increased agility and an opportunity for capacity planning that's similar to the concept of using electricity: it's "metered" based on the usage that you pay for (yes, you'll yell at developers who leave their services running when not in use the same way you do your kids for leaving the lights on in an empty room). In other words, IaaS enables you to consider compute resources as if they are a utility like electricity. Similar to utilities, it's likely the case that your cloud service has tiered pricing. For example, is the provisioned compute capacity multitenant or bare metal? Are you paying for fast CPUs or extra memory? Never lose sight of what we think is the number-one reason for the cloud and IaaS: it's all about how fast you can provision the computing capacity—and this is why we keep urging you to think of cloud as a capability, rather than a destination.

We titled this section with a do-it-yourself theme because with IaaS you still have a heck of a lot of work to do in order to get going. Just like when your kid had an apartment with a stove and a fridge, your team is as far away from writing code or training their neural networks with GPU acceleration using IaaS as your kid was from sitting down with their date and eating homemade pizza.

IaaS emerged as a popular computing model in the early 2010s, and since that time, it has become the standard abstraction model for many types of workloads. Despite the relentless evolution of cloud technologies (containers and serverless are great examples) and the related rise of the microservices application pattern (a cornerstone to the modernization work we talk about throughout this book), IaaS remains a foundational cornerstone of the industry—but it's a more crowded field than ever.

IaaS has a Twin Sibling: Bare Metal

Bare metal is not a 1980s big hair band that streaked at their concerts for a memorable finale, but rather a term that describes infrastructure in its rawest form provisioned over the cloud: *bare metal as a service (BMaaS)*. Think of BMaaS as IaaS's twin —very similar in so many ways, but there are some things that make them each unique. In a BMaaS environment, resources are still provisioned on-demand, made available over the internet, and billed on a pay-as-you-go basis. Typically, this used to be monthly or hourly increments, but more and more pricing models for anything as-a-service is more granular, with by-the-minute (and in some cases by-the-second or service unit) pricing schemes.

Unlike traditional IaaS, BMaaS *does not* provide end users with already virtualized compute, network, and storage (and sometimes not even an operating system, for that matter). Instead, it gives *direct access* to the underlying hardware. This level of access offers end users almost total control over their hardware specs. The hardware is neither virtualized nor supporting multiple virtual machines and so it offers end users the greatest amount of potential performance, something of significant value for use cases like high-performance computing (HPC).

It's a well-known fact that whenever you virtualize anything, you lose some performance. Performance on a bare-metal server will *always* outperform equivalent amounts of virtualized infrastructure. The very essence of the as-a-service model relies on virtualizing away the underlying compute resources so they can be shared and easily scaled. We chose not to delve into these nuances, but if you want the absolute most performance possible right down to single-digit percentage points, you'll want to delve more into the potential benefits BMaaS can offer.

If you're nuanced in the operation of traditional noncloudified datacenters, BMaaS environments are likely to feel the most familiar and may best map to the architecture patterns of your existing workloads. However, it's important to note that these advantages can also come at the expense of traditional IaaS benefits, namely the ability to rapidly provision and horizontally scale resources by simply making copies of instances and load balancing across them. When it comes to BMaaS versus IaaS, one model is not superior to the other—it's all about what model best supports the specific use case or workload.

Noisy Neighbors Can Be Bad Neighbors: The Multitenant Cloud

Before we cover the other as-a-service models, it's worth taking a moment to further examine a fundamental aspect of a cloud provider deployment options: single- or multitenant cloud environments.

One of the main drawbacks to IaaS is the possibility of security vulnerabilities with the vendor you partner with, particularly on multitenant systems where the provider shares infrastructure resources with multiple clients.

Provisioning multitenant resources also means having to contend with the reality of shared resources. Performance is never consistent and might not necessarily live up to the full potential that was promised on paper. We attribute this unpredictability to the "noisy neighbors" effect.

In a shared cloud service, the noisy neighbor is exactly what you might imagine: other users and applications, for a shared provisioned infrastructure in a multitenant environment, and that can bog down performance and potentially ruin the experience for everyone else (think back to our example of a young man hosting a date at a shared residence). Perhaps those neighbors are generating a disproportionate amount of network traffic or are heavily taxing the infrastructure to run their apps. The end result of this effect is that all other users of the shared environment suffer degraded performance. In this kind of setting, you can't be assured of consistent performance, which means you can't guarantee predictable behavior down to your customers. In the same manner that inconsistent query response times foreshadow the death of a data warehouse, the same applies for services in the cloud.

In a provisioned multitenant public cloud environment, you don't know who your neighbors are. Imagine for a moment that you are unknowingly sharing your cloud space with some slick new gaming company that happened to hit the jackpot, and their app has "gone viral." Who knew that an app for uploading pictures of your boss to use in a friendly game of "whack-a-mole" would catch on? Within days, millions join this virtual spin on a carnival classic. All this traffic creates a network-choking phenomenon. Why do you care? If this gaming studio and its customers happen to be sharing the same multitenant environment as you, then the neighborhood just got a lot noisier, and your inventory control system *could* run a lot like the aforementioned game—up and down.

These drawbacks are avoidable in the public cloud and easier to manage or avoid in a hybrid cloud, but you should certainly press any IaaS provider (be they internal or external to your company) on what we've covered in this section.

Cloud Regions and Cloud Availability Zones for Any As-a-Service Offering

You might come across this terminology in cloud-speak: *availability zones* and *regions*. A cloud availability zone is a logically and physically isolated location within a cloud region that has independent power, cooling, and network infrastructures isolated from other zones—this strengthens fault tolerance by avoiding single points of failure between zones while also guaranteeing high bandwidth and low inter-zone latency within a region. A cloud region is a geographically and physically separate group of one or more availability zones with independent electrical and network infrastructures isolated from other regions. Regions are designed to remove shared single points of failure (SPOF) with other regions and guarantee low inter-zone latency within the region.

Different companies use different terminology for this stuff, so we're giving you the basics. For example, some talk about Metros, or have a hierarchy that goes Geography (think North America), Country (like USA), Metro (Dallas, San Jose, Washington DC), Zones (datacenters within the Metros).

We spent a lot of time on IaaS in this chapter despite the fact that the other as-a-service models are getting more attention as of late. This was by design. Each cloud pattern builds upon the other and delivers more value on the stack. Our cloud pattern stack starts with the foundation of IaaS (as shown in Figure 4-2) and will grow as we add more patterns.

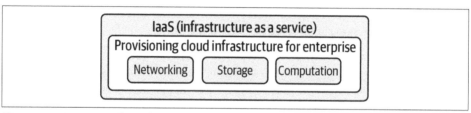

Figure 4-2. IaaS provides a foundational level for any service or application that you want to deploy on the cloud—other as-a-service models build (and inherit) these benefits from here

It might be best to think of IaaS as you would a set of Russian dolls—each level of beauty gets transferred to the next and the attention to detail (the capabilities and services provided from a cloud perspective) increases. In other words, the value of IaaS gives way to even more value, flexibility, and automation in PaaS, which gives way to even more of these attributes in SaaS (depending on what it is you are trying to do). Now that you have a solid foundation on IaaS, it's going to better illustrate the benefits of PaaS and make its adoption within your business strategies easier.

Building the Developer's Sandbox with Platform as a Service

Platform as a service (PaaS) is primarily used for developers to play around (hence the name sandbox), compose (modernization-speak for build), and deploy applications. This pattern is even further removed from the traditional manner in which IT architectures are provisioned because required hardware and software are delivered over a cloud for use as an integrated solution stack.

Quite simply, PaaS is really useful for developers. It allows users to develop, run, and manage their own apps without having to build and maintain the infrastructure or platform usually associated with the process.

This means countless hours saved compared to traditional app dev preparation steps such as installation, configuration, troubleshooting, and the seemingly endless amounts of time spent reacting to never-ending changes in open source cross dependencies. PaaS, on the other hand, allows you to relentlessly innovate, letting developers go from zero to productive in less time than it typically takes to reboot a laptop.

PaaS is all about writing, composing, and managing apps without the headaches of software updates or hardware maintenance. PaaS takes the work out of standing up a dev environment and all configuration intricacies or forcing developers to deal with virtual machine images or hardware to get stuff done (you don't have to prepare the pizza, thinking back to our university student analogy). With a few swipes and keystrokes, you can provision instances of your app dev environment (or apps) with the necessary development services to support them. This streamlining ties together development backbones such as node.js, Java, mobile backend services, application monitoring, analytics services, database services, and more.

The PaaS provider hosts everything—servers, networks, storage, the operating system, software, databases, and more. Development teams can use all of it for a monthly billed fee (which could be billed to a credit card if it's a hobby, a third-party contract for your company, or a chargeback if your company is providing its employees the PaaS platform) based on usage, and users can quickly and without friction purchase more resources on demand, as needed.

PaaS is one of the fastest-growing cloud patterns today. Gartner forecasts the total market for PaaS to exceed $34 billion by 2022 (*https://oreil.ly/ttvxc*), doubling its 2018 size.

Digging Deeper into PaaS

What are the key business drivers behind the market demand for PaaS? Consider an app developer named Jane. PaaS provides and tailors the environment that Jane needs to compose and run her apps, thanks to the libraries and middleware services that are put in her development arsenal through a services catalog. Jane and other developers don't need to concern themselves with how those services are managed or organized under the hood. That complexity is the responsibility of the PaaS provider to manage and coordinate. More than anything, this development paradigm decreases the time to market by accelerating productivity and easing deployment of new apps over the cloud. Are you a mobile game developer? If so, you can provision a robust and rich backend JSON in-memory key value store (like Redis) for your app in seconds, attach to it a visualization engine, and perform some analytics.

The PaaS pattern enables new business services to be built frictionless, thanks to a platform that runs on top of a managed infrastructure and integrates cleanly between services. This is where a lot of work is done for development, even after you've got an environment set up—getting the components you're using to talk to each other. The traditional components of a development stack—the operating system, the integrated development environment (IDE), the change management catalog, the bookkeeping and tooling that every developer needs—can be provisioned with ease through a PaaS architecture. If you are a developer of native cloud apps, PaaS is your playground. CI/CD becomes a reality when your apps and services can be implemented on a platform that supports the full DevOps process from beginning to end.

PaaS offers such tremendous potential and value to developers like Jane because there are more efficiencies to be gained than just provisioning some hardware. Take a moment to consider Figure 4-3. Having on-demand access to databases, messaging, workflow, connectivity, web portals, and so on—this is the depth of customization that developers crave from their environment. It is also the kind of tailored experience that's missing from the IaaS pattern. The layered approach shown in Figure 4-3 demonstrates how PaaS is, in many respects, a radical departure from the way in which enterprises and businesses traditionally provision and link services over distributed systems. Read that sentence again and ask yourself, "Why is the only way I can take advantage of this stuff to have my application on a public cloud?" (It isn't— cloud the capability!) And now you get just how limiting it can be to box your cloud-mindset into thinking of it as a destination, rather than as a capability.

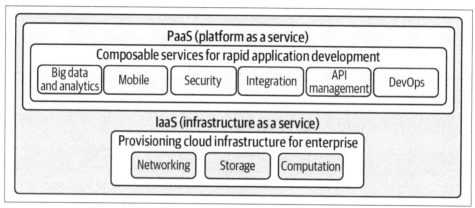

Figure 4-3. PaaS provides an integrated development environment for building apps that are powered by managed services

In the traditional development approach, classes of subsystems are deployed independently of the app that they are supporting. Similarly, their lifecycles are managed independently of the primary app as well. If Jane's app is developed out of step with her supporting network of services, she will need to spend time (time that would be better spent building innovative new features for her app) ensuring that each of these subsystems have the correct versioning, functionality mapping for dependencies, and so on. All of this translates into greater risk, steeper costs, higher complexity, and a longer development cycle for Jane.

With a PaaS delivery model, these obstacles are removed: the platform assumes responsibility for managing subservices (and their lifecycles) for you. When the minutiae of micromanaging subservices are no longer part of the equation, the potential for unobstructed end-to-end DevOps becomes possible. With a complete DevOps framework, a developer can move from concept to full production in a matter of minutes. Jane can be more agile in her development, which leads to faster code iteration and a more polished product or service for her customers. We would describe this as the PaaS approach to *process-oriented design and development*.

Composing in the Fabric of Cloud Services

The culture around modern apps and tools for delivering content is constantly changing and evolving. Just a short time ago, there was no such thing as Kickstarter, the global crowd-funding platform. Today you'll find things as niche as a Kickstarter campaign for a kid's school trip! (When we grew up, our definition for this kind of fundraising campaign was mowing our neighbor's lawn.) The penetration of social sharing platforms (Instagram, TikTok, and so on) that only run on (or are purely designed for) mobile platforms is astonishing. Why? There are more mobile devices today than there are people on the planet—Statista estimated (*https://oreil.ly/b6q5O*) that there would be two for each person to start this year (2021), and that's not including edge devices. We're in the "app now," "want it now" era of technology. This shift isn't a generational phenomenon, as older generations like to think (many young'uns don't care about Facebook, but senior citizens are dominating its signups). Ironically, our impatience with technology today is due to the general perception that the burdens of technology IT infrastructure are gone. (Two of the authors shared a flight to Spain before the pandemic and during the writing of this book recanted how they were complaining about the speed of the internet—over the ocean!)

To be successful in this new culture, modern app developers and enterprises must adopt four key fundamental concepts:

- First is *deep* and *broad* integration. What people use apps for today encompasses more than one task. For example, today's shopper expects a seamless experience to a storefront across multiple devices with different modalities (some will require gesture interactions, whereas others will use taps and clicks).

- The second concept is *mobile*. Applications need a consistent layer of functionality to guarantee that no matter how you interact with the storefront (on your phone, a tablet, or a laptop), the experience feels the same but is still tailored to the device. Here we are talking about functionality that has to be omni-channel and consistent (we've all been frustrated by apps where the mobile version can't do what the web version does), and for frictionless to happen, the customer-facing endpoints need to be deeply integrated across all devices.

- Third, developers of these apps need to be *agile* and *iterative* in their approach to design. Delivery cycles are no longer set according to large gapped points in time (a yearly release of your software, for example). Users expect continuous improvement and refinement of their services and apps, and code drops need to be frequent enough to keep up with this pace of change—thus the allure of CI/CD. Continuous delivery has moved from initiative to imperative. Why? Subscription pricing means you must keep earning your client's business, because it's easier than ever for them to go elsewhere.

- Finally, the *ecosystem* that supports these apps must appeal to customer and developer communities. Business services and users want to be able to use an app without needing to build it and own it. Likewise, developers demand an environment that provides them with the necessary tools and infrastructure to get their apps off the ground and often have next-to-zero tolerance for roadblocks (like budget approvals, getting database permissions, and so on).

Consuming Functionality Without the Stress: Software as a Service

If PaaS is oriented toward the developer who wants to code and build modern apps in a frictionless environment, then software as a service (SaaS) is geared much more toward lines of business that want to consume the services that are already built and ready to deploy.

In a nutshell, SaaS (some people might refer to it as *cloud application services*, but in our experience those people are likely billing you for hourly advice) delivers software that typically runs fully managed and hosted on the cloud. This allows you to consume functionality without having to manage software installation, general software maintenance, the sourcing and sizing of compute, backups, and more. All you have to do to use it is open a web browser and go to the service's dashboard or access the service via an API.

 Nearly everyone is trying to become a SaaS business these days because it's usually tied to a *subscription* license—which means recurring revenues. There is a lot of confusion these days on how subscription licensing represents cloud revenue. For example, we wrote this book using Office 365 (some of us love it, but we won't get into our drama here). We pay a subscription fee for it, but we're not running it in a browser on the cloud (we could, but the functionality isn't the same); we run it locally, which in some ways makes it a hybrid product.

What's more, vendors love the SaaS business model because it's a model that can scale incredibly well from a sales perspective, and once you have paying customers, it's easier to keep them—just keep delivering value.

Even if you're brand new to the cloud, we think SaaS is the most widely recognized type of cloud service because you're likely using it today in your personal lives. Apple Music is a SaaS service—it provides music (obviously) and the management of that music vis-à-vis a rich interface for searching, a recommendation engine, AI-personalized radio stations, and of course your own playlists. Updates to Apple Music are automatic, and your playlists are always backed up; in fact, it was Apple that helped to mainstream music as a service. Never lose your contacts again—thank you SaaS! Google's Gmail is another—you can log in to your email account from any device, anywhere in the world, so long as you have an internet connection. But enterprises are using all sorts of SaaS products too: Monday.com, Salesforce.com, ZenDesk, Mentimeter, Prezi, and IBM all have offerings, as do so many others. Don't get boxed into the ubiquitous SaaS vendors we've mentioned here—there are thousands that encompass all kinds of services, from simple backups to email to project management, to editing a giphy, to tracking a golf shot live on course, and everything in between.

Many well-known SaaS vendors actually buy IaaS from cloud providers like IBM, Amazon, or Microsoft. Why? For the same reason enterprises do! They don't want to concern themselves with things like load balancing, firewalls, and storage—they want to focus on new features to offer their clients (so that they continue paying those subscription fees). Packaging up a SaaS offering on Red Hat OpenShift really opens the aperture of a vendor's offering because they're thinking with cloud capabilities, which allows them to offer up their product on any public cloud *or* on-premises (which some clients might need because of data sovereignty or performance issues).

SaaS consumers span the breadth of multiple domains and interest groups: human resources, procurement officers, legal departments, city operations, marketing campaign support, demand-generation leads, political or business campaign analysis, agency collaboration, sales, customer care, technical support, and more. The variety of ways that business users can exploit SaaS is extraordinarily complex: it can be specific (to the extent that it requires tailored software to address the problem at hand), or it can require a broad and adaptable solution to address the needs of an entire industry (like software that runs the end-to-end operations for a dental office).

Figure 4-4 highlights the fact that SaaS can apply to anything, as long as it is provisioned and maintained as a service over cloud technology (and now that you see cloud as a capability, you can see how powerful it might be to mix public cloud SaaS offerings with internal ones too).

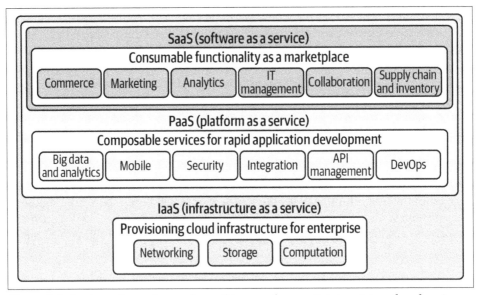

Figure 4-4. SaaS can be pretty much anything—as long as it is provisioned and maintained as a completely frictionless service over the cloud

The Cloud Bazaar: SaaS and the API Economy

We've mostly talked about SaaS as software, but it's important to note that SaaS can be (and is increasingly so with each passing day) delivered vis-à-vis an API. Forget about *Planet of the Apes*—we're watching Planet of the *Apps* and it's all because of today's marketplace trend: the *API economy*. The API economy is the ability to programmatically access anything through well-defined communication protocols (like those RESTful services we talked about earlier in this book). Indeed, today's software delivery platforms have three facets: rentable (like in the public cloud), installable (traditional software), and *API composable*.

API economies enable developers to easily and seamlessly integrate services within apps they compose (or in the case of an end user: services they consume). This is quite a departure from the traditional ways of app delivery, or what you may be used to if you're from a line of business trying to understand how your company fully embraces the digital renaissance thrust upon them amidst a "mobile everywhere," "tech years are like dog years," pandemic-hit economy.

For most people, SaaS experiences are driven by the user experience (UX). Take for example The Weather Company. Many of you might know it as the handy app on your phone that tells you if your family picnic is going to be pleasant (at least from a weather perspective; we have no idea who is going to be there and if you want them there or not). This app is installed on more mobile devices than we're allowed to tell you about, but basically every mobile device in the world has a weather app preinstalled on it; however, that isn't the surprising part. This app gets almost 30 billion API requests a day—the bulk of which isn't from users looking at it hourly, but rather applications pulling weather requests. In one of our keynote demos, we built a cool app that scrapes Twitter for monetizable intents and compares what people are saying, grabbing a Watson API to classify the image if the tweet has a picture; it also uses the location of the tweet to pull a weather forecast closely associated with the person who is tweeting. Why? Real-time promotions. This is a great example of an application that is using an API to get the Twitter stream, another to tell us what's in the image, and yet another to get localized weather—this is why we keep saying today's apps are composed and this is a perfect example of the API economy. Quite simply, more and more SaaS providers are going to rely on API integration of their works into third-party services to drive revenue and traffic *far more* than they rely on a UX-driven strategy for attracting users.

At their most basic level, SaaS apps are software that is hosted and managed in the cloud whose backend stacks mostly look the same: software components are preinstalled (SaaS); the database and application server that support the app are already in place (PaaS); and this all lives on top of the infrastructure layer (IaaS). As a consumer of the service, you just interact with the app or API; there's no need to install or configure the software yourself. When SaaS is exposed as a typical offering, you see it as a discrete business app. However (this is important to remember), under the covers the SaaS offering is most likely a collection of dozens (even hundreds or thousands) of APIs working in concert to provide the logic that powers the app.

Having a well-thought-out and architected API is critical for developing an ecosystem around the functionality that you want to deliver through an as-a-service property. We think this point highlights something amazing: not only is the as-a-service model a better way to monetize your intellectual property, but having the pieces of business logic that form your app be consumable in very granular ways (this API call gets us a zip code, that one does a currency conversion) makes you more agile for feature delivery and code resolution.

Remember, the key is designing an API for services and software that plays well with others—whether you're selling them or creating them for internal use. Don't get boxed into thinking your API audience has to be just for people in your company; potentially, it could be useful to anyone on the value chain. Consumers of the SaaS API economy require instant access to that SaaS property (these services need to be always available and accessible), instant access to the API's documentation, and instant access to the API itself (so that developers can program and code against it).

Furthermore, it is critical that the API architecture be extensible, with hooks and integration endpoints across multiple domains to promote cooperation and connectivity with new services as they emerge. A robust API economy is made possible by a hybrid cloud architecture of well-defined open integration points between external systems and cloud marketplaces from any vendor, without consideration to location —that enables service consumers to focus purely on cloud capabilities, instead of destinations (Figure 4-5).

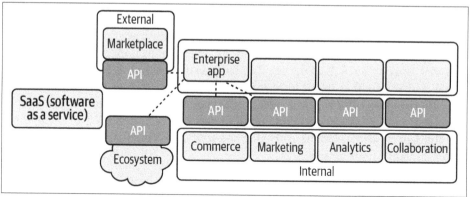

Figure 4-5. A composed enterprise app that on the backend leverages APIs to "round out" its functionality and in turn exposes its line-of-business stakeholders' APIs to support their applications

All You Need Is a Little Bit of REST and Some Microservices

We've talked a lot about RESTful APIs throughout this book, giving you the gist of them to help you understand the discussion in whatever section or chapter you were reading. With that said, since they are so fundamental to the rest (get it?) of this book, we thought we'd spend a little time giving you some analogies and a little more information, because microservices are a key tenet toward modernizing your digital estates.

Let's pretend you're at a superstore like Costco. A REST API consists of various *endpoints* that you access based on things you need. If you're at Costco, most of the things you'll check out and pay for will be processed in the main cashier's line; however, Pharmacy, Optical, and Auto are separate endpoints and those items can't be purchased through the main cashiers. Pharmacy, Optical, Auto, and Cashier are all Costco endpoints where someone is waiting to take your money (a REST API) and service your request. (Unlike Costco, when you consume a RESTful API, you get *exactly* what you came for and leave with just that; you don't walk out spending hundreds of unbudgeted dollars when you just came for one or two items.)

You know how to talk to each of these endpoints, because there's a well-defined standard for doing so—it's akin to human language (well, perhaps today's language isn't so standard, but you get the point). RESTful services talk to applications via their endpoints using their own language called *methods*. Just like we use verbs to describe actions ("Do you have any more ski helmets?"), there are distinct REST API verbs that perform actions too—things like CREATE, READ, UPDATE, and DELETE (tech heads call these CRUD operations). Sometimes those "verbs" are in a different dialect of a method language (like HTTP verbs) and you'll hear them called GET, POST, PUT, and DELETE. It doesn't matter what dialect your dev team speaks with one another, so long as they also know the language (methods) of the service they're programming for.

Each REST API has *one job* (when implemented as a microservice—a best practice) often referred to as the "single responsibility principle." The REST part of that one job is the communication between these separate processes. While REST is how you talk to the API, the execution scope is on running the component code that brings back to the end user what they were looking for. Hopefully you can see how this framework is deeply rooted in CI/CD because the architecture allows you to evolve at different rates (when COVID first started, Costco's Pharmacy service had to evolve much differently than its other endpoints). Building microservices as discrete pieces of logic allows you to granularly evolve different parts of the app over time on their own schedules (for example, look at how many times Uber updates its apps and the reasons for those updates).

With microservices, it's not a single layer that hands an application's data and business logic. You are literally grabbing lots of narrow-minded "bots" that do simple small tasks and wrangling them together for some larger purpose. Microservices are the killers of monolithic apps because you don't develop applications with them; rather, you compose them by pulling together discrete pieces of logic to make an application.

We think that's enough to understand what REST APIs are and the microservices approach, so we'll finish this section with a list of their advantages, summarized in one place for easy reference. The microservices architecture is tremendously valuable because each component:

- Is developed independently of each other—if the service has dependencies on other services (chaining) they are limited and explicit.
- Is developed by a single, small team (another best practice) in which all team members can understand the entire code base—this specialization creates economies of scale, reduces bugs, and creates eminence on the service.
- Is developed on its own timetable so new versions are delivered independently of other services—the team that updates the location logic of the app doesn't have to rely on the team who does discounting calculations in order to effect the change.
- Scales and fails independently—this not only makes it easier to isolate any problems, but also *simplifies* how the app scales. For example, if you're getting more refund requests because of cancelled flights, you can scale refund logic independently of the services that compose the loyalty redemption component.

- Can be developed in a different language—the protocol apps use to talk to each other and invoke (via REST) abstracts away the backend logic and programming language.

GraphQL API

The GraphQL API is a newer type of API that's capturing a lot of attention these days because it was created out of developer frustrations with REST, namely flexibility and inefficiencies. GraphQL is a query language and server-side runtime for APIs that prioritizes giving application pull requests *exactly* the data they requested and no more (or less). As an interesting alternative to REST, GraphQL lets developers construct requests that pull data from multiple sources in a single API call. The neat thing about this API is that you can make all your requests at once. It's outside the scope of this book to delve deeper into GraphQL APIs, but in our Costco example, you could literally walk into the store, ask for your glasses, medicine, a set of winter tires, and fifty pounds of red beets and check out in an instant—it's like a personal assistant. You use GraphQL APIs just like REST APIs (those HTTP verbs we talked about).

It's Not Magic, But It's Cool: The Server in Serverless?

Finally, we get to this mystery called *serverless*. Let's ensure we're clear right off the bat: serverless *does not* mean there isn't a server involved, just like how cloud computing doesn't mean your server is suspended by ice crystals in the sky. If there is one thing we want you to remember about serverless computing, it's that serverless is yet another gear that lets developers focus on writing code.

To understand serverless computing, let's start with the notion that no matter how you're building and hosting apps (traditionally or via REST or GraphQL APIs) there's always been the concept of a dedicated server that's constantly available to service requests. In contrast, the more and more popular serverless architecture doesn't use a live running server dedicated to all of the API calls you're making for your app. And where do you think these serverless servers (even sounds odd to write that) run? They need a distributed, open environment that can easily bring together discrete pieces of logic from anywhere—so naturally, in a cloud of course!

Serverless computing is a new and powerful paradigm, one that naturally has been pounced on by nearly every major cloud vendor in the marketplace today—so you certainly have your pick of providers. The core concern that serverless computing is trying to get away from is the timeless struggle of procuring (ahead of time) correctly sized infrastructure for the workloads you intend to run. With the serverless computing approach, you no longer rent server capacity ahead of time or have to procure a server outright; instead, you pay per computation—without having to worry about the underlying infrastructure at all.

The serverless part means that the serverless framework focuses on scaling automatically to handle each individual request. In short, developers don't have to worry about managing infrastructure capacity to support their service's logic and their associated underlying resources. While IaaS requires that you think about how to provision resources (to support the application and the operating system for that matter), a serverless architecture just needs to know, "How many resources are required to execute your intent?"

To fully appreciate this, let's take a moment to think about today's discussions around cloud (the capability)—workloads are becoming increasingly dominated by containers, orchestration of those containers, and serverless. Looking back, the IaaS pattern we discussed earlier in this chapter was a step in the journey to cloud utopia. While IaaS offers companies more granularity in how they pay for what they use and the time it takes to start using it, as it turns out they rarely paid only for what they use— which is why we often cite that cost savings shouldn't be the primary driver for adopting cloud: it's not a certainty that it will provide them. Even virtual servers often involve long-running processes and less than perfect capacity utilization.

Don't get us wrong. IaaS *can* be more compute and cost efficient than traditional compute, but spinning up a virtual machine (VM) can still be somewhat time-consuming and each VM brings with it overhead in the form of an operating system. The IaaS model of IT is capable of supporting almost anything from a workload perspective but has room for evolution when it comes to certain underlying philosophies and values that make cloud, well, cloud. In many cases, the container has begun replacing VMs as the standard unit of process or service deployment, with orchestration tools like Kubernetes governing the entire ecosystem of clusters.

The crux behind serverless is that you write code that will execute under certain conditions (or code that will run a desired job). When that code is executed, you are only billed for the computational cost of doing the job. You, as a developer, focus on the code and *only* the code. Savvy developers have always endeavored to make their code as efficient as possible. Serverless computing provides an additional incentive for those developers to tighten up their code performance even further—since more efficient code means fewer CPU cycles and therefore (in the case of serverless) even cheaper billing rates to execute their code.

Think about this from another angle: imagine that you have a rarely used service that, when run, is potentially very demanding on local resources. Your system administrator warns you that, should the need to execute this service ever arise (in an emergency), it might adversely affect or even cripple other day-to-day operations running in your environment, simply because of the vast quantities of resources it would require to meet the moment. With serverless computing, your business could host that dust-laden code on a cloud provider to accomplish the job (when necessary), without wasting or risking your own IT infrastructure resources. The burst in resource consumption could be met by the serverless computing environment, allowing your business to address the crisis (should it arrive) without crippling other local services in the fallout.

Serverless is a newer cloud model that is challenging traditional models around certain classes of cloud native applications and workloads. It isn't for everyone, and it has its limitations (which are outside the scope of this book), but if the fit is right—it can be nothing short of a home run. Serverless goes the furthest of any cloud pattern in terms of abstracting away nearly everything but very granular encapsulated business logic, scaling perfectly with demand, and really delivering on the promise of paying only for what you use.

Serverless has a Kid! Function as a Service

We've grossly (perhaps unfairly) simplified it here, but we've been alluding to yet another as-a-service model throughout this chapter—function as a service (FaaS). FaaS is a type of cloud-computing service that allows you to execute code in response to events without the complex infrastructure (dedicated servers, whether they are traditionally dedicated or vis-à-vis IaaS) typically associated with building and launching microservices applications.

Serverless and FaaS are often conflated with one another, but the truth is that FaaS is actually a subset of serverless. Serverless is really focused on any service category—be it compute, storage, database, messaging, or API gateways—where configuration, management, and billing of servers are invisible to the end user. FaaS, on the other hand, is focused on the event-driven computing paradigm where application code only runs in response to events or requests.

Hosting a software application on the internet typically requires provisioning a virtual or physical server and managing an operating system or web server hosting processes. With FaaS, the physical hardware, virtual machine operating system, and web server software management are all handled automatically by the hybrid cloud—which is how we've been describing it.

The Takeaway

Today, traditional IaaS is, by far, the most mature cloud pattern and controls the vast majority of market share in this space. But containers and serverless will be technologies to watch and begin employing opportunistically where it makes sense. As the world moves more toward microservices architectures—where applications are decomposed into small piece parts, deployed independently, manage their own data, and communicate via APIs—containers and serverless approaches will only become more common.

We noted earlier that serverless is great for the right types of applications. From a business perspective, you can start paying for stuff in milliseconds with the FaaS model. Business loves the agility of it all and it reduces the costs of hiring backend infrastructure people (you still need people for IaaS), so it overall reduces operational costs. With that said, businesses have to consider a reduction in overall control of their app at the most granular of levels; furthermore, these apps can potentially be more susceptible to vendor lock-in and disaster recovery can be more complex.

What about developers? Well, they benefit too, starting with the obvious: zero system administration. This means someone (or something) else is handling scalability, which means more time to focus on code, which fosters innovation. That said, developers need to balance this "Zen" dev zone with additional architectural complexity: local testing becomes more challenging; the length of time a built service can run is capped (we didn't cover that here because the book isn't about the details of technology); there is a lack of operational tools; and some other things not worth getting into here.

Wrapping It Up

Now that you're done reading this chapter, we're confident you have a solid foundation around the different cloud patterns that will empower you to decide where to use them and what they are all about. You have a solid understanding on how APIs are shape-shifting app dev in a massive way and how newer patterns (such as serverless and its sibling FaaS) are areas you're likely going to need to explore in the coming months when you're done reading this book.

At this point we know you appreciate cloud as a capability, and how getting yourself (or the people you influence) out of the "cloud as a destination" mindset opens the aperture on all that cloud can deliver to your business. We hope you agree with us that hybrid cloud is the path forward and understand how it can capture the 2.5x value that's been left on the table by the current approach most are using with cloud technology (treating it like a destination).

Before we jump further into details around security, containers, and more, we wanted to give you a solid foundation on those application development epochs we talked about in Chapter 3...so get ready to "shift left" and we'll see you in Chapter 5.

Shift Left

Application modernization is a pivotal moment for information technology, clearly demarcating this generation from those that will follow. In fact, we think it's the only way that organizations can truly capture all the value the hybrid cloud has to offer.

Using containers and orchestration, applications can at last be engineered to realize the "write once, run anywhere" paradigm. For developers, enterprise, and business of all sizes—this means truly unconstrained portability of apps and services. Being able to abstract the process of designing and building applications from the environment(s) they need to run on achieves three goals at once: it unshackles the creativity of developers (who can focus on writing better code with the best tools at their fingertips); it drastically shrinks the time to market for new cloud native (and modernized) apps; and it slashes administrative upkeep that would otherwise be needed to maintain and refactor these apps for new environments over time.

A hybrid multicloud architecture is what makes this level of application portability feasible. The question of where to run applications has shifted from "Here or there?" to one of "Here, and where else?" The plurality of vendors that a business can purchase cloud services from shows that cloud, as it exists today, has transformed from a *destination* into a set of *capabilities*. This holds especially true for vendors that offer cloud footprints that can operate across public cloud, private cloud, and on-premises. Modern containerized apps that follow the axiom of "write once, run anywhere" are able to migrate fluidly across a wide range of hybrid multicloud architectures—and do so in a consistent, repeatable fashion that lends itself well to enterprise.

To "shift left," as developers put it, is to loop back on old processes, identify short-comings within the old ways of doing things, and steadily iterate on those designs to improve them through experience over time. Plenty of lessons are learned each year within the IT marketplace, and the pandemic years are certainly no exception. The disruption underway from this monumental shift in computing, as we enter the new decade, cannot be understated. How can a business have confidence that its choice of technology partner in this new paradigm is the correct one?

Shift Left

The Japanese word ポカヨケ (*Poka yoke*) literally means "mistake-proofing"—its goal is to prevent inadvertent errors and eliminate product defects through early prevention and correction.

For developers, the term *shift left* is a practice intended to find and prevent defects in the software development lifecycle. *Left* reflects the iterative loop that defines such software development cycles, putting forth changes that are tested and evaluated, again and again. It also wonderfully mirrors the same rigorous methodology of revisiting and questioning a null hypothesis using the scientific method. Shifting back to the left—pulling through again with a finer-toothed comb—and continuing to refine on the design (rather than pushing straight through to release with the first working prototype) puts the values of *Poka yoke* into practice.

Monolithic and Microservices

Today, rapid application deployment is a must-have for companies to meet consumer demands or challenges. As you're likely well aware, the quick delivery of capabilities via software to support ever-changing requirements is no easy task.

A real-life example: one of us built a model based on Python's scikit-image library and our script suddenly broke after updating the library to the latest-and-greatest release. Why? The latest version would not accept the `visualize=true` option in our code. Suddenly we had to spell it as `visualise=true` (note the s). We're not sure what Commonwealth English teacher turned open source committer was behind this, but it illustrates the point perfectly: change within the open source community is constant, and in turn these changes can impact (or even break) an enterprise's services just as quickly.

One thing we can unanimously agree on: the faster that a development team can improve their existing applications or find errors in their code, the more time they can otherwise invest in new skills, or use to make better apps.

Separating the Old from the New

A handy way to conceptualize and separate "modernized" applications from those applications that came before is "monolithic" (the old) versus "microservice" (the new) approaches to application design. If both of these terms are new to you, excellent, you're in the right place. If on the other hand you have familiarity with service-oriented architectures, you may be asking yourself how the new approaches to application design are any different than the old—after all, don't they both use services in the end? Indulge us for a moment as we set out to demonstrate exactly why microservices are anything but yet-another flavor of service-oriented design.

For simplicity, let's generalize (generously so) that legacy applications existing within many enterprise organizations today can be described as "monolithic": large, often enormously complex applications, written in a single programming language and frequently running on a single machine. You can see an abstract example of such a monolithic application housed inside a virtual machine (running atop an enterprise hypervisor) in Figure 5-1.

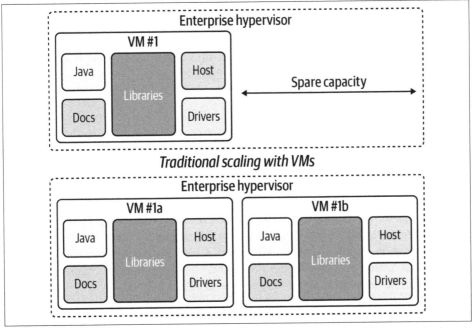

Figure 5-1. Traditional linear approach to scaling up monolithic applications, which is effective, but costly: replicate the virtual machine (and its contents) from the top to what is shown on the bottom with VMs #1a and #1b—both of which are essentially clones of the original VM #1

There are caveats to this, of course—there may be segments of code written in different languages and monolithic applications are not impossible to adapt to distributed systems (although some exceptional feats of engineering may be required). But the reason these are exceptions to the rule (and not the norm) is exactly the reason why we consider monolithic applications to be "legacy" (or at least not modernized). It is precisely because monolithic code is difficult to maintain and challenging to scale that many enterprise organizations are reluctant to modify these apps—not to mention that many of these apps are the backbone of the business and these days a business's risk tolerance is zero. And therein lies the rub: those businesses that are stuck maintaining legacy code are unable to embrace open source innovations, and those organizations unable to scale their mission-critical services are left behind in a marketplace moving increasingly toward hybrid multicloud environments.

Monolithic applications *can* be modular in design, which is why the often-cited description of microservices being "modular" is not always the most helpful way of distinguishing the two design paradigms. A monolithic application usually has a presentation component (HTTP requests responded to with HTML or JSON/XML in turn), a database component (data access objects), business logic, application integration, and plenty of other services. The application might be written entirely in the same language, or it could be split up into pieces—especially with service-oriented architectures, which tend to deploy these monolithic applications across a number of different machines. However, it is still monolithic in design. This will become apparent when we compare how a microservice is constructed and managed later in this chapter.

Microservices Dance to a Different Fiddle

Microservices are often described as the "deconstruction of the monolith," which is a fair assessment of their mission, but may leave you with misconceptions about the methods used to achieve this end state. For example, "deconstruction" implies breaking down into smaller, "simpler" pieces (from a business logic perspective); however, microservices architecture sometimes *adds* complexity, by the mere fact that the composed application is now a distributed service across smaller networked pieces. But what deconstruction provides the developer and business is the decomposition of one unwieldy and large application into more *manageable* chunks of services.

Each of these services, by nature of the way that they are designed, can be developed and worked on (scaled and kept available too...more on that in a bit) independently of one another (now you're starting to see the benefits). This is a tremendous change from the way developers are forced to work on monolithic applications: mainly, having to tackle the entire stack of code at once. The result is that future improvements and refinements to microservices-based applications can be much more strategic ("modular" in the true sense of the word) and collaborative across different teams. As long as you publish the external API of the microservice in a way that other teams or services can dialog with it, teams can work on different components of an application independently of one another.

The extensibility of microservices also means that, for each microservice component within a composed application, developers can use the languages and technologies that they *want* to use—the tools best suited for the focused task at hand—rather than be constrained by the legacy programming languages that at minimum large parts of the monolith would otherwise have needed to maintain. This approach broadens the aperture of open source innovations that can be introduced into a microservices-based application and in turn opens the doors to exciting new workloads your application can tackle.

Scaling: One of These Things Is Not Like the Other

If you manage a set of enterprise apps, scaling up those applications generally means (we're purposely keeping it really simply here) making the application's resource requirements bigger: give it more memory, additional CPU cycles, greater network bandwidth, and so on all the way down the infrastructure stack.

We can already imagine those of you with programming backgrounds shouting at this page, "It doesn't quite work that way!" You're correct, it's not that simple. But for the sake of delineating the differences between monolithic and microservice approaches to scale, let's maintain the notion that in order to scale legacy applications you need only throw more resources at it.

The bottom line: for enterprise organizations maintaining such monolithic applications, the calculus for scaling is a simple one. If you need additional scale, you give the application access to a larger machine. Yes, you can scale out your applications across multiple distributed machines, but that's particularly challenging—and requires more technical chops, so it's not for everyone.

To contrast with the monolithic app, we sketched out Figure 5-2 to illustrate a simplified abstraction of three microservices, each in turn deployed on independent Compute Nodes (servers) from one another. Collectively, they form an application powered by microservices. The color-coded blocks represent modular elements within the microservice that can be modified or developed, scaled, and kept available independently of other elements (stacked blocks of the same color-coded service in turn represent replicas—or copies—of the same microservice). Note the variety of tasks performed by this array of microservices. And yet despite the complexity of the overall application, each microservice is performing only a single (and uniquely essential) task.

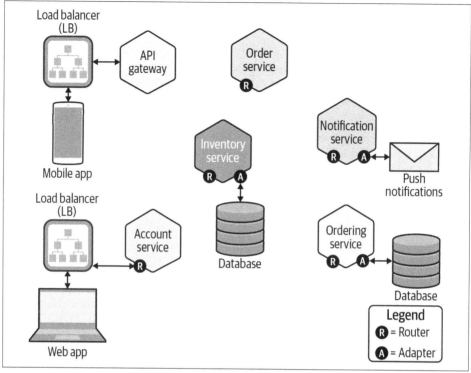

Figure 5-2. A generalized view of how microservices might be arranged across separate Compute (worker) Nodes

In a microservices-based architecture, you scale up by adding more components (or more copies of the same component) to the overall stack. This concept is known as "horizontal scaling," in contrast to the more "vertical" scaling approach used by many monolithic applications. And yet, you could easily make the argument that the two approaches to scaling aren't that substantially different to one another. After all, isn't the solution—throwing more resources and hardware at the bottleneck—essentially the same for both monolithic and microservice applications?

Not quite. We can understand why monolithic applications do not scale well when we look at how it is that developers and programmers go about deconstructing monolithic apps. As we made the argument for previously, an enterprise application "in the old days" was probably written all in the same language. It would have used libraries that were tightly integrated inside of the application. At the same time, there would have been components that existed outside the monolith application—the presentation layer, the database layer, and so on—that are connected by some client or port-adapter mechanism to the monolith.

If you want to scale up a monolithic application, you have to replicate it outright in its entirety—this includes needing to scale everything else that the monolith was dependent on to run (including components like external ports, adapters, and so on). Every copy of the monolithic application would require a replica of its own for each of these external dependencies.

So, what do we want you to take away from all this if you're a business leader looking to bolster your technical chops? When you're scaling a monolithic application, you need to scale all of the enterprise components *together* alongside it. This approach is often rife with wasted resource allocation and complex interdependencies. Certain subcomponents perhaps did not need to be scaled—individually they may have been "keeping up" with demand just fine—but the overall complexity of the monolithic application required that these underutilized components be replicated all the same.

How do microservices approach resource scaling differently? Recall back to the depiction in Figure 5-2 and the matched groupings. Each of these groups are the microservice equivalent to the components (libraries, frameworks, and so on) we described for the monolithic application. There are, however, two key differences. First, external dependencies exist for microservices just as they do for monoliths, but they often communicate over RESTful APIs rather than adapters and are therefore easily modified. Second, the stacked groups of microservice components can be scaled *independently* of one another, as opposed to the wholesale all-or-nothing approach for scaling monolithic application stacks.

An expanded view of our generalized microservice application is shown in Figure 5-3. This depiction revisits the same application we saw in Figure 5-2, only this time scaled up to meet the increasing demand on some of its microservice components. You can see that stacked tiles represent redundant (replica) copies of a particular microservice application or function. Notice that some tiles have more replicas than others—this reflects the way that microservice applications can scale only the components that need to be scaled, independently of the other components.

When you want to scale up a microservices-based application, you simply replicate the individual components (the shaded tiles in Figure 5-3) that *need* to be scaled—and only those components. Think back to the Uber app example we talked about in Chapter 2. It's likely the case that the microservices that provide arrival estimation need more scale (as they are under much heavier demand) than those microservices that provide loyalty point inquiries.

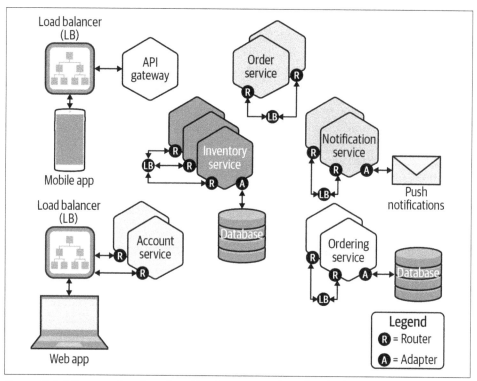

Figure 5-3. Microservices-based applications can scale individual components, independently of one another if need be

Don't overlook this point: the very nature of microservices means that an administrator can be selective in the components they scale (rather than the total approach of monolithic applications), which in turn cuts down on overprovisioning and unnecessary wasted system resources. Microservice components can be treated as separate units and scaled (up or down) independently of each other depending on the component of the app it supports. You can imagine how this modular approach to design, deployment, and scaling lends itself well to a "containerized" worldview that we talked about in Chapter 3.

Teams managing these individual microservice components can therefore work independently of each other, as well. Microservice components can be written in distinct languages from each other, or any mix of languages within the same microservice. As long as that microservice sits behind a well-recognized and documented API interface (such as REST), other components of the microservice application (and external applications) can easily communicate with the component.

Imagine a scenario where a developer has recently been introduced to a team—or perhaps volunteers their programming expertise to an open source community project—and offers to reimplement some component of the microservice application in a much better way than it is currently. The original component was written in PHP, but our astute programmer would much prefer to use Python in order to take advantage of its more efficient programming structures. If this were a monolithic application, this approach to rewriting a component in a different language from the core application language would likely be a nonstarter (or at least significantly more complex to implement). With microservice design, it's no impediment whatsoever! Our programmer is free to select a new language that is much more conducive to their expertise and to the workload that the microservice needs to carry.

Orchestration: Amplifying the Challenges of Scale

One of the design considerations for scaling up microservice applications is that the components themselves should be "stateless" in design. Stateless essentially means that, in the event one of the microservices were to fail (due to hardware loss or other reason), then work can be assigned to any of that microservice's replicas without additional instructions or fiddling around with other instances. If a microservice were to be "lost," then the application will realize it did not get a response to its request and in turn hand off that same request to another copy of the microservice. All of this is managed by handing work to load balancers, which then pick from a pool of the same microservices and hands work off to one of them based on the type of workload. In other words, if microservices go down, any of their replicas should be capable of picking up the slack immediately and the application should carry on without interruption.

The resiliency of microservices to failure is as much a byproduct of their design (which has built-in redundancies and tolerance for failure) as it is a result of the way that microservices manage "state." We won't go into the full details of how they achieve that in this book, but in essence the way that administrators and applications update a microservice is by *modifying* its state. Contrast this with having to explicitly tell a microservice what to do: with stateful applications, these instructions are passed implicitly. Directions such as "I want you to be at *this* state and look like *that*" are relayed without explicit instructions on how to achieve that end state, yet the RESTful API endpoints of the microservice are able to act upon them accordingly. This is different from assuming (or having to figure out for yourself) what state a microservice is in and directly instructing it on what actions to take.

If microservices could speak, their conversations (and their underlying design philosophy) would sound something like this: "Tell me what state you want me in, and I'll make the changes necessary to get there; regardless of the state I'm in at the time, I will make whatever changes are necessary to eventually get to the state that you want." This notion of microservices *understanding* the state they are in, and systems that are able to course-correct to regain this state if necessary, is incredibly useful when you start to consider microservices in the context of containers and orchestration engines.

These concepts are new to many of us—how many of you picking up this book expected to get into discussions about the behavior of applications? It's perfectly alright to feel awash in the possibilities. But know this: these behaviors are fundamental to understanding the essence of all that untapped value we keep telling you that'll remain locked away without a modernized hybrid cloud strategy.

Figure 5-4 depicts orchestration: coordination and communication amongst the nodes and an application's component (microservice) replicas. It is the same application we were just examining previously in Figures 5-2 and 5-3, but now distributed properly across separate hosts. Naturally, the more infrastructure hosts that your app is deployed across, the more fault-tolerant your app becomes and the less disastrous any potential hardware failure will be.

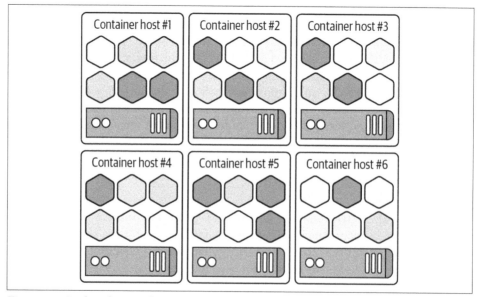

Figure 5-4. Redistributing the same microservices-based application from Figure 5-3 across multiple container hosts: this lends greater resiliency to failure and provides further opportunities for scaling resources as required

Think about it: imagine putting all the same microservices on a single host; while it might scale with the right hardware, if that host were to go down, you would lose all access to those microservices. That's why we advise you to use a pattern that distributes those microservices across hosts in the best manner possible so that they are load-balanced and redundant across multiple servers. The loss of a single physical host would potentially take out multiple microservices, but wouldn't break the application. As the microservices are distributed across other functional hosts, the application continues to run.

In a properly orchestrated Kubernetes (K8s) environment, such as Red Hat OpenShift, there are actively running components that recognize when a microservice has been lost and will immediately deploy additional replicas in response. The platform understands how many replica copies should exist at any one time, and should that number be less than expected, the orchestration platform will act to bring more online automatically. Here's the point: you have to distribute microservices across hosts *first* so that your application remains resilient to failure, and afterwards (on a properly orchestrated platform) can leave the busywork of maintaining that application state to the orchestration layer.

Write Once, Run Anywhere

Up to this point, we've examined what distinguishes a modernized microservices-based application from a monolithic legacy application. But what does it take to achieve this? And more importantly: is the process of modernizing applications *worth* the time and cost of doing so? In Chapter 2, we gave you a framework to help figure that out (the Cloud Acumen Curve); here, we'll give you the rubric for deciding how to place your project along that curve. There are three main stages to approaching container modernization: replatform, repackage, and refactor.

Three Stages of Approaching Modernization Incrementally

We'll start with the "How?"—because the value associated with this process becomes readily apparent once you understand the multitude of ways that applications can be modernized. For each incremental step along the journey of application modernization—from legacy to replatform, repackage, and refactor—there are increasing benefits to users and consumers alike, as marked on the scorecards in Figure 5-5.

A common misconception we often hear from clients is the impression that application modernization is a zero-sum game: the notion that a business must choose to either modernize or stick with the monolith, with no middle ground. Like we said earlier in this chapter, the reality is far different! In truth, applications can be modernized incrementally over time. The pace at which your organization shifts toward microservices-based applications can depend on many factors: the technical staffing and proficiency of skills within your IT department; the complexity and volume of legacy applications that need to be modernized; or even the comfort and level of risk your organization is willing to sustain as you migrate mission-critical workloads toward a new (but ultimately beneficial) paradigm.

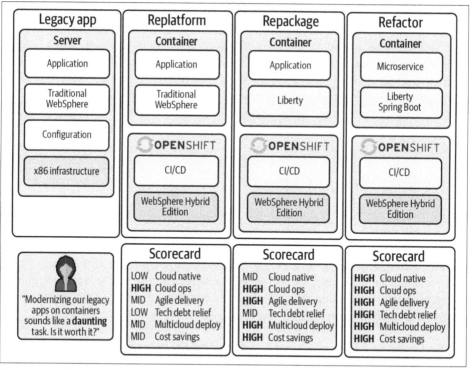

Legacy app	Replatform	Repackage	Refactor
Server	**Container**	**Container**	**Container**
Application	Application	Application	Microservice
Traditional WebSphere	Traditional WebSphere	Liberty	Liberty Spring Boot
Configuration	**OPEN**SHIFT	**OPEN**SHIFT	**OPEN**SHIFT
x86 infrastructure	CI/CD	CI/CD	CI/CD
	WebSphere Hybrid Edition	WebSphere Hybrid Edition	WebSphere Hybrid Edition

"Modernizing our legacy apps on containers sounds like a **daunting** task. Is it worth it?"	**Scorecard**	**Scorecard**	**Scorecard**
	LOW Cloud native	MID Cloud native	HIGH Cloud native
	HIGH Cloud ops	HIGH Cloud ops	HIGH Cloud ops
	MID Agile delivery	HIGH Agile delivery	HIGH Agile delivery
	LOW Tech debt relief	MID Tech debt relief	HIGH Tech debt relief
	MID Multicloud deploy	HIGH Multicloud deploy	HIGH Multicloud deploy
	MID Cost savings	HIGH Cost savings	HIGH Cost savings

Figure 5-5. The stepwise, incremental journey from legacy applications to fully modernized microservices

Turn back and look at the incremental approach shown in Figure 5-5; it transitions from legacy monolithic applications on the left toward fully modernized applications on the right. Quite simply, the journey toward modernized applications exists on a gradient. For every step that a business makes along that journey, they in turn receive increasing benefits to their applications and to the business as a whole—as indicated by the scorecards along the bottom of Figure 5-5.

The first step toward modernizing applications simply is to *replatform* from legacy infrastructure toward platforms designed specifically for containers and Kubernetes orchestration, such as Red Hat OpenShift. Your choice of infrastructure matters here (as it does in all decisions made regarding your IT estate); therefore, selecting infrastructure that simplifies the process of modernizing code can pave the way for a smoother replatform experience. It's important to note here that you're not aiming to change the legacy app's code in the replatform stage, but to merely migrate the monolith into a platform that supports containers and orchestration, as well as continuous integration and continuous delivery (CI/CD) pipelines.

The next phase is to *repackage* the application code. In this phase you have the opportunity to modernize the legacy code of which the monolith is composed. Several vendors in the marketplace today offer services for steering this transformational process in the right direction: first, by automatically assessing the level of effort required to modernize the legacy code with more modern and developer-friendly frameworks like Liberty and Spring Boot; and second, where possible, automatically performing the migration (or providing guidance on how to do so yourself).

The final phase in the journey is to *refactor* the application—the most modernized form as we've defined it, but by no means a requirement for organizations that want to simplify the maintenance and boost the value of their legacy applications (as we've seen demonstrated by the replatform and repackage phases). At this stage, the monolithic application has been refactored into more modular microservices; its code base likely reflects a myriad of open source languages that are tailored to the specific workloads of the app; and the experience of those maintaining the application has been simplified in terms of operations, integrated development environments, and tooling.

Comparing Legacy Applications, Containerized Applications, and Virtual Machines

It is a fitting time to now give containers their due and look at exactly what it is this technology enables and how it relates to the journey toward modernized applications that we've described so far.

Linux containers are the basic instrument—the atomic unit, if you will—of containerization technologies. As you learned about in Chapter 3, Docker is a specific flavor of this technology, which has become nearly synonymous with "containers" in general, but that's merely owing to its popularity. Isolation technologies were developed and popularized first on Linux.

To an operating system, containers are like a process. You can conceptualize a container like you would a sandbox. It uses namespaces, control groups, Security-Enhanced Linux (SELinux), and other Linux security components to keep containerized code secured and isolated. Containerized applications can be remarkably portable: they can run—essentially unchanged—across a number of different cloud providers and types of infrastructure that support this technology.

To a developer, a container is a packaging method: it provides a way to package an application for delivery and ensures that all its dependencies and configuration information are passed along with it.

On the left of Figure 5-6, *traditional* legacy processes run on a single operating system (OS), atop hardware and hosts. They are dependent upon OS libraries, runtime libraries, and possibly special libraries that are required by particular applications. Regardless, it all runs as a stack on that specific host. Applications that are to be ported elsewhere have to be migrated *alongside* (inclusive) of the operating system and dependencies that application requires to run. This is what is sometimes described as the "heavyweight" nature of legacy applications (in contrast to the "lightweight" approach of containerized applications).

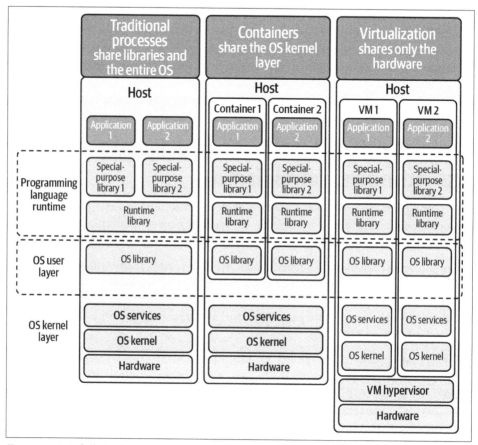

Figure 5-6. A full-stack perspective across legacy applications (left), containerized applications (center), and virtualized applications (right)

The far right of Figure 5-6 shows an example of the approach taken by enterprise organizations for years: *virtualization*. Using this strategy, a hypervisor is built into either the hardware directly or is running as a layer on top. This allows administrators to abstract different operating systems on virtual machines (VMs). In VMs, you are essentially running a full version of the operating system with every instance. This has the positive benefit of allowing every VM to potentially run a different version of unique operating systems from one another—but it also means that potentially every VM will need a bespoke approach to patching and maintenance. (By this way, this doesn't even include the additional storage and resource constraints that running multiple VMs with separate OSes can put on a system!) On top of that are the OS libraries and runtime libraries that accompany every flavor of OS.

Herein lies the double-edged nature of virtual machines. You can have as many of them as your infrastructure is able to support and each VM can be tailored to a specific operating system environment. However, these resource requirements can be difficult to scope, costly to support, and particularly challenging to maintain. These flaws are further exacerbated when it comes to scaling VMs across multiple machines.

In the center of Figure 5-6, we showcase the modern approach toward improving on legacy applications while avoiding the pitfalls of virtual machines: *containerization*. In essence, containers have an OS and services that support the lifecycle of the container. The only contents that a container must supply are the runtime libraries, the application, and the application-specific dependencies that are needed to run that application. This means that all of the containers are running atop the same operating system: Linux.

A container engine runs containers. In the simplest terms, the container engine uses the kernel features of Linux in order to manage and start containers using things like Linux namespaces, control groups, and so on. To help you understand how all of these components come together to enable containers to work, we'll dig into each of these concepts in turn.

Namespaces: What's in a Name?

Namespaces are a Linux kernel feature that provides resource abstraction. They allow users to segregate different applications and set directives on whether those applications can see each other or share data. In effect, namespaces provide an isolation level for different types of resources. For example, if a user has two different namespaces for containers—each of which might have different process ID namespaces—then when that user inspects those containers, they will see completely distinct and isolated lists of process IDs. If they are *sharing* a namespace, that user will see the same list. For users looking to find ways to avoid containers interfering with one another (such as with network interfaces) or those looking to create filesystem constructs that are not seen by other containers, namespaces are the tool of choice.

Shared operating systems in general function because files and other objects (processes) have permissions to say who can run them, open a write to file, use a file, and so on. What permissions *don't* tell you (or the operating system for that matter) is the context for how that object is supposed to be used.

Security-Enhanced Linux (SELinux) was mentioned earlier—it is fundamentally important to the way that Red Hat containers secure and isolate themselves from each other. SELinux provides a much more complete and comprehensive set of policies and tags that get applied to objects and processes, which essentially start to label them as, "What is this and what is it supposed to be used for?" Developers get to write the rules that say: "Processes with this tag can do X, Y, or Z to files or other objects that have tag A." SELinux allows the administrator to set the minimum privilege required to work with objects, and to disallow (especially in situations of hacking or intrusion when a process is overtaken) processes from being used with something it was not designed to be used for.

For example, an Apache process with a tag `httpd_t` is illustrated in Figure 5-7. An SELinux configuration file exists on this container that states that "assets with tags can perform functions with assets of the same policy tags." There is a policy that says that `httpd_t` services are allowed to work with files that have a tag of `httpd_sys_con tent_t` or `httpd_log_t`, but no others. The absence of a policy automatically disallows that interaction from taking place. There is no stated policy, for example, to allow `httpd_t`-tagged services to work with `postgresql_db_t`-tagged directories or files from *home/user*; therefore, the Apache service is disallowed from interacting with the PostgreSQL database. Anything not explicitly set as a policy is fundamentally denied which enables the Zero Trust security model (we will discuss further in Chapter 6).

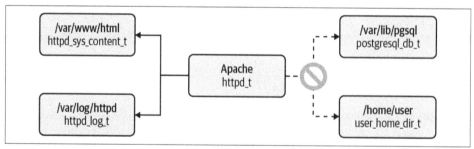

Figure 5-7. A depiction of SELinux "context" at work in securing an Apache HTTP server application with regard to permitted access routes (the /var/ directories on the left) and disallowed routes (Apache cannot access the PostgreSQL database on the right): context is set on every object across the system

One powerful feature within SELinux is mandatory access control, which may be a term familiar to those of you who have worked with security clearances before. People and objects are defined with security parameters, and these parameters dictate who is allowed to read top-secret documents and so forth. Mandatory access control, therefore, can be thought of as a labeling system. If your label (or pair of labels—the way in which you label is arbitrary, so long as you are consistent with how you do so) does not correspond to the level of access required by an object, you are disallowed from interacting (or perhaps even seeing) that object.

Another security feature is known as Control Groups or "cgroups," another construct of the Linux operating system. Control Groups provide a way of setting up different collections of processes and determining rules for how resources are assigned to those groups. It is critical to explicitly set out these policies precisely because processes are capable of "spawning" child processes from parent processes. Control Groups ensure that these child processes are forced to share (and are limited to) the resource limits set on their parent processes. Limitations and caps can be set on aspects such as the bandwidth available to a process, the CPU cycle time that process can occupy, memory constraints, and much more. Control Groups in effect prevent rogue or hijacked processes from running rampant across your container platform resources.

At this stage, we're ready to elevate the conversation another level: from containers to orchestration. Specifically, let's talk more about Kubernetes and Red Hat OpenShift Container Platform (OCP).

Within OCP itself, Red Hat has put in tremendous amounts of work to rearchitect the platform in order to place Kubernetes at the very core of the offering itself. What you will see as we delve deeper into the platform is that OpenShift adds significant value (and prevents significant headache) compared to cooking up a Kubernetes orchestration platform in-house using open source components. We certainly won't claim that it's impossible to build your own Kubernetes orchestration platform—it began as an open source community project, after all! But after you look into the technical burden you'll need to assume, the vulnerabilities that the open source tooling is exposed to, and the complexity of wrangling all of these components together, we are confident you'll view the choice this way: "Sure, we could build our own—but why would we want to?"

Building an Operating System for Containers

Kubernetes retains the honors of the container orchestration layer for the Red Hat OpenShift platform. The features of K8s are vast. But for our purposes, we need only understand that these features include service discovery and load balancing—both of which are built into OCP natively. K8s also handles horizontal scaling (a replication controller concept), which can be used manually or be given parameters to work automatically—either from a command line or from a web console interface. Along the same line, K8s can actually check to see if containers exist; if they are down, it will restart them (similar to horizontal scaling: it knows there are supposed to be certain quantities of them, and it will clean up and replace those that fail).

Why does load balancing suit the distributed nature of containers so nicely? A requesting service only needs to know the target's DNS name. This means that behind the scenes, an administrator can change the IP addresses and locations of that service (for example: a container could go down, be replicated, or be brought back online)—yet still map back to the original DNS name. As such, external applications or services can continue to reach out to the same DNS name consistently and not concern themselves with the potentially fluid and dynamically changing underpinnings of the containerized environment.

Kubernetes can recognize when underlying base images have changed, and update containers based on those changes. Afterwards, it can roll those out to production so that users tapping into your services are not detrimentally impacted by the rollout. If you take down services to replace them, users will complain that they cannot access the tooling they've come to depend on. Kubernetes does rollouts intelligently to ensure that it is only replacing a certain number of services at a time (instead of an all-or-nothing approach); furthermore, if rollouts of specific replacements fail, K8s knows how to recall those changes and bring back the previous iteration (without losing it for good). It's a smart upgrade capability for your applications.

Kubernetes is designed for high availability and resiliency against failure—which happens more often than you might think in cloud and distributed systems. But a functional Kubernetes cluster also needs to be able to maintain state for the cluster and the applications running atop it, so OpenShift Container Platform also includes an etcd database (an open source distributed clustered key-value store used to hold and manage the critical information that distributed systems like K8s need to keep running). If certain nodes go up or down, you still have consistency in the configuration.

The purpose of this kind of store is that, for each of the resources making up the objects and entities belonging to the cluster, that definition for the "proper" state of these resources is maintained and stored in etcd. These include deployment configurations, build configurations, and more. The cluster uses that information to know how to restart application containers again, whatever the circumstance. This also applies to containers that are cluster services infrastructure. OpenShift Container Platform itself is built upon containerized services—it's not just the applications that OpenShift users deploy that are containerized! OpenShift and Kubernetes run as containers themselves.

The operating system underlying all of this is CoreOS. With version 4 (and above) of OpenShift, Red Hat now uses the CoreOS container operating system in place of Red Hat Enterprise Linux (RHEL). It is a tightly integrated refinement of the RHEL operating system designed specifically for containers. Within that operating system, Red Hat has included the CRI-O engine, which is an Open Container Initiative (OCI)–compliant runtime that handles all of the container startup and management on top of CoreOS.

The most important concept introduced with CoreOS is the idea that the operating system is immutable (can't be changed). When you boot up a CoreOS node, you cannot make changes on it. More specifically, any changes made on it are thrown away—so if you reboot the operating system again, you'll receive the same level of consistency when it redeploys. The operating system itself underneath cannot be hacked or manipulated while it's running. It also means that when you're managing it, you'll have to learn new techniques for how you are managing it. The entire operating system is updated as a single image, instead of using RPM packages. It is designed and tuned *specifically* for running containers. And everything, including system components, runs as containers on top. Red Hat OpenShift Container Platform knows how to perform updates to RHEL CoreOS, so there are proper procedures for maintaining the cluster itself.

Within Red Hat OpenShift, there are three types of load balancing working together: external, HAProxy, and internal. External load balancing depends on what types of load balancers and environments are available within your datacenter, and it performs the duties of managing access to the OpenShift API itself. HAProxy gives users and services an external-facing route to applications. Internal load balancing is handled using Netfilter rules (another Linux concept), which can be used for security and other path management between applications inside of the cluster; however, it has no control over outside users getting into the cluster. OCP understands how to perform automated scaling and does so by examining the amount of traffic coming in across the load balancers ("being handled" by the cluster); correspondingly, it adds or terminates containers as needed in order to handle the load.

OCP ships with logging and monitoring capabilities built in, which includes Prometheus (which we tell you all about in the Appendix). The combination of Prometheus and OpenShift's alerting system gives administrators the ability to proactively respond to anything that happens within the cluster. They can keep track of the health and activity of the cluster and then take actions based on that information in a timely manner. OCP integrates the Elasticsearch/Kibana logging solution, which handles the aggregation of logs across all of the nodes and applications in the cluster. It also handles storage and retention of those logs.

Application management in OCP involves OpenShift Source-to-Image (S2I) for automatic build and deploy capabilities. Simply, Red Hat stores images that can be reused and can create configurations that automatically take source information, figure out what needs to be done with it, create a build set of instructions, and execute on those build instructions to deploy the application—all in one long flow. S2I can take any application that is source code (even when it comes from a Git repository or code from your local machine directory) and convert that code into a deployed containerized application. Once you've designed that workflow and performed it, the build config and the deployment config from that workflow are available to repeat the same containerized application again in the future.

Extensibility in K8s takes advantage of the orchestration layer's fixed set of services, which includes an extension mechanism where providers like Red Hat can add features on top of the upstream K8s code. Red Hat provides package extensions that include Operators for ease of installation, updates, and management. Red Hat also has an Operator lifecycle manager that facilitates the discovery and installation of application and infrastructure components. Many other companies (not named Red Hat) have seen the advantages of using Operators and there has been momentum for standardization of publicly available Operators, resulting in OperatorHub.io, which was launched as a collaboration between IBM, Red Hat, Amazon, Google, and Microsoft.

It's OK to Have an Opinion: Opinionated Open Source

So far we have discussed what it means to modernize applications, the technologies that make containerization possible, and the componentry underlying an orchestration platform such as Red Hat OpenShift. To pull these pieces together and take us home, let's examine how each component—microservices, containers, and orchestration platform—enable modernized application services that are ready for the hybrid multicloud world.

Putting It All Together

As a way of thinking, Kubernetes defines a cluster's state. Administrators and developers are keeping track of all the information in the etcd database. Kubernetes is running the controllers that monitor these resources, checking what their state is, and if the state is different from that which has been declared, it will take action to bring those resources to the state that they are supposed to be in.

OpenShift Container Platform (OCP) runs on essentially two types of nodes: masters and workers. Master nodes run the API; provide the interface for the web console, command line, and many other API endpoints utilized for internal and external cluster communication; host the etcd database that maintains the state of the cluster; and execute all of the internal cluster services needed to maintain cluster operations. This list is not exhaustive, but for our purposes it gives a comprehensive idea of the importance of the Master nodes to a K8s cluster. Master nodes are configured so that they cannot be scheduled for end-user application pods. In other words, when you deploy applications and they are looking for nodes to be scheduled on, the Master nodes are specifically marked as being unavailable for use as general-purpose (Worker) nodes. Worker nodes, or Infrastructure nodes, can be scheduled as application pods for deployment of containers. Administrators can determine how many Worker nodes they expect will be needed to handle the resiliency and redundancy requirements for their applications (with consideration given to how many Worker nodes the cluster infrastructure can support, of course).

Administrators supply the compute nodes, networking infrastructure, and a sufficient amount of storage to supply the storage volumes and space for additional disks within containers—not just the space to run the containers themselves. Figure 5-8 illustrates the orientation of these services and technologies across the compute, network, and storage componentry of the OCP cluster. These variables need to be set up (or made available) before the cluster is provisioned, much like you would do for any datacenter.

Sitting atop the architecture stack depicted in Figure 5-8 are Worker nodes, on which teams schedule all of the user applications and containers that are to be built. You can easily scale Workers by adding more of them; furthermore, OpenShift can scale these Workers automatically for you should demand for services outpace what they are outputting at the time.

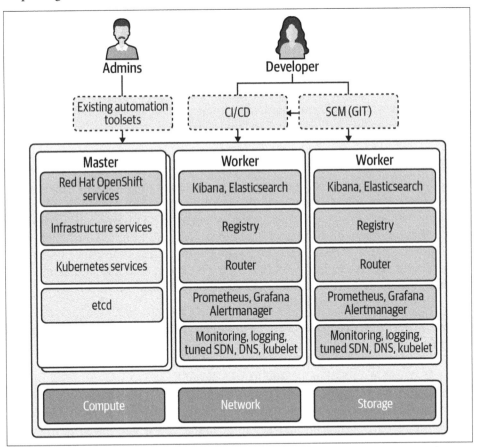

Figure 5-8. A simplified view of the OpenShift Container Platform stack and an abstraction of Kubernetes at the core of the platform

The Master node(s) are usually set up in groups of three for high availability and to achieve a cluster quorum. User workloads never run on the Master. An etcd service is running on the Master node, which keeps track of the state of everything in the cluster, including which users are logged in, where workloads live on the cluster, and so on. Master nodes also play host to the core Kubernetes components: Kubernetes API server (overseeing APIs to get at the cluster management services), Scheduler (for scheduling across nodes), and Cluster Management (handles the cluster's state via the etcd database). On top of that we also have OpenShift services: OpenShift API server, Operator Lifecycle Management (integrated to give administrators access to automatic cluster upgrades), and Web Console. A number of internal and support Infrastructure Services also run on the Master, which make containers easier to run at scale, including monitoring, logging, SDN, DNS, and Kubelet. All of these come integrated and operational out of the box with the Red Hat OpenShift cluster.

OpenShift has a cluster management solution that includes Prometheus, Grafana, and Alertmanager. Each of these components has been enhanced based on work done by Red Hat's own engineering team, which applied lessons learned and best practices from Red Hat's experience managing OpenShift to improve the monitoring capabilities for its customers. These cluster management tools make it possible for administrators to understand the health and capacity of the overall OpenShift cluster and empowers them to take actions based on that information.

Logging capabilities are based on Fluentd, Elasticsearch, and Kibana—making it easy to visualize and corroborate log events. This is immensely valuable when you have applications that can scale to many, perhaps hundreds or thousands, of instances. In such a scenario, an administrator would do anything to avoid having to read through 100 disparate logs; they would much prefer having access to a single aggregated log per application. Many of the features described here also tie into OpenShift's role-based access control (RBAC) features, allowing administrators to control who gets access to what services within the cluster. In the case of operational logs, administrators have the ability to control and make sure that the right individuals see the logs (and only the logs) that they are meant to have access to.

Regardless of whether people consuming this platform are administrators or developers, the web, command-line, and IDE integration tools support people working in whatever way they want or need to. As you can infer, all of the components we've discussed so far come together to simultaneously improve the quality of life of the administrator, while bolstering the security and stability of the platform as a whole. And, naturally, they accelerate the journey of businesses deployed on the platform toward fully modernized applications that are hardened for the challenges of hybrid multicloud computing.

CHAPTER 6

Hackers, Attackers, and Would-Be Bad Actors: Thoughts on Security for Hybrid Cloud

All software, proprietary or open source, has long been a target for cyber hackers, attackers, and would-be bad actors. We want to ensure we set the right tone for this chapter: we aren't suggesting that open source is inherently less secure than products built in a proprietary manner—not at all. But there is something to the old adage "You get what you pay for." (And as we'll explore later, there's a world of difference between building systems for pet projects versus designing for the needs of enterprise.) Kate Compton (*https://oreil.ly/xnt1v*) makes the delightful comparison of "free" (open source) software to the curbside donations you might find after a move or when the college dormitories empty out come spring: "mattress-ware." Sure, it's free, but like with so many things in life you're generally getting what you pay for. "Mattress-sourced" software might be the byproduct of an academic project or a developer's Friday night whimsy. Making project code "open source" is a potential way to give new life to the project, but it comes with the expectation that there's a fair bit of cleaning to do (of software bugs or literal bedbugs) before you would consider putting it "into production." The point we want you to remember is that open source software for the enterprise requires much consideration and effort. You're almost always better off partnering with an enterprise open source vendor.

One of the best parts about open source is the number of developers that can put eyeballs to software problems and the speed at which innovation can get to market with so many hands to keyboard. With that said, open source is not without its shortcomings. We've had firsthand experiences with getting open source projects up and running that date back to when Linux first came out decades ago, to standing up our first Hadoop instance in the early days (where it took months to properly get the full ecosystem working). The constant innovation is astonishing, but nevertheless it can wreak havoc on the stability of any company's solutions—large or small. Often, you'll find documentation is lacking. Finally, you need some pretty deep skills to support any open source project.

It's also important to keep in mind that open source isn't about a single solution; in fact, open source organizations don't care if there are competing projects created for the same goals. What they *do* care about is ensuring that there is a sustainable development community behind the project. Quite simply, open source *is about fostering open innovation through the commitment of a community; it's not necessarily a standards-based organization.*

It's quite evident that the open source model has taken off. In fact, we'll boldly tell you that most innovative companies are using enterprise open source software. Because of this, you'll see a number of vendors integrate open source software into their product (like using Spark for data wrangling and cleansing), companies formed with committers of an open source project to offer paid support for it, and others that are a combination of both as they contribute to, make easier, and harden these open source solutions for the enterprise (like IBM).

What is enterprise hardening? It's all the things a vendor can do that makes open source software more appropriate for enterprise deployment. It can take the form of "fit-and-finish" work like closing unused ports and firming up access controls, to enabling secure default configurations that make the project more secure, easier to install, more manageable, simpler to upgrade, and more.

Success can bring windfalls for your company, but it can just as easily lure in bad actors. Now more than ever, cybercriminals are wreaking havoc in the open source community and preying upon the very attributes that make open source technologies so attractive to developers: ease of access, modification, and redistribution. In this chapter we will explore some of the more common security concerns, dive a little deeper into container security, and give you some of our top recommendations to enhance your cybersecurity posture in a hybrid cloud model. This is not meant to be a comprehensive guide to hardening your hybrid multicloud environment, but it will put you on the right path and prime you to see the vulnerabilities (and opportunities) that may exist as you enable your business with cloud capabilities.

Just to Level Set: What's This Open Source Stuff?

If you're a business leader, chances are you've picked up on open source software (OSS), what it is, and why you should (*must*, really) care about it. To level set and get us all on the same page, here's what open source means to us (and why it should matter to you).

OSS can be thought of as code that has been made publicly available by its original creator or authors. The concept behind OSS is a decentralized software development model that encourages open collaboration among a vast developer community. Often, developers will share their projects for peer review and further refinement by the community at large. This level of collaboration introduces a way of working that reaches far beyond typical proprietary software development methods. It provides for more flexible and less expensive up-front cost solutions that—for successful open source projects—outlast those solutions from proprietary software, precisely because they are built and maintained by software *communities* rather than a single *company*. Most OSS solutions began as a project in one of the many online code repositories, such as GitHub or GitLab. These repositories have large communities of developers that contribute code to existing projects, fork (open source lingo for taking a copy of something and then making it your own and taking it in a different direction—for example, MariaDB was forked from MySQL), and create new projects. The more developers engaged on a given project, the better the innovation pool becomes.

 Some open source projects go on to be wildly successful and become foundational to the enterprise. Linux and EnterpriseDB are great examples. Others never really take hold—there are literally thousands of open source database projects, and we've seen many customers start on one only to realize the open source project was abandoned by its original committers within a year. Finally, some projects take off like rocket ships (Hadoop), look like they're set to change the world, and then peter out. The Kubernetes open source project is a fundamental anchor to cloud as a capability and we're certain it will become an enterprise foundation building block.

As enterprises adopt agile development methodologies, OSS becomes increasingly valuable. In fact, the Linux kernel itself has seen a significant rise in adoption over the last decade and we expect even broader adoption with the growing popularity of Kubernetes (which we briefly talk about throughout this book, but go into detail in the Appendix). Each year we see an increasing number of commercial applications (distributed and sold under proprietary licensing) with embedded OSS as well. These trends show no sign of slowing—the trajectory toward broader adoption of OSS and community-led projects is a clear one.

With that out of the way, you might be asking yourself, "If everyone has access to the code, is OSS secure?" The answer isn't always straightforward. We'll suggest that OSS projects have the benefit of having an enormous base of developers committing code (particularly the more popular projects), which imparts a great deal of innovation, scrutiny, and expertise. However, not all OSS projects receive equal attention, which means they don't all have thousands of developers reviewing the code for bugs and vulnerabilities in equal measure or have vast experience in enterprise enviroments. Generally speaking: your experience and quality-assurance levels may (and will) vary. You need to do your research before pulling any code down from your favorite repository. Let's dive into what we mean by this.

Data Breaches, Exploits, and Vulnerabilities

You'd have to be asleep at the proverbial wheel if you haven't seen the commonplace news about cyberattacks that have been launched over the last few years; as we've said throughout this book, they continue to increase at a steady (and alarming) pace. These attacks range in scope and severity: from data breaches and ransomware attacks at major financial institutions; to attacks on states, local governments, and federal agencies; and disturbingly, on health institutions (disproportionately targeted during the current COVID-19 pandemic). Because of their proliferation and integration into proprietary offerings, OSS technologies have become popular attack vectors for cybercriminals.

The Ponemon Institute's "Cost of a Data Breach Report 2020" (*https://oreil.ly/WLyw4*) summarized a vast number of in-depth interviews conducted with 525+ organizations across 17 countries who all share a common thread—they all experienced data breaches between August 2019 and April 2020. As the pandemic boosted work-from-home patterns during on-and-off again lockdown protocols, Ponemon followed up with supplemental interviews with these same sample groups.

Ponemon's report revealed that the average cost of data breaches has gone down (slightly)—likely representing established protocols and playbooks around handling such events. The report also shined a spotlight on the threat vectors where most attacks originate from and which types of breaches were shown to be increasingly on the rise. The study goes on to point out that the trend in malicious attacks has risen steadily over the last five years, making it the leading cause of security breaches today. As you can see in Figure 6-1, the third most common threat vector that often led to a data breach was "Vulnerabilities in third-party software," including OSS code.

One discovery that caught our attention (but seemed obvious after it did) was the use of OSS tools to carry out these attacks. OSS, it seems, is a sword that can cut both ways: like so many technological inventions, it can be used for tremendous good—but it can also be wielded as an instrument of ill intent and harm. A perfect example of this conundrum is the dark web. You get on the dark web using an open source browser that enables anonymous communications (called Tor) and law enforcement may use OSINT tools to find bits of information about the kind of interactions going on there.

We recommend following Ponemon's security work to continue to learn information about data breaches after reading this book. They've been doing it a long time and have become one of our most trusted sources for data breach information. We'll also note that data breach reports are out of date the moment they are published; the numbers keep going up, so it's worth keeping up with the newest reports.

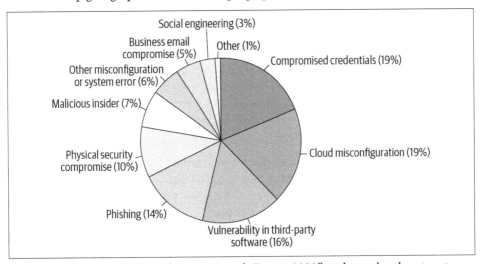

Figure 6-1. Ponemon's "Cost of a Data Breach Report 2020" and popular threat vectors used for data breaches

Hackers Don't Care Where You Work: Public Cloud and Security

Digital transformation goes hand and hand with the rise of cloud computing; in fact, it acts as an accelerator for cloud as organizations seek to modernize their IT infrastructures and apps. Looking to take advantage of the flexibility and potential cost savings of moving workloads to a cloud service provider (CSP), some organizations often view the public cloud as being more secure. They may feel that CSPs are better equipped to provide more elaborate security controls and policies, which might prevent attacks from the outside world, either because of a concentration of knowledge or economies of scale applied to such operations.

To quote Thomas Gray, author of "Ode on a Distant Prospect of Eton College": "ignorance is bliss, 'tis folly to be wise." The reality is that malicious attacks against misconfigured cloud environments (look back to Figure 6-1) *have been and remain* one of the leading causes of data breaches, tied for first with stolen or compromised credentials. One could surmise that these two leading causes go hand in hand: a malicious attack on a misconfigured cloud environment leading to compromised credentials. CSPs may be better equipped to withstand an attack provided they've invested in the proper tools, processes, and skills, but there are other risks and variables you need to consider before hosting your business applications and data in a public cloud.

For starters, placing all of your trust into another entity doesn't relieve you from the responsibility of safeguarding any personally identifiable information (PII), sensitive personal information (SPI), or IP assets that you may have been entrusted with. Passing the buck on to someone else is not a strategy. Being a good data steward should still be a top priority for every organization. This means becoming familiar with and taking an active role in reviewing security controls, policies, threat awareness, and audit report reviews of any CSP you choose to partner with. Think about even the most basic example: access control lists (ACLs) for database authorizations. Misconfigured ACLs follow you to any cloud destination. Now think back to the concepts we discussed in Chapter 2 where we referenced how some public cloud administrators can access your encryption keys—that makes a security posture more complex (and potentially more exposed), doesn't it?

In the context of public cloud, an additional concern is that your organization could potentially become collateral damage in a targeted attack against another company (or the public cloud vendor itself) that could leave your data assets inadvertently exposed. This is becoming especially concerning with the rise of attacks on public cloud infrastructures, where cybercriminals are finding new ways to exploit vulnerabilities on the surface in order to gain access to the underlying cloud platform. Once breached, attackers can gain access to move laterally across public cloud environments from tenant to tenant.

Security professionals often talk about an *attack surface*—all the potential points of entry where unauthorized access can be obtained. If you were to think of this in the physical context of a home or office building, think about doors, windows, ventilation systems—any conceivable point of entry would come to mind. *Attack vectors* describe methods used to breach the surfaces of IT estates: compromised credentials, software vulnerabilities, rogue insiders, misconfiguration, phishing, ransomware, and so on. Attack surfaces and attack vectors have steadily increased over the last few years, and public clouds (as well as hybrid cloud deployment models) have contributed to much of that increase. While we've not seen a 2021 year in review report yet, we think it's a pretty safe bet to suggest there will be spikes in these methods of attack given the massive shift toward working from home and moving to CSP infrastructures.

Many of the common attack vectors that existed with traditional IT infrastructure deployments still apply (in a modern cloud and hybrid cloud deployment model), but the attack surface itself has increased. Take APIs as one example. There are hundreds —potentially thousands—of publicly exposed APIs that a single CSP may host. These APIs, by design, regularly serve up application logic and data. If not properly secured, they can lend themselves to malicious remote code execution (RCE), yielding a point of entry to a now-compromised system. If this goes undetected, this can lead not only to a single attack, but potentially *multiple* attacks. In the cyber underground and black markets, such access can be sold repeatedly before a data breach event actually takes place. Now think back to Chapter 2 where we talked about how applications are composed by stitching together various microservices—you might aggregate those from multiple vendors and (in many cases) those built by and hosted by your own organization…this gets more complex in the cloud, not less.

The Ponemon report also details the average cost and frequency of malicious data breaches associated with their root cause vector (Figure 6-2). Digging into these, we found some pretty telling facts within those findings.

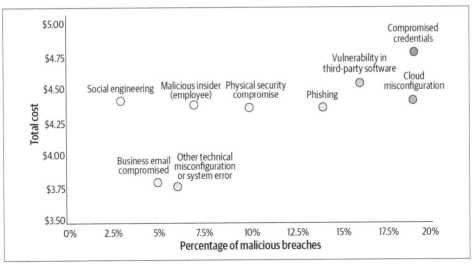

Figure 6-2. Average cost and frequency of malicious data breaches by root cause vector

Let's say you're breached because of a misconfiguration or system error…that will cost (on average) $3.86 million to manage. What we highlighted earlier warrants repeating here: Ponemon's report noted how *cloud misconfiguration tied for the most common threat vector along with compromised credentials.*

But there's something else that really caught our attention (and should catch yours too): the average cost of a data breach associated with a cloud misconfiguration is $4.41 million—that's a 14% premium to deal with a configuration breach based on the destination!

Our book is about using cloud as a capability in multiple destinations. We're not detailing these findings with you to push you one way or another, but rather to dispel some of the common myths and pitfalls we've seen clients fall into around cloud destinations and their instincts (like an instant cost-savings button). Whether looking at public clouds, private clouds, or the hybrid model we're sure you'll put to use, security is security and there are nuances you need to be familiar with for any destination. From access to your encryption keys to costs and more, flush them out and choose the appropriate cloud destination for supporting the workloads (and capabilities) your business needs.

Finally, something to keep in mind while studying Figure 6-2 is that misconfigurations often lead to compromised credentials. Any attacker who is seeking to exploit misconfigured cloud systems, in order to gain access and further compromise the system, will almost certainly begin by looking for ways to illicitly obtain credentialed access to the system. The holy grail for an attacker is to move laterally through a victim's network by utilizing compromised credentials, elevating privileges, and going undetected to either steal as much data or inflict as much damage as possible.

A Case Study in Exploitable OSS

Arguably, one of the most prolific data breaches of the last decade began with bad actors exploiting a remote code execution vulnerability in a common OSS development tool for web applications known as the Apache Struts Web Framework (a tool used by thousands of websites globally).

> Details of this vulnerability can be found under the CVE-2017-5638 record (*https://oreil.ly/EVnlG*) listed on the National Vulnerability Database (NVD) and by referencing US Government Accountability Office (GAO) report GAO-18-559 (*https://oreil.ly/YKQ61*).

The Common Vulnerabilities and Exposures (CVE) report for this breach goes into all kinds of techy details about the code and the exploitation itself. All you need to know is that this vulnerability allowed an attacker to send malicious code wrapped in a content-type header and tricked a web service into executing its malicious code. Once exposed, this vulnerability permitted an open door into an otherwise protected network perimeter (we cover perimeter security later in this chapter).

Over time, news of this data breach caught the attention of media outlets, federal government agencies, and business leaders around the globe—but most shocking of all was the way that an OSS vulnerability exposed one of the world's largest consumer credit reporting agencies to attack. At the time of the attack, this agency (which we won't name here) collected and aggregated information on over 800 million individual consumers and more than 88 million businesses worldwide. Until this breach, a majority of consumers entrusted these agencies with their most sensitive and confidential information.

According to the NVD, the vulnerability in Apache Struts was first discovered in March 2017 and given the highest possible severity rating (10/10) because of the ubiquity of Struts and the fact that this vulnerability could be exploited without credentials, essentially making this a very easy attack vector. The good news is the community rallied around the vulnerability and created a remediation. The bad news? Hackers started exploiting the vulnerability on unpatched servers just days later.

Here's what you need to know: there are lots of security fixes available but not yet implemented—this is one of the issues with the "roll your own" (RYO) approach to open source and befalls many open source practitioners. It's hard as a developer to keep up when fixes don't come pre-packaged and maintained by someone else for you. Regardless of whether you are using open source or proprietary software, it's essential to maintain great security hygiene. Our experiences tell us that all in all, it's harder to do this without a partner and solely relying on your team and stock open source software.

But there's another lesson here: criminals are rewarded when you don't have good security hygiene (think of the "1234" password on an ATM card). The CVE and NVD are publicly accessible resources that can be used for *good or bad*. Hackers will use it to look at easy attack vectors on vulnerable code (the bad) and you can use it to keep abreast of issues and create linkages to vulnerability scanning tools that can immediately warn you of these kinds of vulnerabilities (the good).

The agency in this example lacked both good security hygiene and these linkages and it resulted in over 40% of the US population discovering that their SPI (names, SSNs, addresses, driver license numbers, etc.) had been compromised in the breach—some even had credit card numbers compromised.

Over four months elapsed from the initial intrusion to when the breach was finally discovered, after the organization updated a digital certificate during a network inspection (which had expired 10 months earlier). Once updated and upon restart of the network scanning tool, administrators began seeing abnormal activity and initiated further investigations.

One strange anecdote about this data breach is that none of the compromised data seems to have made its way to the dark web. In many recorded cases where a data breach has occurred, the attacker did so for financial gain and immediately sought to sell the compromised data on the dark web—often to the highest bidder. However, in this breach there has been no evidence of the 143 million plus records resurfacing. This raises the question—what was the motive behind this high-profile attack? Fast forward to February 2020 and reports began to surface that the US Department of Justice was able to link a nation state to this data breach, charging them with computer fraud, economic espionage, and wire fraud. Their motive? Presumably it was an effort to build a massive data lake of information on American citizens that contained PII and SPI classified data, including financial information on high-ranking government officials. (Source: *https://oreil.ly/ekojL*.)

This data breach, though large in scale, contains a number of mishaps that could have been prevented: usernames and passwords had been stored in the clear (without encryption), vulnerabilities in OSS applications were not immediately patched once identified, and there were what appears to have been relaxed security policies that allowed unabated lateral movement between systems and databases. We'll talk more about the importance of proactively mitigating these risks and a concept called Zero Trust security later in this chapter (since we only briefed touched on it in Chapter 2). Each of these blind spots are commonplace in many organizations that are embarking on their digital transformation. Today, Chief Information Security Officers are dealing with IT environments far more complex than from even five years ago, so much so that standard perimeter security methods alone will prove to be grossly inadequate in the years ahead.

Digging further into cloud native and containerization, the risks persist. In 2020 there were 240 CVE records associated with the Linux kernel and 29 for Kubernetes that had been identified. Of the 29 associated with Kubernetes, almost one third were given a base severity score of high, but only one was given a base severity score of critical. Keep in mind this represents only two key OSS components out of what are likely hundreds that could be running in your "cloud the capability" environment. It's not something that organizations should gamble on—for exactly the reasons demonstrated by the case study we just examined. A full list of those CVEs can be found at *https://cve.mitre.org/about/index.html* or in the National Vulnerability Database at *https://nvd.nist.gov/vuln/search*.

Did You Leave the Container Door Open?

Using privileged escalation to escape running pods. Moving laterally through a cluster and across tenants. Man-in-the-middle attacks against public services leading to leaked credentials. Remote execution commands executed against exposed APIs with malicious intent. What do these exploits have in common? Each vulnerability has surfaced within Kubernetes (K8s) and the underlying Linux kernel. The good news is that almost all of these vulnerabilities were discovered by the developer community and received fixes almost immediately. The challenge for security teams is to spot these holes and apply patches to them using vulnerability scanners and remediation procedures as part of a well-defined and automated playbook for tackling security threats.

You may be asking yourself: "Why spend the time discussing these examples if only some of them have led to real-life data breaches?" We can't emphasize enough that securing workloads from unauthorized access, whether it is from internal or external threats, is *critical*. You can invest time and resources into nailing down the user experience design (UX), only to lose your customer's data to a breach. If that happens, the UX for these customers won't be great no matter how wonderful your designs are—not to mention your company's reputation in the aftermath. Security is critical and no organization is fully immune to cyberattacks.

So where should you focus your company's efforts to secure modern enterprise IT estates (cloud, distributed, or hybrid), which often have physical boundaries? Focus on what you can control: data. This also happens to be your most prized asset, and you should control access to the data relentlessly. It's the one asset that your business likely cannot survive without (and would fetch a shocking ransom to get back if lost or compromised). Let's explore a few areas where you can prioritize on protecting your data assets in the next section. We are going to cover a lot of ground here and since this is a book on hybrid cloud, we will begin with what should be the foundation of all hybrid cloud deployments—the *Zero Trust* security model (a concept we first introduced you to in Chapter 2, but will delve deeper into here).

Zero Trust in a Hybrid Cloud World

There is no doubt about it: digital transformation and the move to hybrid cloud is changing the way that companies do business. Now more than ever, data and resources are increasingly accessible to anyone—and with that ease of access comes the perilous responsibility of ensuring that only the right person (at the right time) is granted the right level of access to both data and resources. How that level of access is defined will vary business to business, team to team; however, we might suggest that the appropriate level is only what a user (or application) needs to complete their task for that moment in time, and not one rung higher up the ladder than is necessary. There is a common security design principle that best describes what we mean here—the *principle of least privilege* (POLP). This is the idea that any user, program, or process should have only the bare *minimum privileges* necessary to perform the intended function.

What was once considered "outside" of the network is now "inside" the network, a traditional IT network perimeter line that is further blurred by multicloud architectures. Many companies subscribe to multiple services: software as a service, platform as a service, infrastructure as a service, and so on. More often than not, a business places its trust for its most-prized assets (its data) in someone else's hands. In short, the traditional ways of managing IT security—which has largely focused on building a perimeter wall and keeping bad actors out—is no longer sufficient. Are firewalls and other network barriers still important? Absolutely. However, the best security practices will always assume that those barriers can and will be breached. The concept of "don't trust anything or anyone, and always verify" could mean the difference between a minor event and a major breach—it can also mean the difference between the destination choices you have for your cloud applications.

By definition, Zero Trust is an IT security model that emphasizes strict identity and integrity verification on every person and device attempting to access data or services —regardless of if they are inside an established network perimeter or or on the outside. Quite simply, it means *trust no one.*

Every attempt to access a service or data must be verified before being authorized. This applies to all networked devices irrespective of their connectivity to a managed corporate network. The Zero Trust security model serves to protect sensitive data, critical services, and devices while enabling end-user productivity. This is a major paradigm shift in IT security where although trust was once implicit within the internal network, the Zero Trust model is now seeing a marked uptick in adoption. This is particularly critical in an era where cloud services have blurred the perimeter lines and employees work from home on an increasing (or in some cases permanent) basis.

Context is key to applying a Zero Trust security model and it relies upon an established governance model for sharing context between security tools. Having shared contextual awareness is key to protecting the connections between users, data, and resources. Figure 6-3 gives a highly simplified side-by-side comparison of the traditional IT and Zero Trust security models.

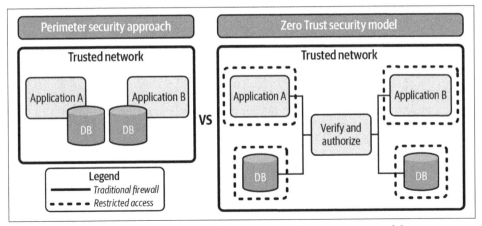

Figure 6-3. Traditional perimeter security versus Zero Trust security model

In Figure 6-3 you can see the importance of having perimeter security as the main line of defense to malicious network attacks no matter the approach you take—that's a given. The Zero Trust approach is based on establishing firewalls within a network to establish a "safe zone." Communications between users, applications, databases, servers, and other devices within this safe zone are considered secure. Identity and access management (IAM) methods and tools often exist within this model, prioritizing protection of network perimeters (and everything encapsulated within it). With the Zero Trust security model, you will see that the network perimeter still exists; however, new lines of defense have been established for each application, database, and server (the dashed lines surrounding the architecture pieces in Figure 6-3). The Zero Trust approach employs the notion that *all requests for access* must be verified before being authorized.

Implementing a Zero Trust security model in a modern cloud architecture is shown in Figure 6-4. Such an implementation often includes a mixture of hybrid cloud, distributed and multicloud, and traditional on-premises services. With multiple technology services spread across multiple datacenters, networks, and providers, the number of perimeters increases—and so too does the number of potential holes in those defenses. The traditional perimeter security approach is simply not enough. Like we said earlier, a vulnerability allowing access to one network can quickly bleed over into other cloud infrastructures.

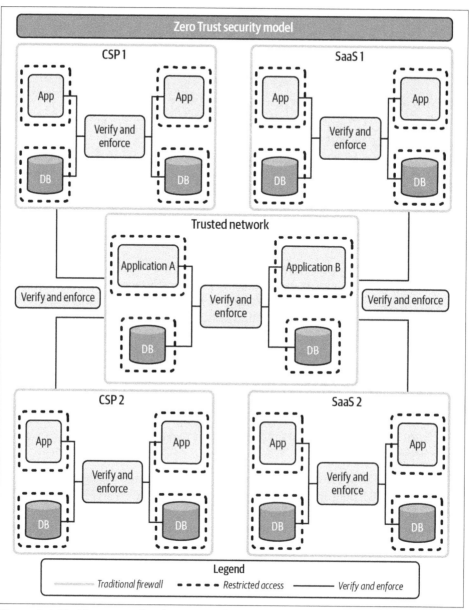

Figure 6-4. Verification and enforcement of permissions and access control is critical: in a hybrid multicloud architecture, the integrity of these checks must be maintained between applications and databases, between Software as a Service (SaaS) providers, and between cloud providers, as well as between the aforementioned endpoints and trusted networks

Implementing a Zero Trust security model will limit risk exposure by restricting access, which in turn limits the ability for a threat to move laterally throughout a network.

A key element to implementing Zero Trust security in a Linux-based hybrid cloud enterprise architecture is *Security-Enhanced Linux* (SELinux). Linux systems have a very tight approach to access control; however, escalating privileges to root (the superuser of Linux operating systems—a "go to" move for many to get things done like a data scientist using pip to add a Python package to a server) access could easily compromise the entire system if not properly implemented. In order to provide an extra layer of security to IT environments within the US government, the United States National Security Agency (NSA) created a series of improvements to the Linux kernel using Linux Security Modules. That work was released under the GNU General Public License (GPL) in the year 2000 and was adopted upstream in 2003. SELinux was born out of this set of security modifications provided by the NSA and was adopted by various Linux variants, including Red Hat Enterprise Linux (RHEL).

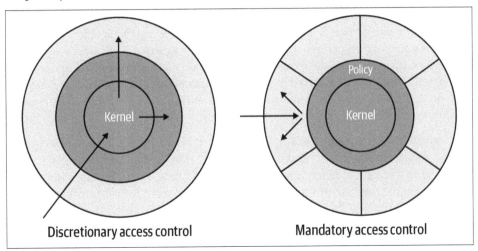

Figure 6-5. *A security exploit that grants privileged access on a system using discretionary access control (DAC) will expose the entire system, while with mandatory access control (MAC), kernel policies (SELinux) block access even when running with privileged access, preserving the system integrity and firewalling the compromised service from the rest of the system*

To understand the benefits of SELinux you need to understand how the traditional Linux access control system works. Linux's traditional access control systems use a *discretionary access control* (DAC) system, which was defined by the Trusted Computer System Evaluation Criteria to provide access control that restricts access to objects based on the identity of the subjects (or groups which they are part of). If you are the owner of that object (or part of a group that owns that object), then you have control of that resource or object. Simple, right? Most of us are familiar with this model even with our own home laptops. But enterprise computing isn't our home laptop.

Let's explore a common IT scenario to illustrate: a service *httpd* running under an *apache* user where a user account becomes compromised. This then empowers the attacker to successfully escalate instructions and commands to *root* level (super powers on a Linux system) access by exploiting vulnerabilities in the *httpd* web server code. Not only are the contents of that service now compromised, but so too is the entire system—DAC provides access based on ownership. Since *root* is omnipotent (meaning unlimited powers) on a DAC model, it immediately has the highest level of ownership (and therefore access) possible. You can imagine the havoc that could be unleashed on such a compromised system. This is where SELinux shines and helps mitigate the risk of (or completely prevent) such scenarios from arising.

SELinux is an implementation of *mandatory access control* (MAC), which complements the traditional access control (DAC) *but* also enforces a specific set of control policies. There are different ways to deploy SELinux: a strict mode and a targeted mode. Strict mode denies all access by default such that every single object is required to have a policy set up beforehand in order to perform work. This makes enterprise use very restrictive and is the impetus for having an alternative targeted mode available as well. Think of the targeted mode as a "guards at the gate" approach, where you only protect the objects that *could* be exploited during a successful security breach; this follows a more prescriptive approach to security, rather than a blanket approach.

Let's return to our previous example, where the object (service) that runs as the *apache* user is compromised and the attacker is able to escalate privileges to *root* access. With SELinux in place, administrators would have a set of policies in place to prevent even the *root* user (in the case it was hijacked) from inflicting any additional damage to the system. The *apache* hijack would only compromise the objects that the particular *apache* service would traditionally have access to, thereby restricting the pool of targets and limiting damage to the system. This is all possible because a set of rules were previously created that defined the objects that the web server has access to. Everything else that is not explicitly defined by the policy becomes untouchable, as the SELinux mechanism will enforce access control rigorously (even if *root* access is granted from that particular service). In other words, even if you're a superhero with all the powers in the world at your disposal, SELinux has some Kryptonite in case a hero turns bad. In practice, the kernel must query and authorize against SELinux policies before each system call to know if the process has the correct permissions to perform a given operation. SELinux policies are, in a nutshell, a set of rules that authorize or forbid operations no matter who you are.

It's also important to mention that DAC controls ownership plus permissions (like read, write, and execute). The users can change these permissions and, historically, the *root* user is omnipotent. With MAC, policies are predefined and locked in. Even if you try to change DAC permissions, if the policy was not written to enable access to an object, it will be blocked by SELinux.

For orchestrated multicloud environments, containers will continue to play a much bigger role. Having a secure, trusted platform foundation for containers is paramount to building a successful cloud implementation. As containers are nothing more than a process running on a Linux system, it shares the host kernel with other containerized processes. Each of these containerized processes are isolated from one another using kernel spaces. We won't go too deep here, but the point we need to make is that *container security is Linux security*—which means that SELinux plays an important role when we are talking about containers as well.

Red Hat CoreOS, for example, is based on a trusted and mature Linux distribution known as Red Hat Enterprise Linux (RHEL) and inherits all of its robust security attributes as the basis for a secure operating system for container orchestration platforms. Each process on Red Hat CoreOS has an associated context and set of rules defining the scope of interactions permitted by the process. You might have wondered: "What does *context* mean in the scope of SELinux (and operating systems in general)? Essentially, when you have a file or directory that you want to create policies for, you typically require some sort of mechanism to label it (a way to map it to a set of SELinux policies). For example, for a file to be acted upon, it must belong to a specific label that identifies the SELinux policies governing permitted actions upon that file.

Let's explore another scenario: a service running inside a container has a code bug that allows the attacker to gain shell access to that container. Thanks to *cgroups*, that kernel's namespaces will restrict the attacker from observing or interacting with any other containers on the same CoreOS systems. However, if the attacker is able to take advantage of a kernel bug, they might be able to escape from that container environment—as multiple containers will be running as the same user. Having SELinux enabled (which Red Hat CoreOS activates by default) ensures that the Linux kernel restricts the attacker in this scenario from compromising any other containers running on that system. Each container carries a uniquely contextual security policy to deny cross-content access and prevent any further damage from occurring. In plain words, SELinux would prevent any further escalation. This is a big deal: think back to the Arriver's Guide we introduced you to in Chapter 1 and the things containerization requires you to think about in a new way: security, resiliency, performance, and more.

Many attacks have been stopped or mitigated by simply having SELinux enabled, which is why having Red Hat CoreOS as a foundation for any hybrid multicloud platform is so beneficial—CVE-2016-9962 (*https://oreil.ly/YJpCL*) is one such example. On Red Hat systems with SELinux enabled, the dangers posed by hijacked containers with privileged access are greatly mitigated. SELinux prevents container processes from accessing host content, even in cases where those container processes manage to gain access to the actual file descriptors.

Another example: CVE-2017-7494 (*https://oreil.ly/BdSvr*) addressed a vulnerable Samba client.[1] A malicious authenticated Samba client, having write access to the Samba share, could use this flaw to execute arbitrary code as *root*. When SELinux is enabled by default, the default security posture prevents the loading of modules from outside of Samba's module directories and therefore mitigates the flaw. This is just one example of many. We could go on and on about the ways that SELinux technology plays a vital role in today's IT environments. If nothing else, we hope our examples illustrate the benefits of kernel-level security and explain the rationale behind Red Hat's strategy of embedding CoreOS at the center (where it has resided since the release of version 4 and onwards) of the Red Hat OpenShift Container Platform.

Beyond enabling Linux Security Modules for the Linux kernel itself, there are a number of additional solutions that provide value and can increase an organization's security posture, such as the products behind the shield of IBM Security. It caters to the Zero Trust security model and thus offers contextually aware access control for identities and services, regardless of where those happen to reside (on-premises, off-premises, or a hybrid blend of the two). These tools offer a centralized approach and focus on understanding users, data, and resources in order to create coordinated security policies that are aligned with the initiatives of a business. By centralizing identity management and providing contextual awareness organizations can begin to automate the verification and enforcement procedures, enabling conditional access to data and services without friction.

Let's face it: the current cybersecurity market is a crowded space with thousands of software vendors and OSS projects offering a plethora of tools. Many of these technologies still cater to traditional monolithic apps running on-premises, with a few new entrants that focus solely on the hybrid multicloud container market. They run the gamut from endpoint management to IAM, vulnerability scanning, threat detection, threat intelligence, and so much more. Many of these tools are often siloed or niche, making it incredibly difficult for security administrators and analysts to effectively perform their jobs. Many gaps exist in this often-segregated approach, which can alarmingly produce a false sense of security. Consider again the data breach example from earlier in this chapter: that organization felt they had all their bases covered. As soon as they were alerted to the vulnerability with Apache Struts, the security team scanned and patched all of their systems—or so they thought. The breach didn't happen from a lack of skills alone. In fact, there was no evidence

---

1 Samba is a standard Windows interoperability suite of programs for Linux for file sharing and printer services.

pointing to any one person's inadequacies or incompetence. Rather, it was the tools and processes that supported the security apparatus that fell short. Placing heavy reliance on tooling is commendable, but having a well-established process for how they are managed is key.

Importance of Sec(urity) in DevSecOps

Let's talk about DevOps and its role in ensuring a solid security strategy for deploying containers in a hybrid cloud environment. DevOps is a methodology that pulls together development processes, technology, and people with IT Operations. This is not to say that these historically disparate organizations now share only one unified toolset, process, or collection of resources. Not at all. DevOps is more about increasing the collaboration and transparency between the two groups. The end game is to build a cohesive system that is made of the people, processes, and technologies regardless of team or discipline. In the past, development teams have worked independently of IT Operations teams (and vice versa). In fact, each of these groups often created "silos within silos," working independently of one another (and often pointing the blame to each other for anything that went wrong)—from the design phase, all the way to product release.

The DevOps methodology has in many ways simplified the entire development process. What would once have taken months or years to design, develop, package, and release now might only need days or weeks to implement. This has increased business agility dramatically, allowing companies to bring new services to market very quickly. These advances are particularly important in today's economy, as it's not always the biggest companies that succeed but rather (it seems more often than not) that success goes to the fastest and most innovative. Speed of innovation is a competitive differentiator that turns new market entrants into market incumbents.

There are downsides, however, to rapidly churning out new code in the form of rapid releases, updates, and patches. On occasion, a lengthy and sometimes egregious development process can lend itself well to catching bugs, defects, or other issues that could potentially lead to code vulnerabilities (and therefore risk to new adopters). Additionally, with longer production cycles IT security teams will generally have more time to prepare for and audit production rollouts. With DevOps practices, security teams are typically left out of the equation during the initial design and development phase. In the context of cloud native, leaving security out of DevOps can result in costly mistakes that are discovered much further downstream (potentially only after the damage has already been done).

In Chapter 5, we discussed the phrase "shift left" in the context of application development, but can it also be applied to security? The notion of incorporating both operations and security earlier into the development cycle is what we refer to as *DevSecOps*. The challenge for implementing the DevSecOps methodology can be a big culture shift, primarily due to IT security being viewed by many developers, operations staff, and business leaders as an inhibitor to speed and agility. Remember: speed of innovation drives business in today's economy (and anything that applies friction to that velocity is often scorned). To make matters worse, a significant number of software developers have not been adequately trained in the concepts and best practices of security, creating a massive knowledge gap. Developers are often under tight deadlines to deliver and security often becomes someone else's problem (or at least an afterthought). This mentality, whether it be a conscious effort to avoid delays in release cycles, or just a simple lack of understanding, can be a challenging cultural obstacle to overcome for many organizations.

We've found that by training development teams on the importance of adopting security principles and best practices, they are often able to move beyond the mindset or preconceived notions of security being an inhibitor to speed and innovation. Developers realize that their efforts to apply security best practices and collaboration with IT security teams early on in the project lifecycle can dramatically mitigate the risks and impacts of security vulnerabilities. These security holes, if exploited, have the potential to consume a developer's time and resources in the future if ignored. Adopting a DevSecOps methodology early on in a project's lifecycle will pay enormous dividends down the road.

When we speak with clients, one of the most common inhibitors preventing them from running production workloads in a container environment is the lack of acquired security skills. Many organizations that find themselves in this category believe that they can overcome the skills and process gaps through the use of tooling and automation (which can certainly help); yet simultaneously, they remain apprehensive because of unfounded concerns that the container security market is "too new." Many such organizations are finding themselves leap-frogged by smaller, more agile companies who are willing to assume the risks and recognize the tremendous potential of containerization.

How do organizations overcome this stigma and risk apprehension? Our response is to look at what you already have in place from a technology perspective. What are the capabilities of the products you use today? Do those vendors have a strategy for how they will address container security at any stage in the lifecycle? Do they collaborate with other vendors to enrich their capabilities and add value for their clients? Do they have a well-established ecosystem of partners whom they work with to advance their products? You may find that many of the tools that you've already invested in either have plans to address these gaps or may in fact already address them. The key here is understanding that there are only a few security software vendors that can adequately address every phase of the lifecycle for container platforms. Others will come close; some will remain niche and you will be left to reconcile the pieces. This is why it is incredibly important to prioritize selection of vendors that are known collaborators with other companies in the market; focus on ones that build their solutions to open standards and seek to expand their offerings across the entire marketplace.

Container Security Visibility 101

Containers represent a new paradigm to IT security where traditional methods for securing the enterprise are no longer adequate (new worlds come with new rules, right?) What makes container security a challenge for IT organizations is linked to the very attributes that make containers so valuable. This paradox exists because:

- Container images themselves are immutable (they can't be changed—if you change a container image, you are essentially creating a new one), meaning any vulnerability within the container image will persist for the life of the image.
- Containers are rapidly swapped and scaled, creating a lack of visibility into their attack surface.
- Container configurations are vast—lots of knobs and dials raises the potential for misconfiguration (not to mention complexity is the top reason for outages).
- Containers tend to be short-lived, making forensic investigations as well as compliance reporting a challenge.

At a high level, there are five key areas (shown in Figure 6-6) to focus on as you look to build out your container security strategy. It's important to note that code scanning prior to the container build process is equally important.

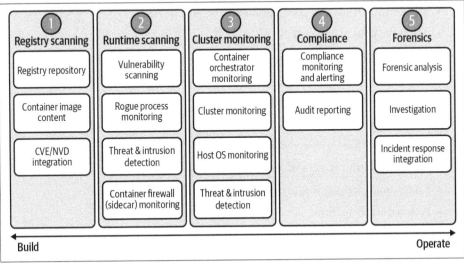

Figure 6-6. Gain security visibility across five key areas of your container deployments

Providing visibility into the health and security of your container environment is key to preventing, mitigating, and remediating cyber threats, so we've put together a basic checklist that will serve you well for years to come:

1. Registry and Container Image Vulnerability Scanning
   - Secure the repository itself
   - Securely store push/pull secrets
   - Scan image contents for known vulnerabilities and malicious code
   - Integrate with CVE/NVD for real-time vulnerability updates and establish known CVE baseline
   - Predictive analysis

2. Container Image Runtime Vulnerability Scanning
   - Container runtime scanning
   - Threat and intrusion detection
   - Container firewall (sidecar—some code on the side) monitoring
   - Anomalous execution
   - Predictive behavioral analysis
   - Integrate with CVE/NVD for real-time vulnerability updates and establish known CVE baseline

3. Container Orchestration and Cluster Monitoring
   - Misconfiguration and configuration drift monitoring
   - Threat and intrusion detection
   - Identity access
   - Privileged account monitoring
   - Container network monitoring
   - Pod monitoring
   - Predictive behavioral analysis

4. Compliance Monitoring and Reporting
   - Continuous access monitoring
   - Anomalous detection
   - Privileged account elevation detection
   - Configuration drift
   - Audit reporting across all

- Predefined industry templates for internal and external regulatory compliance, including PCI-DSS, GLBA, SOX, NERC CIP, HIPAA, etc.

5. Forensics Analysis and Investigation

- Post-event analysis
- Integration to incident response

Placing emphasis on both registry and container image vulnerability scanning followed by container runtime vulnerability scanning and threat detection can help close a big gap. This is still an evolving market with many point products to choose from; choosing a point product for any one area may lead to gaps in the attack surface of your container environment—press whomever is selling you a solution to give you an end-to-end discussion on this topic.

Together, Red Hat and IBM have built an open ecosystem of technology partners to help close these gaps. Many of these ecosystem partners continue to focus on the areas where they are strong, while Red Hat and IBM seek to bring their solutions together into an integrated offering. For example, Red Hat Quay is a private container registry that allows organizations to store, build, and deploy container images. Red Hat's Security Container Module is supported by Clair—an open source project that provides a tool to scan each layer of container images stored in Quay and delivers proactive alerts based on vulnerabilities such as configuration defects, embedded malware, and clear text secrets (passwords and API key licenses in configuration or code files) detected. Clair is configured to import known vulnerabilities from a number of sources, one being the CVE database mentioned earlier in this chapter (as well as the National Vulnerability Database). Our pro tip: *provide vulnerability scanning early in the development lifecycle, as it raises awareness about potential vulnerabilities before code leaves the registry for deployment.*

Runtime vulnerability assessments, container orchestration, and cluster monitoring provide exactly that level of proactive awareness. Having visibility into your Kubernetes orchestration engine and its configuration (including network, storage, and workload isolation settings) is imperative. Most containers are transient in nature, which quite simply means they tend to have a short life span. This makes it very difficult for traditional IT vulnerability scanning, threat detection, and intrusion detection tools to effectively work with a containerized environment.

Technologies such as StackRox (a Red Hat company) cater specifically to evaluation of containerized runtime environments by measuring baselines for process activity and providing runtime anomaly detection (and response) for anything that falls outside of those expected norms. StackRox can also monitor system-level events within containers and invoke prebuilt policies to detect privilege escalation, cryptomining activity, or other common exploits that might be running afoul within your Linux distributions and Kubernetes orchestration. There are a number of other capabilities provided by the StackRox platform, including compliance monitoring, network segmentation, risk profiling, and configuration management. Each of these capabilities is key to securing your enterprise container environment, giving you the tools to perform investigative analysis in the event of a breach (or to prove compliance if asked).

Finally, compliance monitoring, reporting, and forensics analysis are a critical capabilities for anyone—and also required by law for many industries under tight regulation. Whether implemented by regulation or due diligence, all organizations benefit from the ability to apply industry-specific compliance policies for their container-native environment and the ability to monitor any changes to the environment against that policy baseline. This also applies to scenarios where it's necessary to provide evidence of compliance for auditing purposes using reporting capabilities provided by the tooling. Trust us on this: without this level of monitoring and reporting, fines will likely follow (not to mention brand erosion, loss of trust, and more).

With regards to forensics analysis and investigation, in the event of a breach it's critical to quickly identify which systems have been impacted. This requires the ability to go back in time and retrace any potential anomalies that occurred, such as a privilege escalation, rogue containers, lateral movement between clusters, and so on. The Security Information and Event Management (SIEM) system must integrate several core areas when an incident occurs. There must be quick event correlation and historical analysis, and your incident response system must link known vulnerability attributes to identified suspicious behaviors. SIEM security teams provide tracking, insights, and visibility into security-related activities within IT environments.

Without this level of visibility, you can only assume that your entire container environment has been compromised (although in reality it may not have been—you just can't be certain enough to discredit the possibility without full visibility). This can lead to unnecessary public disclosures, remediation, and discovery work—which is a waste of precious resources. Of course, the opposite can also be true: without the visibility provided by a combination of these capabilities, a breach may be missed entirely, leading to data loss. These become painful experiences for victim organizations and their end users—disasters that often could have been minimized or mitigated with the correct security strategy and tooling.

We began this chapter by discussing what OSS is and how cybercriminals (and on occasion nation state attackers) use exploits in software to expose vulnerabilities for financial gain (or for use against federal governments). The foundation for hybrid cloud is based on an open platform and new architectural model that many traditional IT security methods simply do not adequately address. To combat rising threats in containerized hybrid cloud environments, organizations need to take a new approach based on Zero Trust to protect systems and data, as well as a more collaborative approach to managing the software development lifecycle through a cohesive DevSecOps operating model.

CHAPTER 7

Data Gravity

The COVID-19 pandemic has affected each of us in many different ways. But in the scope of business and IT, what specifically made 2020 (and most of 2021) so particularly challenging? A question that we routinely ask our clients is, "Who is leading your digital transformation?" Oftentimes, the answer has been "our CIO," "our CFO," and so on. But in 2020, more often than not the answer was "it's COVID-19." There have been massive impacts across employees, partners embedded within companies, and end-user digital experiences as a whole. Increasingly, everything needed to be available and accessible online. Companies accelerated their drive toward cloud, and their customers were pushing urgently for all-digital availability of services.

Our experience during this time as IBMers was an interesting one, to say the least. The nature of our work and the diversity of our client interactions meant that we had the broadest aperture possible to the range of ways businesses have been impacted by and have responded to the pandemic. We have observed businesses that have struggled, but likewise there have been clients that have flourished in the "new normal" (recall the thrivers, divers, and new arrivers we talked about in Chapter 1).

From the perspective of containerized storage (and IBM Storage in general), we've recognized three major trends:

Management and control
> In the past, administrators would have procured more storage (in support of applications and users), as needed, from the datacenter—we're talking about a time well before the advent of cloud. Often the datacenter would in effect be spread across two or more sites: one serving as the primary hub and the other being a smaller satellite for disaster recovery and business continuity services. In these early configurations, storage allocation would be managed by system administrators entirely through the primary site (from which they would also remotely control the satellite locations). With COVID-19, we've seen a flip

toward working from home—and as such, all of these system administrators are now scrambling to find ways to manage *all* of their datacenters (the central hub *and* the satellites) entirely from their remote (at-home) workstations.

Availability and reliability

Many businesses wish to become a 365x24x7 company, but COVID-19 pushed them into making that level of availability more than a sound byte in an earnings call—it became a necessity, not merely a luxury. Digital transformations were already well underway across the industry at the start of 2020, which naturally applied stress to the digitized services running off-premises. In turn, this put additional stress on the high availability (HA) and disaster recovery (DR) components of those containerized and cloud-centric services. COVID-19 further accentuated that stress because of the push toward contactless, socially distanced, always-online experiences.

Cyber-resiliency

Cyberattacks continue to rise and escalate in severity with each passing year—and once again, the push toward digital experiences owing to COVID-19 has created an ample supply of untested vendors and businesses (in other words: ripe pickings for an attack) for these malicious entities to target. 2021 is proving this to be true each day: it's not simply about keeping the "bad guys" out or tracking the attackers down. Sometimes—speaking anecdotally based on what we've heard or seen firsthand with clients—your business may not even be aware an attack has occurred until weeks or months *after* the intrusion has taken place (you'll recall we touched in this in Chapter 6—almost every report we've seen suggests that it takes almost six months before you're likely to discover malware inside your company). If your enterprise doesn't have cyber-resilient and well-secured storage in place before your containerization and digital transformation strategy begins, the damage may already be done before you're even in a position to recognize and react to it. This is one big reason why air-gapping and Safe Guard copying your backups—think of it like an offline-only copy of your data that can only be accessed in case of emergency—is a prudent part of any modern data protection strategy.

Another trend around securing containerized and cloud native applications is the increased sensitivity, among businesses and consumers alike, toward data residency: where does your data reside today, and where (if anywhere) can it move to once generated?

How do concerns and legislation regarding data residency impact those businesses that are looking to adopt the hybrid multicloud approach that we've been evangelizing thus far? For example, if a Canadian business is contemplating using three or four different cloud vendors, and one of those vendors does not have a datacenter within a province (or state) covered by that country's data sovereignty laws, then that vendor cannot be selected (for data storage purposes) by that business. There are multiple countries around the world with similar legislation in place as well. As you evaluate different cloud-first vendors, you need to be cognizant of the fact that no single cloud vendor has a datacenter within the borders of every country on the planet. Therefore, when plotting out your digital transformation and application modernization strategy, you *absolutely* must take into consideration an on-premises component for data retention, as well as cloud.

This really hits on the theme of our book: *you need cloud capabilities at all destinations.* It's precisely why we believe that an on-premises/off-premises (hybrid) blend of several vendors (multicloud) is essential for every business—all of whom will need to be increasingly sensitive to application and customer data residency moving forward. Even though the new (ab)normal is fraught with challenges, there are tremendous opportunities for those that give weight to the data gravity conundrum, which is the residency of data and the challenges of moving it to the cloud, and opportunities for those that strategize toward a blend of on-premises and off-premises, multivendor solutions to those challenges.

Thinking of cloud as a set of capabilities, where any business can harness the powers of multiple vendors and technologies, broadens your organization's ability to innovate with speed and reach new audiences. That level of agility, resiliency, and adaptability is precisely what the "new normal" of a post-COVID-19 marketplace demands. But it is equally incumbent on organizations to not fall into the trap of thinking of the public cloud as *the* destination for all of their data. As noted earlier, we can't change the laws of physics—moving petabytes of data to the cloud will always be a challenge that few can stomach. Likewise, while we aren't fortune tellers, we're certain there will be even more demanding and unique challenges relating to data residency and privacy that 2021 and beyond will usher in. One thing we can promise you: establishing a hybrid multicloud strategy premised around secure containerized data, multivendor support, and vendor-agnostic technologies will put your business in the best position for success in the new (ab)normal's marketplace.

Data Gravity: More Formally Defined

A key consideration for workloads in hybrid multicloud environments is *latency*. For applications with data dependencies that businesses are looking to modernize, planning and consideration must be given to the ways that distance and distribution over containers (and cloud platforms) may impact these services.

The inconvenient truth is that much of an enterprise's crown jewels (data) today resides in storage which is not easily adaptable to—or might even be seen as antithetical to—the unique storage requirements of modernized and containerized applications. These challenges are further exacerbated by the fact that containers were not originally developed with persistence and long-term storage in mind. These technologies were conceived with a "build it and bin it" mentality in mind (for rapid development and testing), an "ephemeral" approach to application design. As such, the technology (and vendors that support it) have had to gradually evolve adaptations to these requirements over time.

You can't change the laws of physics. Data that needs to move between distributed systems is inevitably going to suffer from latency or performance drags. The alternative is to constantly move data back and forth across premises to replicate that data into distributed cloud systems. But how then do you maintain, secure, and preserve the integrity of data during such a migration? What happens to the mission-critical business processes on-premises that generated that data in the first place? If synchronization between the endpoints were to break down, how would that impact the applications running across the disconnected sites?

We refer to complex workloads such as these, with deep data dependencies and high volume, as being subject to *data gravity*. Data's "weight" on-premises can make it difficult to burst to the cloud, and the further you move that data away from the on-premises IT core of your business, the more tenuous that connection (the gravity) between your data and mission-critical systems becomes. This relates to the connectivity, resiliency, and security challenges of ground-to-cloud operations. Before your business can break free of data's gravity and boldly set out in search of new ventures, you need the correct storage strategy to accelerate your modernization journey and overcome the "stickiness" of the legacy data dependencies that are dragging you down.

Container-Ready and Container-Native Storage

Chapter 3 introduced you to IT container technology and the curious ways in which the containerized application revolution echoes the shipping container revolution of centuries past. Very often when talking about containers in the IT world, there is an adjacent picture of a container in the physical world (like a shipping container you might see stacked alongside a port). For example, containers in both worlds (logistics and IT) exhibit characteristics of efficiency, organization, standardization, and security. But is there any real value in this metaphor of containerized goods and container-based shipping? Or is it merely a play on words?

Solving Challenges of Business Continuity in a Containerized World

Global container shipping and local road delivery to the doorstep is now well-known across the world thanks to the ubiquity of companies like Amazon and UPS. Their widespread success couldn't have happened without three essential shipping container innovations or rules:

- Containers are *orchestrated* (translated into normal English: organized) and marshaled according to their intended destination and priority.

- Handling facilities are standardized—they simply would not work without standardization.

- Freight handlers don't need access to the contents of containers in order to ship them (they are secured from the point of origin to the place in which a customer unloads them).

Orchestration describes the process by which containers get to where they need to be. Just as a physical shipping container can be moved by different forms of transport (rail, ship, and so on), IT containers can be deployed on different types of cloud destinations (on-premises, public cloud) using the same cloud capabilities. In the same way that a manufacturer or distributor loads a physical container with the goods they are sending, DevOps teams can describe and build container images prior to their deployment because there are standardized ways for distributing, receiving, and running containerized workloads in the environment where they are finally deployed.

Traditionally, IT servers were sized for their peak workloads. This required enormous amounts of upfront work to understand the app being supported; it's akin to predicting the future, and don't forget the countless hours finding consensus across the mutual business and IT stakeholders that the architecture was meant to serve. We all know how things go when planning turns to practice: peak capacity demand might only be reached a few times a year; maxing out your capacity in those days was generally thought of as "the exception," rather than "the rule" of today. Keeping level of service up and running meant that storage was typically directly attached (or locally networked) to those servers, along with specialized data protection, high availability (HA), and disaster recovery (DR) solutions. Satisfying business continuity could be challenging because you needed different solutions for HA and DR to satisfy those needs—particularly if the secondary operating site was a significant distance away from the primary site.

Procurement and management of these bespoke systems required operations staff with specific sets of skills. Within these businesses were glaring inefficiencies such as spare computing capacity and unused networking and storage resources, which very often were underutilized or sitting idle (but nevertheless paid for) much of the time. You're probably starting to get the picture of how this worked, and to be honest, many of you are quite familiar with it. Traditional architectures require lots of work, plenty of skill, resources you're willing to sacrifice (at times for potentially no gain), and reams of preventative measures to mitigate risk.

Returning to the example of shipping and logistics: end users are typically happy if their goods are delivered to them in a single, secure package, where the contents of those shipments are just as they were when they left their point of origin. However, in the domain of goods transport, infrastructure operators recognized that further efficiencies were possible if multiple containers could be loaded onto a single transportation platform. Rapidly, long trains and large ships requiring fewer labor resources entered the mainstream and became the *de facto* method for global container shipping with economies of scale. Today many parts of this process are automated with analytics and AI, making it even more efficient.

In a very similar way, IT containers are engineered to integrate with the deployment infrastructure (what we'll call "hosts") in such a way that requires fewer resources than a traditional virtual machine (VM). Multiple guest operating systems and the hypervisor that controls them (the approach used by VMs) are replaced with a single container engine, which also relies on specialized isolation capabilities to ensure that the containers it supports are lightweight and secure. Even the simplest operating system of a VM might require 2 GB of operational space per instance. Every one of those instances needs operational management for security patches, upgrades, and so on. By contrast, a containerized application could strip away the bloat of unnecessary OS libraries and dependencies, only packaging the absolute minimum needed to run the service.

VMs are frequently allocated to individual application users and may also require asset management business processes; containers, on the other hand, are typically not allocated to individual users. Containers are created dynamically in order to provision a service that users need, and then subsequently disappear after the container's lifecycle has ended. Containers don't need asset management, only a descriptor so that they can be assigned to a workload when required. Finally, developers love containers because they can be confident that their applications will be deployed with the right libraries, in the correct configuration, every time, on any architecture. Just like a physical container, in the IT world a container image can be made secure so it cannot be deployed or used until it is accessed by a permitted system that has the right key to unlock its capabilities (and contents).

Why Storage? Why Now? The Curious Evolution of Persistence for Containers

Recall that one of the early application development and architecture challenges was dealing with business continuity. The portability of containers addresses two significant operational challenges:

- The standardized specification of containers means they can be easily moved, running in a business continuity site as soon as they are needed.

- When the server hardware on which a container is running needs maintenance or replacement, another copy of that container can be quickly deployed on different hardware while the upgrade is done—without any service interruption.

Figure 7-1 breaks down the foremost pain points that organizations experience when needing to find storage solutions for containerized applications. As you can see, many (if not all) of these pain points have their roots in the "weightiness" of data—be that the latency and time-to-delivery impacts from moving data across the wire, strict regulatory and data sovereignty laws, or the friction generated when agile innovation rubs against disaster recovery and availability requirements.

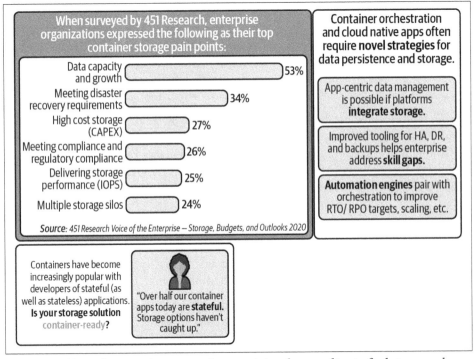

Figure 7-1. Typical pain points enterprises run into when needing to find storage solutions for their containerized applications

Performance is a key requirement for any business application, even those running via (relatively lightweight) containerized microservices. As memory and CPU resources become cheaper and more ubiquitous, legacy hard drives that read one block at a time are becoming a performance bottleneck for data-intensive applications (see Figure 7-1). Built with multiple channels and flash devices, solid state drives (SSDs), and storage class memory (SCM), today's storage is inherently parallel and able to provide orders of magnitude higher internal bandwidth compared to traditional hard drives. In addition, for clients looking to use file storage, leveraging parallel filesystems (like Spectrum Scale based on the General Parallel File System, or Lustre) can provide a huge boost to performance as well. One thing to never forget when you design your cloud architectures: *all servers wait at the same speed for the data!*

From an availability perspective, when your team moves containers, you need to be on the lookout for industry-leading storage capabilities that include automated, policy-driven data movement, synchronous and asynchronous copy services, high availability configurations, and intelligent storage tiering. You want six 9s (99.9999%) uptime for data assurance and resiliency, as well as 100% data availability guarantee with multisite options.

Manageability is another big challenge for your running containers. Ensure your team looks for easy-to-use tools to manage your containerized applications. These tools should provide capabilities to easily deploy, manage, monitor, and scale applications. They need to be integrated with environments that provide a private image repository, a management console, and monitoring frameworks to seamlessly hook containerized apps and services into your broader application ecosystem.

To round out this list of concerns we want you to be aware of, think about data protection for containerized applications. There are many aspects of a containerized environment that need robust backup and disaster recovery routines, as well as contingency planning in place for protecting the state of the cluster, container image registries, and runtime (state) information.

Containers for one reason or another will inevitably need to be *reconstituted* (brought back into their operational state) after a hardware failure, crash, or software maintenance to their image layer. Although containers are resilient against such failure conditions, it does require architects and designers to consider how a containerized application will retain any data between reconstituted container environments.

Figure 7-2 illustrates the challenges associated with application data storage (stateless or stateful) for containers (ephemeral or persistent, respectively).

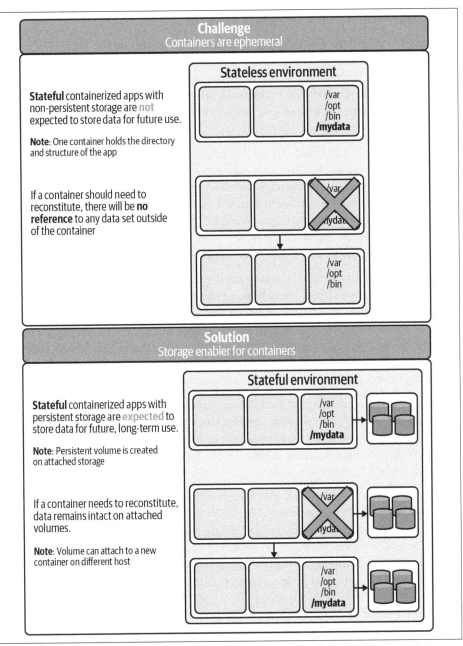

Figure 7-2. It's not a question of if an outage will occur, but when: these are the challenges associated with application data storage for different kinds of containers

Container: May Ye Live Long and Prosper

By default, containers are inherently ephemeral environments. Any information about their state that is created over the course of a container's lifecycle will be deleted (lost) when that container's lifecycle is complete—think of it as amnesia. This includes each time a container is restarted, such as for an update, migration into a new environment, or because of a stoppage. We refer to this default container behavior as *stateless*.

Persistent storage is the means by which data that is created by application usage is retained throughout the lifecycle of a business process, allowing the entities it manages to change state. A stateful containerized environment is one that persists and retains data across sessions in a permanent fashion—in other words, by using persistent storage. Using external storage devices, a containerized application can persist its data throughout and beyond the lifecycle of the container, meeting the needs of long-term business processes (not merely short-lived or technical processes).

Persistent storage for "stateful" containerized applications has proven particularly difficult for the industry. Unlike monolithic applications—which reserve storage resources once—containers and microservices bounce in and out of existence, migrating between machines at breakneck speeds. The repeating cycle of coding and testing, followed by agile production deployment, further exacerbates the data storage challenges for containerized applications. Data services fashioned for traditional application architectures must now serve a new, very transient data paradigm.

The unit of storage capacity that a container can make use of is called a *volume*. There are mechanisms built into container orchestration environments that allow these volumes to be named and attached as required. Kubernetes allows containerized applications to request storage, locating the best match from available resources, and delivers a volume (a place to store your data).

Red Hat OpenShift elevates the management claim to provide a catalog of storage providers from which the most suitable can be easily chosen by a cluster administrator. Microservices are no longer tied to a single implementation of business logic and storage access libraries. They can be deployed in a loosely coupled fashion with the most appropriate technology for their needs, while DevOps tools allow storage to be presented using a consistent approach through the whole of the release lifecycle. As a result, only those storage solutions capable of providing shared storage to both existing (virtualized and bare-metal application infrastructures) and container-native applications with a consistent set of data services are likely to survive.

Container-Ready and Container-Native: Reinventing Storage for Containerized Applications

Persistent storage for containers is generally defined in two categories: container-ready storage and container-native storage.

What benefits does container-native storage confer over container-ready storage types? First, it simplifies management: a single control plane within your K8s containerized environment is able to manage the integrated (native) storage. Second, both internal drives and external storage can be leveraged, giving further flexibility in terms of where application data and state are persisted. Third, this architecture paradigm is consistent with the "hyper-converged" approach for containerized applications, in which storage and compute are able to scale independently of one another.

 The early days of public cloud-backed data lakes and data warehouses taught vendors some tough lessons about certain Hadoop as a Service (HaaS) offerings that soon became HaaS-been (get it?) offerings. Imagine needing to buy more storage capacity and being forced to bundle that with purchasing additional CPU and memory, every time (on a system where you've already got plenty of excess processing power)! Today, many data warehousing SaaS offerings have adapted in response to these lessons learned to allow for independent scaling of compute and storage.

What do we mean by container-ready? As customers are moving to container-based environments, they are able to use storage as a persistent storage layer for both block and file architectures. For example, storage is container-ready today, while many vendors are still in the early stages of delivery for container readiness (alpha or beta versions of their storage plug-ins as of the time this book was written). It unifies traditional and container storage, and provides cloud native agility with the reliability, availability, and security to manage enterprise containers in production.

Container-ready storage includes devices such as Storage Area Network (SAN), Software Defined Storage (SDS), and Network Attached Storage (NAS). These devices support capabilities such as backup/snapshots, clones, and data replication. Another benefit to choosing amongst these options is that they often allow clients to leverage existing investments that they've already made in infrastructure (either in networking or storage), processes, management, and monitoring solutions. IBM Spectrum Virtualize, IBM Spectrum Scale, Heketi with GlusterFS, and IBM Cloud Object Storage are products that clients may have invested in previously, which can be *immediately* made available as "container-ready" storage options.

Container-native storage is deployed directly with containers. It is immediately available in the cluster catalog and appears to the administrator in a very similar way to how storage would be in an appliance. Red Hat OpenShift Data Foundation (ODF) is an example of container-native storage. It is capable of provisioning block, file, and object storage—which a variety of applications might require. It operates using the same management control plane as the Red Hat OpenShift platform on which it runs. With ODF, both internal and external drives can be configured. Data persistence is available right in the heart of the container environment itself, where applications need it most readily. Yet both the compute and storage solutions can still scale independently in order to meet changing demand or workload requirements. Container-native storage won't let you down when it comes to data protection or resiliency. It is usually deployed in a mirrored or replicated architecture, and it supports the same snapshot capabilities as container-ready storage.

Adding Storage for Containers...The Right Way

OpenShift has many prebuilt containers that can be used to assemble applications, but it's important that you fully understand the differences between ephemeral and persistent storage. What does it look like to provision a containerized service with available storage?

If you're working from the command line, you're working with *Podman* commands. Red Hat originally used Docker infrastructure, and due to some design limitations in the way that Docker works—in particular, the single process background daemon that is a bottleneck, and more—Red Hat switched over and designed a new daemonless container engine for handling the starting and management of containers: Podman. (Don't get confused. As we said earlier, K8s runs Docker containers—all containers that adhere to the standard OCI, really—we're specifically talking about the past reliance on the Docker command interface.) This is Red Hat OpenShift's container engine and also the command line for communicating with containers. If you are familiar with Docker syntax, Podman is essentially the same. Podman works with all Open Container Initiative (OCI)–compliant containers on Linux systems. Containers with Podman can be run either as root or in rootless modes—running containers created by Podman seems indistinguishable, to us, from those created by any other common container engine that we've played around with.

To start, stop, and work with containers, you'll likewise use Podman. It contains all of the subcommands needed to create and manage containers. There are different commands related to different types of objects or states. Essentially, you are searching against external registries: first you must pull containerized images from the external registries into the local storage (disk space—not the internal registry), and afterwards those images are then made available on the local machines for deployment. Conversely, when you go to do a run, it pulls it from the local storage; it doesn't have to go out to an external registry to first retrieve it (as it already exists in local storage.)

Commands such as `images`, `inspect`, and `history` are all executed against the node local storage in this manner.

When you have a running container and you `stop` it, it goes to a "stop" state (of course) but it still remains in memory. If you are accustomed to working with processes, you expect that when you stop/kill a process that it will disappear from the system memory. *Containers are different.* When you run containers, they take up memory and they perform tasks; when you stop a container, it stops but it continues to reside in memory.

There's an important reason for this logic: containers are designed to be stood up, perform a task, and then be thrown away. This is unlike enterprise services or VMs, which store their information on some persistent storage device. Without creating persistent storage, the container will be completely ephemeral and stateless. So when it goes away, you've lost everything it's done and any knowledge it ever had about anything, including itself.

One of the reasons why containers stay resident in memory after they have been "stopped" is so that you retain the ability to query them afterwards. For example, if a container were to fail or disappear, you'd lose the container logs (which are also in-memory); so how would you be able to dissect what went wrong afterwards? By keeping stopped containers in-memory, administrators and developers can still query those stopped containers (using Podman logs, as an example), debug containers, and troubleshoot them.

Stopped containers are *not* like VMs. They don't pick up where they left off. In fact, stopped containers are like imposters when you think about it. For example, if you restart a container it actually cheats or misleads you, so to speak, by throwing away the old container and instantiating (creating) a new one with the *old* process ID that it had been using beforehand—while it *does* make a new container, it's disguised as the old container using the *same* process ID (this is typically done for a restart Podman task).

Red Hat conforms to the Container Networking Interface (CNI) open source project to define standards for consistency for software-defined networking for containers across many platforms and clouds. Based on this, Podman attaches each container to a virtual bridge that Red Hat can manipulate and add richer capabilities to (including security), and then uses that to assign to each container a private IP address and makes it accessible (not necessarily externally, but this is internally how networking and connectivity work). You have to make a container available to the outside world by mapping a port. What we want to do is declare a container port that maps to a host port, so that we can connect to the host and get to the container.

Seven Best Practices for Securing Containerized Data and Applications

We cover security throughout this book because we think it is important. Many of the concepts suggested in this section provide the foundation for what we discussed in Chapter 6. This isn't an either/or suggestion—you need both. Containerized applications make it easy to ensure consistency of development, consistency of testing, and consistency of deployment—across physical servers, virtual machines (VMs), and public and private clouds. But does this level of consistency also extend equally to concerns like security? Organizations are keen to know the answer to such questions (and rightly so). However, the answer is not always immediately obvious; likewise, your results may vary depending on your choice of containerization platform and the vendor supplying it.

How you go about securing a container, and the approach you take to achieve this, depends on the background of the person you ask. For example, if your background is in managing infrastructure, you may perceive a "container" as a lightweight alternative to VMs, such as a sandboxed application process, that shares a Linux operating system (OS) kernel with other containers. Alternatively, if your background is as a developer, you might conceptualize a "container" as a packaged bundle of an application (like you would a JAR file in Java) and all of its dependencies, provisionable in seconds within any environment of your choosing, and readily enabled for continuous integration and continuous delivery (CI/CD).

Regardless of whether you subscribe to the application-builder or infrastructure-manager perspective on containers, there are seven key elements essential to securing any containerized environment, which are summarized in Figure 7-3 and explored in more detail in the following sections.

Containers (and container-ready storage) make the portability of data easier than it's arguably ever been before—and that's something to be wary of, particularly for those of us operating in environments with strict data sovereignty and regulatory compliance laws that must be met. Under these conditions and within these countries, the pull of data gravity is ironclad. Likewise, the controls and safeguards built into your hybrid multicloud environment must be equally solid in order to ensure your business doesn't run afoul of these laws.

From our time spent working with clients operating under these strict data guidelines, we've compiled a list of seven elements that encompass each layer of the container's solution stack (like you would do for any running process)—from before you deploy and run your container, to the lifecycle of the containerized application once it has been placed into production. We'll dig into each element and provide you some lessons learned on how to prepare your hybrid multicloud for the realities of containerized data and applications.

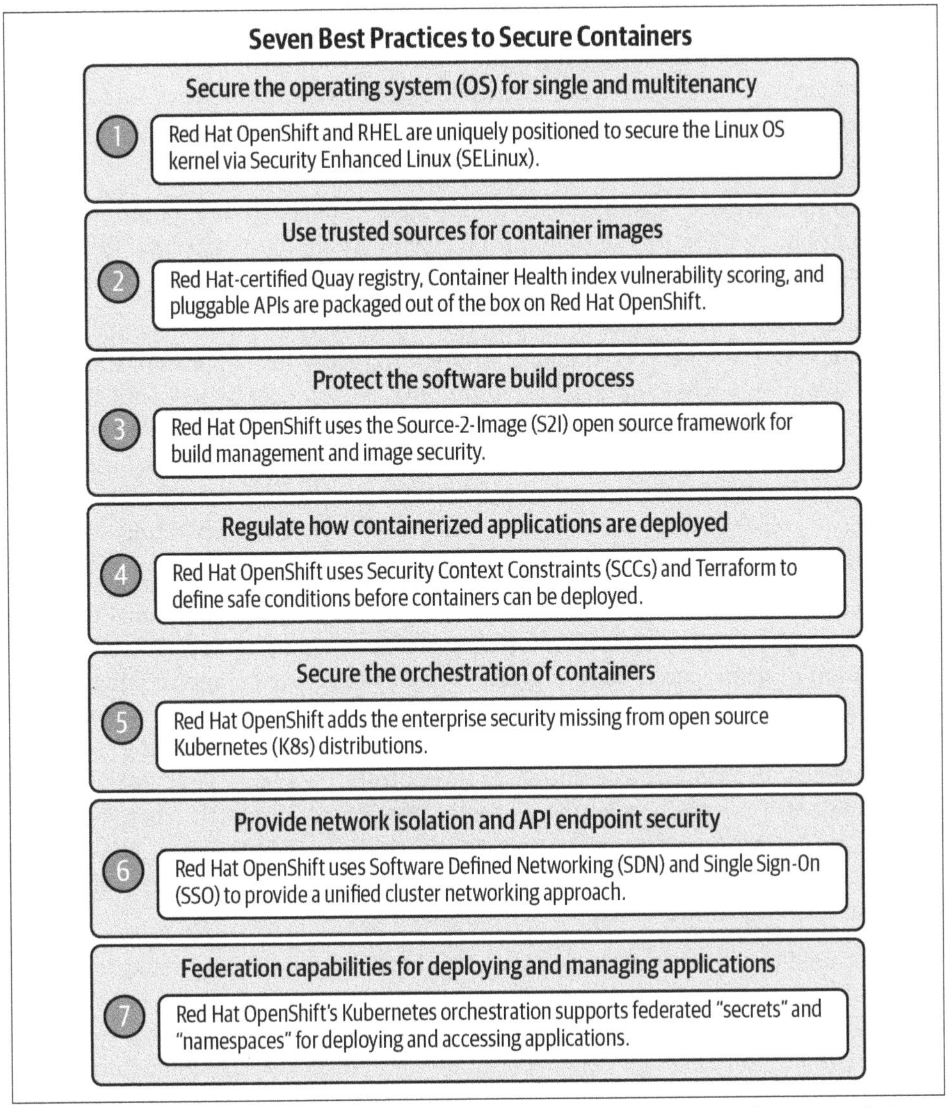

Seven Best Practices to Secure Containers

Secure the operating system (OS) for single and multitenancy

(1) Red Hat OpenShift and RHEL are uniquely positioned to secure the Linux OS kernel via Security Enhanced Linux (SELinux).

Use trusted sources for container images

(2) Red Hat-certified Quay registry, Container Health index vulnerability scoring, and pluggable APIs are packaged out of the box on Red Hat OpenShift.

Protect the software build process

(3) Red Hat OpenShift uses the Source-2-Image (S2I) open source framework for build management and image security.

Regulate how containerized applications are deployed

(4) Red Hat OpenShift uses Security Context Constraints (SCCs) and Terraform to define safe conditions before containers can be deployed.

Secure the orchestration of containers

(5) Red Hat OpenShift adds the enterprise security missing from open source Kubernetes (K8s) distributions.

Provide network isolation and API endpoint security

(6) Red Hat OpenShift uses Software Defined Networking (SDN) and Single Sign-On (SSO) to provide a unified cluster networking approach.

Federation capabilities for deploying and managing applications

(7) Red Hat OpenShift's Kubernetes orchestration supports federated "secrets" and "namespaces" for deploying and accessing applications.

Figure 7-3. The seven best practices any organization can apply toward securing their containerized applications and services

1. Multitenancy and the Unusual World of Container Host Operating Systems

We mentioned before how containers simplify work for developers by allowing containerized applications to be conceptualized as a single bundle of your code and *all* of its dependencies (a single "unit," if you will). This has a knock-on effect—multiple containerized applications are able to run on a shared host, as all containers can be deployed in a multitenant fashion on the same machine without cluttering or polluting the underlying operating system with conflicting binaries or other dependencies. With containers you also eliminate the need for traditional VM hypervisors or guest OSs, further decreasing the complexity and size footprint that would otherwise be placed on hardware with virtualized machines.

The linchpin therefore becomes the OS that these containerized applications share and run upon. The host OS kernel *must* be able to secure the host kernel from container escapes and it *must* be able to secure containers from one another.

Decreasing risk to the shared OS begins with how you design your containerized application. For example, you should drop privileges from the application where you can (or assign only what you need at minimum) to create containers with the least number of OS-level permissions possible. (Security aficionados tend to group this concept into something they call the *principle of least privilege*—a cornerstone of any security playbook.) Run and execute applications as "user" rather than as "root," wherever possible. The second task is ensuring that your Linux operating system is surrounded by multiple levels of security.

Red Hat CoreOS and Red Hat OpenShift are positioned to secure the Linux operating system through a combination of SELinux, available as a part of CoreOS and RHEL, for isolation of namespaces, control groups (cgroups), secure computing mode (seccomp), and more. Namespaces provide a level of abstraction inside a container to make an application appear as though it is running its own OS inside of the container —with its own dedicated allocation of resources from the global pool. SELinux isolates containers from the host kernel, as well as containers from each other. Administrators can enforce mandatory access controls (MAC) for every user, application, process, or file. This serves as a net of protections if the namespace abstraction of a container is ever breached or exploited by an attacker.

Compromised containers running on the same host OS is a common vector of attack for those looking to exploit unsecured networking between containers not running on SELinux. Utilizing cgroups can place limitations on the resources that a container (or collection of containers) is able to consume from the host system, mitigating their ability to "stomp over" other (healthy) containers. Seccomp profiles can be defined and associated with a container, restricting the system calls available to it.

2. Trusting Your Sources

You must be mindful of any packages or external code that you bring into your environment. Can you guarantee that the container you're downloading from a third-party repository won't compromise your infrastructure or contaminate other containers running in the same environment? Does the application layer of the container have vulnerabilities that could be exploited? What is the frequency with which the container is updated? And who authors those updates? (Think of all the reasons why you shouldn't go hunting for movies from a BitTorrent site—aside from the fact it's illegal—you just don't know what's in the file you're downloading.) Our pro tip? Hardware can help here with the cross-container memory contamination protocols we are starting to see (for example, on IBM Power 10).

Containerized software from public repositories, even highly reputable ones such as Docker Hub or GitHub, carries the same potential risks. The unavoidable fact is that if your organization is working with containers published in these repositories, you are ultimately inheriting code and work performed by others, almost certainly from people you've never met. This is not to suggest that code from public repositories is riddled with malicious code—far from it! But there is always the risk that the containerized code may inadvertently come with vulnerabilities that the original developer(s) failed to recognize.

Modern software projects are enormous undertakings and might contain upwards of thousands of different dependencies and libraries. If you're working with someone else's code (or another person's container), some of those dependencies won't be fully under your control. Data gravity once again rears its ugly head with the "pull" these containerized apps and repositories have on us: the reliance we (as developers) have on extending the open source projects of others; and the need to include *dependencies* within our projects over which we have limited (or no) control.

One way to mitigate the risks is to work with trusted and established vendors when sourcing containerized application code. For example, Red Hat has been packaging and delivering trusted Linux content for years in RHEL, and likewise they now do the same via Red Hat–certified containers that run anywhere RHEL runs, including OpenShift. Red Hat's *Quay* container and application registry can also provide additional levels of secure storage, distribution, and deployment of containers on any infrastructure, for those who might need that.

If you want to use your own container scanning tools to check for vulnerabilities, you can also leverage RHEL's and OpenShift's pluggable API. This makes it simple to integrate scanners such as OpenSCAP, Black Duck Hub, JFrog Xray, and Twistlock with your CI/CD pipeline.

3. Protecting the Software Build Process

For containers, the *Build phase* of an application's lifecycle occurs when application code is integrated with runtime libraries and other dependencies. One of the key hallmarks of containers is the repeatable, consistent manner in which they deploy across any infrastructure. Consider the frictionless portability of these containers and the multitude of environments that one container might be deployed over the lifecycle of its code (and the utility it provides). The gravity of the legal and privacy situation in the European Union (and increasingly across the globe) demands that businesses and individuals maintain tight control over data ingress (data in) and egress (data out) over national boundaries. Defining what and how a container is deployed (the Build process) is critical to securing a container that may be deployed dozens or hundreds of times over its history.

The *Source-2-Image (S2I)* open source framework provides build management and image security for containerized applications and code. As developer code is built and committed to a repository (such as Git—a version-control system for tracking changes) via S2I, a platform such as OpenShift can trigger CI/CD processes to automatically assemble a new container image using the freshly committed code, deploy that image for testing, and promote the tested image to full production status.

We strongly recommend that your organization adopts integrating automated security testing and scanning into your CI/CD pipelines as a best practice. Making use of RESTful APIs allows your business to readily integrate Static Application Security Testing (SAST) or Dynamic Application Security Testing (DAST) tools like IBM AppScan or HCL AppScan, among others. Ultimately, this approach of securing the software build process allows operations teams to manage base images, architects to manage middleware and software needed by your application layer, and developers to focus on writing better code.

4. Wrangling Deployments on Clusters

Tools for automated, policy-based deployments can further secure your containers, beyond the software Build process and into the production Deployment phase. Consider this in the context of the regulatory compliance and data sovereignty issues we discussed earlier. If the country or market in which your business operates demands that data-generating applications or PII records stay within a particular boundary (some countries and regions have stronger gravitational pull than others, it turns out), then it is absolutely critical that you have reliable control over how apps and services are deployed. It becomes doubly important if those deployments depend on semi or fully automated orchestration engines, or if those applications are easily portable (such as with containers).

An important concept to Kubernetes orchestration is Security Context Constraints (SCCs), which define a set of conditions that must be met before a collection of containers (sometimes referred to as a "pod" or, in essence, an application) can be deployed. SCCs were contributed back to the K8s open source project by Red Hat, to form the basis of K8s "Pod Security Policy," and are now packaged as part of the OpenShift Container Platform. By employing SCCs, an administrator can control a variety of sensitive functions, including running of privileged containers; capabilities that a running container may request; allowing or denying access to volumes (like host directories); container user ID; and the SELinux context of the container.

In terms of where containerized applications deploy and how those images are deployed, OpenShift and IBM Cloud Paks use open source Terraform (recall from

Chapter 3 that Terraform is an infrastructure as code software toolchain) for deployment to any public or private cloud infrastructure, as well as open source Helm Charts (a collection of files that describe a related set of K8s resources) for consistency of operations.

5. Orchestrating Securely

Modern microservices-based applications are made possible in large part because of orchestration services like K8s, which handles the complexities of deploying multiple containerized applications across distributed hosts or nodes. However, as is the case with any large open source project that we've ever been involved in across our aggregated century of IT experience, rolling your own version of Kubernetes is *hard* to implement from scratch and rife with challenges. Why do it yourself when you can adopt a platform with enterprise-hardened Kubernetes orchestration already engineered at the core of the solution?

One of the key tenets of any successful orchestration platform should be access to collaborative multitenancy between all members of a client's workforce, while still ensuring that the self-service access to the environment remains secure. To once again use OpenShift as an example, the platform was fully architected around K8s in order to deliver container orchestration, scheduling automation, and containerized application management at the scale and with the rigidity needed by enterprise. That last point about enterprise is important. Naturally, enterprise organizations are subject to stringent regulatory and compliance requirements that go above and beyond what smaller shops may need to adhere to. However, we believe that it is in the interest of *every* business (from enterprise, to "ma and pa" brick and mortar) that OpenShift secures K8s in a multitude of ways over the RYO *stock* (100% free) edition. For example, OpenShift enterprise hardens K8s in many ways including: all access to master nodes is handled over Transport Layer Security (TLS); API server access is based on tokens or X.509; etcd (an open source key-value store database) is no longer exposed directly to the cluster; and the platform runs on Red Hat–exclusive SELinux to provide the kernel-level security that we discussed earlier.

When you think about it, selecting a container orchestration platform (on top of which will run your data, services, applications, and users) is akin to determining the center of critical mass for your modern IT estate. It is a center of gravity for your hybrid multicloud architecture, if you will. This platform will serve as the nexus of the future investments of your business, the hub for both your workforce and customer base, and naturally will be where data from both of those sources accumulates and resides. Selection of an orchestration platform with enterprise-certified container security already built into the Kubernetes layer puts your organization in the best position moving forward.

6. Lockdown: Network Isolation and API Endpoint Security

When working with containerized applications that are deployed across multiple distributed hosts or nodes, it becomes critical to secure your network topology. Network namespaces usually assign a port range and IP address to a collection of containers, which helps to distinguish and isolate containerized applications (pods) from one another. By default, pods of different namespaces cannot send or receive data packets —unless exceptions are otherwise made by the system administrator. This is helpful for isolating things like dev, test, and pod environments within the same infrastructure.

A container orchestration platform that uses software-defined networking (SDN) to provide a unified cluster networking approach to assigning namespaces (for pods) can simplify this architecture immensely. A platform that is able to control egress traffic (outbound data moving outside of the cluster) using a router or firewall method will also allow you to conduct IP whitelisting (explicitly stating which IP addresses are allowed and denying access to all others), for further network access control.

Red Hat OpenShift supplies all of these tools that are well known in any best security practices playbook, as well as numerous other network security measures, in abundance. Chief amongst the API authentication and authorization services it provides are Red Hat Single Sign-On (RH-SSO), which provides SAML 2.0 (Security Assertion Markup Language) and OpenID Connect–based authentication. Furthermore, Web Single Sign-On and federation services are also available via open source Keycloak. RH-SSO 7.1 also features client adapters for Red Hat JBoss, a Node.js client adapter, and integration with LDAP-based directory services. API management tools such as Red Hat 3scale API Management can also be readily added to OpenShift to provide API authentication and organization.

7. United Federation of Containerized Applications

Federation is invaluable when deploying and accessing applications that are running across multiple distributed datacenters or clouds. Kubernetes orchestration supports and facilitates this in two different ways: *federated secrets* and *federated namespaces*:

- Federated secrets automatically create and manage all authentication and authorization "secrets" (sensitive information like API keys that serve as license files, passwords that get buried in configuration files, and so on) across all clusters belonging to the federation. The result is a globally consistent and up-to-date record of authentication secrets across the whole of the cluster.

- Federated namespaces create namespaces in the federation control plane, ensuring that K8s pods have consistent IP addresses and port ranges assigned to them, across all federated environments in the cluster.

Readying Data for the New Normal

Back in 2010, Dave McCrory (an engineer at GE Digital) coined the term *data gravity* in an attempt to describe the natural attraction between data and applications. (In "millennial speak," apps swipe right on data every time.) We think that McCrory's turn of phrase couldn't be more apt, coming at the start of a decade where more data was generated and collected than all previous years of recorded human history *combined*.

This trend shows absolutely no signs of wavering in 2021 and beyond. In fact, we believe that the COVID-19 pandemic only further accelerated the explosion of data capture—as more and more work moves to remote, digitally-delivered experiences and processes. Whatever the future holds—from edge computing, to AI, to cloud-born startups offering you fantastic new ways to post something about anything—it all means huge growth in enterprise and personal data.

Following the techniques and strategies outlined in this chapter will enable your organization to overcome many of the challenges associated with data gravity, as we all grapple with how to adapt to the hybrid multicloud paradigm shift. We'll say it again: there's no changing the laws of physics (not outside of Hollywood, at any rate). There will inevitably be friction against such changes: the substantial gravity of legacy and on-premises data will drag performance and time-to-delivery for systems spanning public and hybrid clouds; regulatory and security concerns for newly containerized data and applications will require proactive care to mitigate risks; and even the culture within your enterprise or business may be slow to adapt to the new ways of operating in a hybrid multicloud marketplace.

Yet it is our firm conviction that the momentum toward cloud is far greater than the drag from legacy application services that have yet to be modernized for blended off- and on-premises ways of doing business. The techniques covered here (and throughout the book) can give your organization the boost needed to overcome such friction. Data gravity will keep us grounded, but it won't hold us back.

CHAPTER 8

Ecosystem for Automation

Automation, in the scope of technology and its applications for the world of IT, aims to unburden humans from mundane tasks so that more energy and time can be focused on higher-value endeavors— much in the way that automation has applied to other fields and industries. For technology, this can include tasks like business process automation, IT automation, personal applications like home automation, and more. The goal isn't to get rid of humans, but to pull them from away from time-consuming tasks that could otherwise be handled more efficiently and consistently by a machine. We like to describe the world of automation as having two branches: business automation and IT operational automation.

Whichever branch you're interested in, there are types of automation you could apply to either:

Basic automation
> Simple, rudimentary tasks are automated by centralizing and removing the friction associated with those tasks. Robotic Process Automation (RPA) and Business Process Management (BPM) are good examples, but so too is learning to manage the deployment of infrastructure, or route service tickets, and more.

Process automation
> This type of automation manages business processes for uniformity and transparency. It is typically handled by dedicated software and business apps. Using process automation can increase productivity and efficiency within your business. It can also deliver new insights into business challenges and suggest solutions. Process mining and workflow automation are types of process automation. From an IT Operations perspective, this automation can build on basic automation tasks to pull together multiple tasks: deploying a service, applying software patches, crafting access control lists, and managing networks.

Integration automation

Machines mimic human tasks and repeat the actions defined in rule sets. One example is the digital worker. In recent years, people have described digital workers as software robots (the kind you're likely thinking about) that are trained to work with humans to perform specific tasks with a specific set of skills. This type of automation is growing fast across all industries: from agriculture, to warehousing, to maintenance, to delivery—the way many field workers do their jobs is going to change drastically in the coming years.

AI automation

This is the most complex level of automation. The addition of AI means that machines can "learn" and make decisions based on past situations they have encountered and analyzed. For example, in customer service, cognitive assistants can reduce costs while empowering both customers and human agents, creating an optimal customer service experience. On the IT Operations of the house, having access to AI-assisted observability for cloud-native apps is going to become the standard for modern application performance management.

This chapter is about one of the best process automation-based IT technologies in the world: Ansible. Organizations are using it to flatten the time to value of repetitive and complex configuration management tasks, cloud provisioning, software deployment, intra-service orchestration, and more. But it's more than that—Ansible bolsters developers and operations teams with a standardized approach to IT automation (using a single skill set) that works across almost any endpoint you can imagine. With Ansible, teams no longer need to go to every endpoint and install software on every device to reap the benefits of automation.

Imagine a single skill to configure or patch myriad server architectures across an enterprise. Is your business loaded up with IBM Z, x86, IBM Power, and 5G endpoints? Shout it out loud: "Ansible!" Take a single skill and empower organizations to create consistent deployment processes across the board, which is ultimately going to save resources for more important tasks like training for niche skill's, reduce overall management costs (the endpoint example above), and free up IT to pursue higher value projects.

Red Hat's strategic acquisition of Ansible in 2015 would become a cornerstone in the company's OpenShift Container Platform (OCP). It speaks to Red Hat's commitment to open source technologies at the core of everything that they do. But it also demonstrates the company's foresight in recognizing industry trends toward hybrid multicloud environments. In hindsight we can say that Red Hat's gamble on automation paid off handsomely, but what brought the company to see the value in the Ansible technology?

One intractable problem for taking *any* project and delivering it at scale is how to manage, maintain, and continue growing once the efforts of your labor start to take off. Silicon Valley may have started in suburban garages in the South Bay, but clearly it doesn't operate that way today. Technologists have been solving the problems of *scale* for decades—and in many ways, cloud (the capability) is the most successful expression of overcoming the challenges of scale to date. We call the solution to challenges of scale *automation*.

If automation is old hat at this point, then why dedicate an entire chapter to it? And more importantly, why did Red Hat make such a gamble on it in 2015 by making it a key cornerstone of their flagship platform as a service? After all, doesn't Kubernetes and orchestration solve many of these challenges already?

Advancements in technology are always incremental (sometimes by leaps, but consistently on an upward climb), and through stubbornness or necessity we find better ways of accomplishing old tasks. For cloud—and hybrid multicloud in particular, where you're working across different vendors at mind-boggling scale and across entirely different premises from the four walls of your own business—automation represents one of those leaps (you might even call it *one giant leap*) forward.

In acquiring Ansible, Red Hat gained a formidable tool for performing orchestration across vendors and across premises. Orchestration—now there's another word we've seen a lot of before. "Hold on," you might ask, "so is Ansible just another alternative to K8s?" And the honest answer is that both technologies are in fact looking to solve challenges of scale through automation; however, the key distinction between the two is in *how* they do so and in the particular *domains* that they apply automation toward.

We've already seen throughout this book the ways in which Kubernetes performs orchestration (the how) of containerized applications and microservices (the domains in which it commonly operates) for hybrid multicloud environments. Sounds a lot like automation—and it is! But while Kubernetes is geared toward automation (orchestration) of containers and microservices across distributed systems, Ansible is principally concerned with the automation of the environments (physical infrastructure or cloud-based servers) that those microservices and containers run upon.

Kubernetes and Ansible, therefore, are complementary means to an end: an end to the challenges of scale, made ready for the era of hybrid multicloud architectures. This was a key motivation behind Red Hat's investment into Ansible (placing it near to the core of their Kubernetes-based orchestration platform) and is likewise why Ansible has such tremendous adoption within the marketplace today.

Automation of nearly any infrastructure endpoint with minimal amounts of code has immense practical value to a world increasingly dependent on clouds operated by different vendors, in varying countries, across multiple premises. Furthermore, these automation capabilities translate to a number of benefits for you and your business: reduced storage and resource burden placed on the machines to be automated; a much smaller footprint on these endpoints that could be hacked or exploited by malicious users; and most importantly, a greatly simplified approach to automation. Likewise, as environments change and operating systems advance over time, the automation jobs Ansible is running can be easily modified in lockstep as well. Adaptability and extensibility are key ingredients in the longevity of any technology—and fortunately the automation tooling for the hybrid multicloud era has those in abundance.

Ansible aims to commodify the automation of everything else that applications, services, and containers need to run upon: infrastructure provisioning, server deployments, IoT edge devices, script execution, and lots of other things that operations teams spend their time doing to "keep the lights on." It makes automation available to everyone with the lightest touch of human-readable, undaunting snippets of code. More importantly to us, it makes automation of nearly everything needed to deliver the capabilities of the cloud possible, regardless of the destination.

Rethinking Automation for the As-a-Service Era

Ansible doesn't exist in a vacuum, of course. As we mentioned earlier, the challenges of automation have been a known problem for decades. That said, it's far from being a "solved" problem. Fifteen years ago, open source technologies like Puppet and Chef appeared in the marketplace to tackle these challenges—although with a far different philosophy and approach toward automation than more modern tools like Ansible, which will become more apparent as we dissect the technology. All three stacks (and others not mentioned here) are in heavy rotation throughout the industry today. If you've ever dabbled in some level of automation at any large IT shop, it's very likely you've worked with (or taken advantage of the work done by) one of these solutions.

As we dig into each more deeply, it'll become apparent that none of these options are inherently flawed or the *wrong* place to start; rather, we expect you'll see that each has its niche part to play. But ultimately each solution is a byproduct of the era for which they were built (from the days of cloud as a destination, to the age of cloud as a capability).

One particular quality to call out regarding precursor technologies like Puppet and Chef, compared to alternatives like Ansible, is their congruency (or lack thereof) to modern-day approaches to cloud. Fifteen years ago, nascent cloud was very much designed for and architected around as a destination. The notion of cloud as an as-a-service set of capabilities, understandably, hadn't entered the lexicon—and this is very much reflected in the design decisions that technologies like Puppet and Chef made toward automation of cloud endpoints and infrastructure. This is a repeating problem for lots of software as enterprises move to cloud-native. For example, most vendors in the Application Performance Management (APM) space provide monitoring tools built with the "cloud as a destination" philosophy in mind and they struggle enormously trying to observe loosely coupled applications built cloud native.

When we say that Ansible adheres to our vision of cloud (the capability, not the destination), we really mean it. Ansible is an "agentless" architecture, so there's nothing unique that needs to be running on any endpoints for Ansible to start managing them. This means that there is much less of a footprint required on the machines that are to be managed, compared to alternative approaches. That's how Ansible delivers automation to nearly any endpoint, regardless of where that target (destination) happens to be.

Puppet and Chef, alternatively, use agents to invoke automation on their endpoints. A key difference between these technologies and cloud-centric ones such as Ansible is the need for Puppet and Chef to pre-install libraries of code on the endpoints (the machines) that are to be automated. This is a decidedly more heavyweight and less agile approach to take, but it makes sense in light of the times in which Puppet and Chef came to prominence: when cloud was viewed as a destination and configuration management of these endpoints was the priority.

Fast forward to the present day—while configuration management is still a key facet of cloud administration, the advent of fully managed cloud services has greatly reduced the managerial burden placed on IT. Instead, those looking to tap into the capabilities of cloud are less concerned with managing their resources and more focused on ensuring that those capabilities are available in the premises where they're needed most (as soon as they're needed). Being able to rapidly provision and deploy those capabilities via automation to any cloud or premises as needed has been a key driver in Ansible's success over Chef or Puppet.

From an in-house IT culture perspective, you can draw similar distinctions between the three technologies as well. Requiring agents to be installed and managed ahead of time on automation endpoints has repercussions on how your organization executes on its automation ambitions. In a nutshell, it increases the operational burden on your team. As your inventory of automated endpoints grows, so too must your Puppet or Chef administrator team grow with it—and so too does the complexity and interdependencies of the code used to manage those automation tasks and agents. Following an agent-driven approach to automation also dampens your team's agility: resources cannot be automated unless they are configured and accessible ahead of time, which doesn't always play nicely in a world where cloud infrastructure and services are often deployed on an ad hoc basis. Getting "access" to endpoints (to install the agents and perform the management) can be problematic as well, particularly with so many cloud-based vendors moving to fully managed (in other words—fully out of your hands) services and delivery models.

Terraform is another entrant into the modern automation space, geared specifically toward providing "infrastructure as code" technology using a declarative style very reminiscent of what Ansible uses. Terraform will take instructions from an administrator (for some state or result an administrator wants to achieve) and interpret the most efficient way to realize that state, without burdening the administrator with the complexities of how exactly to bring it about.

The "infrastructure as code" distinction is an interesting one, particularly in light of how we have positioned Ansible for you as an "everything as code" solution for providing the infrastructure, servers, and management needed to run today's orchestrated containers and microservices. Can't Ansible do the same? And the reality is that yes, both technologies (Ansible and Terraform) have the potential to automate infrastructure with code. As we said early on, adaptability and extensibility are the keys to the longevity of open source technologies—Terraform represents yet another branch in the evolutionary tree of tools built toward solving the challenges of scale, with a particular emphasis placed on automation of infrastructure. We don't see these as competitors, per se; rather they are fit-for-purpose tools that can often be used in conjunction with one another for delivering well-honed cloud capabilities. We'll explore examples of how Ansible and Terraform can be used together later in this chapter.

An expression we've run across in the marketplace is that if you need to perform automation of configuration management, choose Chef or Puppet; if you need automation of infrastructure provisioning, choose Terraform; and if you need automation of both—to make automation of everything as code—then choose Ansible.

IBM and Red Hat (and even some of the authors of this book) have done configuration management using scripting for a very long time. The problem with this approach is that scripts only work for a specific situation that's been defined or foreseen ahead of time. Move beyond those parameters, however, and things rapidly begin to cascade and fall apart. So how does Ansible's approach to automation differ from a do-it-yourself approach that we (and perhaps many of you) have followed until now? After all, automation isn't a *new* technology or concept, so why is this latest generation an improvement over those that have come before?

In general, Ansible is an open source IT configuration management, deployment, and orchestration tool. It delivers productivity gains via automation, to enable faster time-to-market for IT projects with predictable and consistent deployments. Ansible supports the orchestration of multitier workloads—including infrastructure, networking, operating systems, applications, and services—across hundreds (or even thousands) of nodes. Ansible's automation makes use of "Yet Another Markup Language" (YAML), with automation tasks written in easy-to-understand "Playbooks" that allow your entire organization to benefit from automation. Developers, lines-of-business professionals, and system administrators can have an equal and powerful part to play in building and maintaining powerful automation processes within your business using Ansible.

Hardcoded automation scripts may do great work, but they're difficult to maintain and even more challenging to adapt further. Very often, teams will be forced to abandon legacy automation scripts and write new ones altogether—as adapting older scripts might simply be unfeasible. Ansible upends that concept. When you write an Ansible Playbook, you're not writing a script. You're instead defining an end state of how you want the world (your IT landscape) to look after Ansible has put in the work —through automation—to bring about those changes. Your expectation, as an administrator and user, is that Ansible understands how to reach this end state without needing to be explicitly told (in all the gory detail) how to do so.

Ansible, therefore, gives its automation engine a lot of flexibility and room to maneuver in determining how best to execute the instructions given by the administrator. What is important to understand, however, is that the *ordering* of the instructions (complete task A before moving to B and later C) will be executed in exactly the order they're written. This approach contrasts sharply with alternatives like Chef and Puppet, where the execution order of jobs as written is not necessarily the order in which the automation will be carried out. Chef and Puppet automation scripts won't always begin from the same start state each time and it's possible that, on repeat runs of the same job, they may not arrive at the same end state either.

Essentially, this is configuration management applied to the management of IT estates. Instead of having a hardcoded script that instructs exactly how to move from task A to task B, you're creating a Playbook that lays out the expected end state and asks Ansible to figure out the delta between the current and end state. But critically, Ansible will not move on to task B until all of the conditions required by task A have been satisfied. This has two profound implications for Ansible clients. First, it removes any ambiguity from the automation process (Ansible will execute your instructions in exactly the order you've assigned). Second, it places the burden of deciding *how* to achieve the end states of tasks A and B on the automation engine itself, rather than requiring the user to explicitly define all the gory details themselves.

Automation with Ansible becomes a matter of simply defining the state of the world you want to achieve and the steps to get there, then leaving the heavy-lifting and complexities of how that state is achieved up to the automation engine.

More Agency with Agentless Design

Ansible's "agentless" design is ideal for high security or high performance environments alike. Agentless tools operate via a "push" model, meaning that no software or tooling is required to be installed on the remote machines that Ansible interacts with. Instead, all communication and management is handled remotely over SSH (Secure Shell for Linux and UNIX) or WinRM (Windows Remote Management). Furthermore, this agentless design can also be leveraged in an IBM Z (mainframe) environment. By utilizing an interface known as Zowe CLI to remotely execute tasks on z/OS, mainframe administrators can apply the same automation across heterogeneous environments. This also means that no resources are consumed or abused unnecessarily on managed machines, as Ansible has no software bloating the target systems; likewise, no background processes are being run when Ansible tasks are not being executed on those machines. Remote management frameworks like SSH and WinRM already exist natively on their respective operating system platform, and provide a secured means of communication between Ansible and the infrastructure it is automating. You, as the end user, are simply leveraging the capabilities and resources *that are already a part of your IT estate* to further amplify the value of your business services with automation.

What does "agentless" design mean in practical terms? On the infrastructure that is to be automated and managed, *no* administrator access is required, and *no* dedicated users need to be created in reserve ahead of time for Ansible. Ansible can leverage any user credentials already set up to work with the targeted infrastructure. Ansible uses the credentials that the user (or application) supplies, and with those credentials set it will "push" the desired instructions to the target infrastructure. Furthermore, machines that Ansible is automating cannot see or affect how other machines are configured; they are only interacting directly with Ansible itself. This greatly reduces the risk of a jeopardized machine being able to hijack or eavesdrop on other machines in the cluster.

Granted, having a serialized order of tasks defined within a Playbook may sound like a procedural (or even imperative) style of programming; however, the nuance with Ansible's declarative approach is in the way those sequential statements are interpreted and executed by the Automation Engine. "Imperative" paradigms are much more explicit and literal, but harder to scale and automate. Let's consider a scenario where you require a service to be up and running. A declarative approach would be to tell OpenShift that "Service X" should be in a state of "running." When you consider what it means for a service to be running, you realize that this encompasses quite a lot: if the service has yet to initialize, it must first be launched; if it is already launched and running, then it must be maintained and kept stable; and so on. With the declarative approach of OpenShift and Ansible, an administrator does not need to explain to the system explicitly what all of these duties are or how they should be carried out. An administrator simply expresses a desired state ("Service X should be running") with a minimal number of commands, and the packaged Module and implicit understanding within Ansible sees to it that this desired state is achieved.

Alternatively, with an "imperative" approach, an administrator would start up Service X by hand—but of course, this only satisfies one objective. It does not account for the ongoing maintenance of the service's lifecycle, for example. We're sure you can appreciate just how quickly this manual process can become unsustainable at scale; imagine if Service X needs to be launched repeatedly hundreds of times across thousands of hosts!

Consider Figure 8-1, which illustrates the diversity of roles that participate through the lifecycle of an automated process for provisioning servers. In this example, a system administrator can simply author an Ansible Playbook with a full set of instructions on how to create, patch, secure, and deploy some infrastructure. Using Ansible Playbooks to configure the broad automation strokes (and leaving the gory details to Ansible Automation Engine to figure out) can dramatically cut down on the complexity of setting up these jobs for the administrator.

Ready-to-go configurations of OpenShift (for nearly any customer use case or workload) are readily available from open communities supported by Red Hat, so administrators may not even be required to write a Playbook themselves—it may very well be as simple as choosing the Playbook configuration appropriate for their organization, and then leaving the rest (in a declarative paradigm fashion) up to Ansible Automation Engine. The heavy lifting is carried out by Ansible, but there is plenty of opportunity along the way to incorporate other members from the organization into the lifecycle.

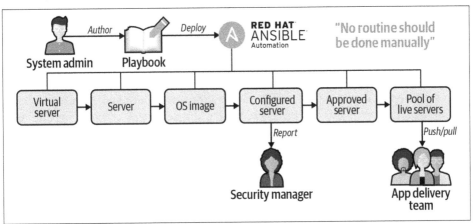

Figure 8-1. The lifecycle for provisioning and deploying infrastructure through automation with Ansible Playbooks

From a user's perspective, the emergence of declarative systems for performing automation have reduced operational oversight, complexity, and costs significantly. Processes become more scalable, instructions are carried out in more consistent ways, and ongoing tasks become more resilient to failure.

What's the Play? Architecting for Automation

Ansible Playbooks are the means by which users interact with Ansible to create and manage automation tasks that the service is to carry out. Playbooks (as we mentioned) are defined in YAML files, which have a number of advantages to other automation languages available in the marketplace. YAML files are easy to read by both humans and machines, with automation instructions for all the endpoints that Ansible can work with—infrastructure, services, users, and so on—clearly expressed with an explicit order of operations. This nontechnical, unambiguous way of creating automation tasks reflects the declarative approach to automation that we described earlier: a clear set of instructions on the state of the world the administrator wants to achieve, and the instructions for Ansible on how to reach this goal.

Your developers and administrators first translate your business procedures into Playbooks, and then apply those Playbooks to specific devices. Playbooks understand and know how to maintain a number of different devices. Many vendors in the marketplace have signed on to the Ansible way of working—helped quite a bit in part by being a core part of the Red Hat ecosystem, meaning that the technology has immense support within the community.

Playbooks ensure that dependencies only need to be declared once and managed centrally within the YAML file. Furthermore, these Playbooks are executed sequentially from top to bottom (the explicit order of operations we mentioned earlier), ensuring that no dependency is missed. Before acquiring the next item or executing the next instruction in the YAML Playbook, the Ansible Automation Engine requires that all previous instructions have completed successfully. (It's like taking money out of an ATM...it either came out or it didn't. In the tech world, this concept is referred to as *atomicity*; you'll hear it a lot in the database world, but it's applicable here too). If an operation fails, Ansible will retry it; fail at this task too many times, and Ansible can be made to "fail gracefully," terminating the automation task altogether and preventing any botched (or potentially dangerous) work from being applied to the automation targets.

We've discussed at length so far how Ansible commodifies the automation of everything—infrastructure, applications, and code—to make automation ubiquitous across the enterprise. If you ask businesses where they are leveraging Ansible and automation today, the answer you'll often get back is "everywhere and anywhere." For some organizations, they're looking to streamline and modernize their existing on-premises investments with automation; others may be looking to do the same, only with born-on-the-cloud ventures.

Streamlined Automation for the Hybrid Multicloud Era

By now, you have a firm grasp on *how* a declarative approach to automation works, but *what* do those capabilities actually translate into for IT teams? After all, it seems like we're placing a lot of trust into automation engines to interpret our automation tasks and pull them off in the best possible way. Is that really the best way to go about provisioning and configuring an enterprise-grade cloud?

Let's consider this question from several angles: how a declarative approach to automation fits the multicloud paradigm of working with multiple vendors; how declarative systems work (or don't) at scale; and how declarative systems might keep your developer's heads above water (and not drowning in minutiae).

Automation for Multivendor Stacks

Kelsey Hightower (one of the most prominent and respected faces in cloud computing and open source software—famous for his guru knowledge of Kubernetes), has nevertheless voiced caution about assuming open technologies are immune to vendor lock-in. In 2020 he posited on Twitter (*https://oreil.ly/AMTw8*) that "even open source can actually put you in a situation where you get locked out of moving forward, because you've decided to go too far deep into the thing you have, even if it is free and open source." The takeaway we should all glean (and what we've seen firsthand examples of in practice during our years spent working with clients) is that expanding the scope of technologies—and the vendors supporting those technologies—that your organization depends on can *significantly* reduce your risk of lock-in. Think of it in the same way that you would plan your financial market investments: the more diversified your portfolio (software stack), the less likely your success will be hemmed (locked) in by any one part of the portfolio turning sour (switching to a proprietary model, losing support of key contributors, and so on.)

Sounds great, but as we've talked about earlier in this book, not all open source projects adhere to the same open standards—and likewise not all vendors (on the cloud or elsewhere) are as easy to work with as others. On one hand, that lack of homogeneity is a good thing for the industry: it prevents the type of lock-in that Hightower is cautioning against, by supporting a healthy array of alternative providers, APIs, and licensing models instead of one all-encompassing hegemony. But on the other hand, that wealth of vendor options can be incredibly challenging to develop across and align your business services to work with. The more vendors you work with, the more interfaces (proprietary or open) there are to design around, and the more complex the solution ultimately becomes.

Building consistent, repeatable patterns for working with hybrid on-premises and off-premises, multivendor collections of services is the perfect fit for automation. We've discussed the "philosophy" behind agentless architectures and human-readable automation "scripting," but how do these things translate into more effective tooling for working across multiple vendors and premises?

Agentless architectures, such as Ansible, radically simplify the calculus you need to make in deciding which vendors your automation needs to support. No additional installation or configuration is required on the managed endpoints—which, if those endpoints are coming from a public cloud vendor, are likely being deployed and maintained outside of the four walls of your own business—meaning the up-front work you need to perform to automate those endpoints is significantly less. The only question you need to ask yourself (and the vendor in question) is: does your service support SSH or WinRM? If the answer is yes: superb! Agentless automation services such as Ansible can readily support it.

Up next is the question of how your business goes about patterning ways for your automation architecture to perform work on those hybrid multicloud vendors. Once again, technologies such as Ansible make this process far less daunting than it might first sound. The automation tasks to be carried out on some collection of public cloud services or infrastructure (the set of hosts defined in the Inventory manifest) are organized into a series of Plays within a YAML-based Playbook.

Take a look at Figure 8-2, which illustrates how a Playbook—one which is easily parsed and understood by nontechnical users and machines alike—establishes connectivity across multiple endpoints and vendors. Without much explanation at all, you can understand how the Playbook defines an application (`Apache httpd`) that is to be deployed across endpoints (webservers) via automation. The "Plays" within the Playbook consist of one (or many) "tasks" that target some (or all) of the Inventory hosts that you wish this automation performed on. "Tasks" supply the intent (the declarative instructions) for what Ansible is to do: simple "tasks" might include installing a software package on a host machine; updating a configuration file; or more complicated work like spinning up an entire set of infrastructure from your approved hybrid cloud vendor.

```
1    --- SAMPLE YAML FILE ---
2
3    - hosts: webservers
4      vars:
5              http_port: 80
6              max_clients: 200
7              remote_user: root
8
9      tasks:
10       -        name: ensure apache is latest version
11              yum:
12                      name: httpd
13                      state: latest
14
15       -        name: write the apache config file
16              template:
17                      src: /srv/httpd.j2
18                      dest: /etc/httpd.conf
19              notify:
20                      - restart apache
21
22       -        name: ensure apache is running
23              service:
24                      name: httpd
25                      state: started
26
27      handlers:
28       -        name: restart apache
29              service:
30                      name: httpd
31                      state: restarted
```

Figure 8-2. The configuration of a YAML Playbook is remarkably simple and intention-
ally designed to be easily readable for both machines and humans

The sample YAML file in Figure 8-2 defines three tasks called yum, template, and
service (denoted on lines 11, 16, and 23, respectively)—with a brief name descrip-
tion/pointer and a series of variables encapsulated within each respective task. Take
note of the restart apache instruction on line 20: this instruction is part of the
"template" task's definition, which will invoke the restart apache service handler
(definition beginning on line 28). This demonstrates how you can easily chain multiple tasks and services together to craft more complex and nuanced automation Playbooks. Consider the benefits this has to the scenario we described earlier about
designing consistent, repeatable patterns for automating across multiple premises and
vendors.

Critically, the explicit instructions defined in a Playbook are easily read (and the logic contained therein easily followed) by nontechnical and technical professionals alike. This is an important distinction of Ansible that differs from other attempts at automation and orchestration software—which often require a high degree of technical know-how to understand and work with. Ansible's straightforward and nontechnical approach to defining even complex automation tasks is core to its popularity and is why Ansible's automation has become a ubiquitous and powerful tool in today's IT arsenal.

Another key component in Ansible's architecture are Modules. Think of a Module like you would an API or any kind of abstraction—a complex set of instructions, encapsulated within a function that you can invoke with a single (simple) command. Modules allow you to easily achieve some desired state that you want Ansible to automate; furthermore, the conditions of the desired end state are codified within the Module, such that it is able to achieve and verify that the desired state is reached, without needing further instructions or input from the user on how to do this.

Think of Modules as a preconfigured, ready-to-go method for rapidly plugging into some of the most popular cloud vendors and hybrid (on and off) premises in the marketplace today. Essentially, having access to these tools mitigates (or even eliminates altogether) the up-front work your business needs to do when configuring automation to work with a hybrid multicloud IT estate. Today, Ansible supports an ever-growing collection of 450+ Modules for complex and simple tasks alike, including configuration management, device networking managers, and deployment of infrastructure specific to any of the major cloud vendors. If a Module exists for a vendor or cloud that your business needs to pattern automation for, it's very likely you'll need to do only a little (or even no) configuration before you can immediately start taking advantage of those endpoints.

There is a plethora of packaged Modules for Ansible users to explore out of the box, but for those of us who still need to craft bespoke automation tasks, the process of modifying and extending Modules is relatively trivial. Modules can be adapted and written in Python, PowerShell, or any other language that can accept JavaScript Object Notation (JSON) documents as input (and likewise are able to produce JSON documents as output)—the only caveats that Ansible places on modifying its Modules.

For example: your business may wish to change default behaviors within Ansible—such as how it handles callbacks, connections, or lookup operations—by writing new plug-ins to modify runtime behavior. Alternatively, you may want an available infrastructure (host nodes and so on) from a public cloud vendor to be discoverable at runtime, rather than statically defined ahead of time, thereby enabling a "dynamic inventory" via scripting. The script is run at the time that you execute a particular Playbook—essentially, at runtime. Instead of working against a static (and therefore possibly out of date) inventory list, Ansible's dynamic inventory script will retrieve the available servers and endpoint hosts that exist *at the time* the script is run.

You may notice a pattern beginning to emerge. Agentless automation technologies like Ansible make the process of defining automation tasks for essentially any cloud vendor simple (if it supports SSH or WinRM, it works) and packages these jobs into Playbooks. If a Playbook contains multiple "tasks" that together achieve some singular goal or purpose, you may want to group these tasks into a single reusable unit: for example, a string of "tasks" might provision infrastructure for separate development, test, and production clusters from a cloud vendor. Patterns for automating endpoints from these vendors can be codified into Modules, supported by Red Hat and the Ansible community at large. And finally, collections of Playbooks (invoking published Modules or custom Modules that your business has tailored for itself) can be shared; these collections or recipes of Playbook "tasks" are known commonly as Ansible Roles. In other words, a Role is a blueprint of "tasks" frequently used together to achieve some goal that you want to make repeatable or shareable with others. Roles are frequently published on the Ansible Galaxy community site (*https://galaxy.ansible.com*). Via communities such as Galaxy, thousands of Roles are available for Ansible users to use within their own Playbooks.

Collectively, these Playbooks, Modules, and Roles form a comprehensive ecosystem of business and community-driven support for patterning automation to work with the broadest range of vendors, technologies, and clouds.

Automation for Cloud-Scale Deployments

As so much of this book is dedicated to the hybrid multicloud reality of a modernized marketplace, let's take a pause for a moment to examine where else the economies of scale and simplification of management that automation (and the "everything as code" philosophy) might also be applied: mainly, virtual private clouds (VPCs).

A VPC is a public cloud capability that provides you the ability to find and control isolated cloud networks, and then afterwards deploy resources into those networks. Your experience with how you go about *defining* and *deploying* a VPC, however, can be wildly different depending on the approach you take. Let's examine how to create a private cloud (using public cloud infrastructure) using the two most common approaches—traditional and virtualized cloud networking—to see how your mileage may vary.

How have organizations traditionally deployed networks into a standard public cloud infrastructure? A network administrator would often start by first defining a "backbone" to carry all of the network traffic in that cloud. There will be some segmentation in that backbone to create separation between clients, separation between different applications for the same client, and so on.

Once segmentation is defined, a network function is needed—called a router—for communication between those segments. This creates the ability to decide where traffic is permitted (and not permitted) to flow between segments via the router. This filtering on the segment traffic is called a *firewall function*.

Now that the cloud has been isolated across different segments and is regulated internally by firewalls, it needs connectivity to the broader internet at large. To do this, you'll require another network function called Network Address Translation (NAT). NAT is an important feature of gateway (dual home and screened subnet) firewalls. They ensure that private network IP addresses are *not* advertised to external networks. The NAT is responsible for translation of internal (private) addresses to external (public) addresses. In addition, you likely have applications in the public cloud you're defining (or will in the future) that need to be able to transfer data from your on-premises enterprise systems to off-premises systems in the public cloud. To do so, you'll build a virtual private network (VPN) function to create a secure tunnel between the enterprise and the public cloud endpoints.

With traditional public cloud networking, almost all of the public network functions we've been describing so far are often accomplished using *appliances*. These appliances require infrastructure and network administrators to log in to them (using proprietary interfaces) to define all of the flows, functions, and controls we've mentioned thus far. It's granular and often mundane work that is difficult to scale.

The difference with virtualized cloud networking is that all of the same capabilities you would receive with a traditional public cloud are—with the virtualized approach —delivered via an as-a-service model. Virtual cloud networking allows users to create the functions, define segmentations, and utilize all of the other components we described thus far—but instead via a user interface (UI), command-line interface (CLI), or API. Operational teams can say "We want 4 of these networks, and we want to define our own custom segmentation for applications A and B, with connectivity to the enterprise through a VPN and connectivity to the internet with a ready-to-provision service (instead of needing to define the NAT ourselves)."

Teams get an equivalent level of control as with the traditional approach, but without needing to know the proprietary networking interfaces of legacy appliances in order to make these connections or meticulously define the flows across the network. This approach sounds very much like the declarative paradigm to automation that we discussed at length before, doesn't it? Administrators retain control over how connectivity across the network is architected and defined, but the gory details of implementation (like the APIs, protocols, and pathways specific to any one vendor's cloud) are offloaded by the automation built into the virtualized cloud network.

Having defined the general idea for how a virtual cloud network is defined, you can begin to see the advantages it has for VPC networks as well. VPCs make so much more automation available to any team: defining segmentations, deploying routers, establishing firewalls, creation of VPNs, nearly any task that you can think of is accessible through some degree of automation. Furthermore, because VPC networks have built-in isolation—where these components are discretely isolated from one another until an adminstrator allows them to communicate with one another—your organization also gets tremendous security benefits over public cloud networks.

Since virtual private cloud networks bypass the need for appliances and it's all delivered via the capabilities of the cloud, it can be done at scale. It's also customizable to your needs as a developer and flexible enough to change the scope of your capabilities (or size of your deployment) later on down the road. In other words, a virtual private cloud allows developers to become more agile in the ways that they work—all because of the "everything as code" and "as-a-service" delivery model of hybrid multicloud vendors.

Automation for Stress-Free DevOps

Earlier we asked whether automation was the best way to go about running an enterprise-grade cloud for today's multivendor, hybrid premises marketplace. By now, you have a firm grasp on how a declarative and agentless approach to automation can streamline development when working across multiple vendors, as well as how it can simplify provisioning of resources for even the most complex of private cloud networks. But can it also benefit the workforce? After all, it is the teams of DevOps, engineers, and developers within your organization that will actually be putting hands to keyboard and working with these automated cloud environments. How does automation benefit them?

At this point, you're armed to the teeth with automation concepts and the technologies underlying tools like Ansible. But what are some ways that you can apply Ansible toward solving (or at least mitigating) some of today's cloud DevOps responsibilities? One prime example of how tools like Ansible can solve (or at the very least mitigate) some of today's cloud DevOps complexities is illustrated in Figure 8-3.

Imagine a team managing and performing work on 300 different servers across a mix of different processor architectures (such as deploying a common application across each of those servers), it's wiser to stagger the deployments over a few servers at a time rather than perform all 300 jobs in parallel. That might seem obvious to a developer or engineer with years of expertise, but to the layman trying to cobble together an automation task from scratch, that foresight might be missing. Configure the job incorrectly and your 300-server environment may come grinding to a halt as it struggles to cope with executing the request. Approaching the same problem (deploying the same application across 300 servers) with Ansible is markedly different. A developer tells Ansible the following: "Here's a list of machines that you're going to work on, but I'll leave it to you [Ansible] to decide the most efficient and safe way to perform this work." That's it! (That's not *actually* it—there are minimal amounts of scripting inside the YAML file to define the endpoints to be managed, instructions on how to access and deploy the application, and so on—but the net effect is the same.)

Traditionally, network provisioning and configuration have been handled by a completely separate team from the group of IT specialists that manage infrastructure provisioning. Furthermore, very few traditional IT automation tools offer a networking automation capability at all! Using Ansible, the team responsible for automating infrastructure provisioning can also provide networking automation using the same tooling. Ansible customers today are often using Playbooks to automate networking with major vendors such as Cisco, Juniper, Hewlett Packard Enterprise (HPE), IBM, and Cumulus, among others.

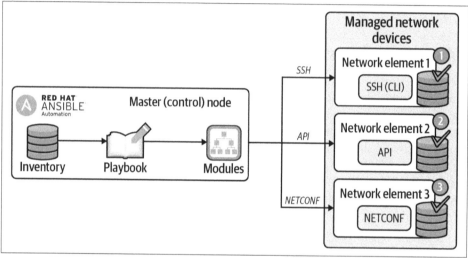

Figure 8-3. Configurations for network switching and VLAN (virtualized local area network) setup for new services, as an example, can be codified in just a few simple tasks within an Ansible Playbook

Another popular use case for Ansible is automation of cloud (public or private) and infrastructure provisioning. The Playbooks, Modules, and Roles we described earlier in this chapter can be rapidly configured to perform automation against public and private cloud endpoints, agnostic to any particular vendor. The extensibility of these structures allows tools like Ansible to work uniformly with IBM Cloud, Amazon Web Services (AWS), Microsoft Azure, Google Cloud Platform (GCP), Rackspace, VMware, and OpenStack—simply select the vendor that best fits the strategic goals of your business. Provisioning can encompass nearly everything your organization might have to ordinarily go about instantiating by hand: compute, storage, networking, and more. As the provisioning process is automated and programmable, you can ensure that the current provisioning request—as well as all subsequent requests made via the Playbook you crafted—will be handled by Ansible predictably and consistently, every time.

Let's take a moment to think about how clients can automate patching of an IBM AIX cluster of servers using Ansible Automation Engine (Figure 8-4). There are two fundamental units in any Ansible deployment: the Ansible "Controller" (running Ansible Automation Engine) and Ansible "Clients" (the host nodes of the Inventory). Controllers follow Playbook instructions and invoke Modules to configure and effect the desired end state on the client node Inventory. All clients are "agentless"—with no special software or libraries installed locally on the nodes—and therefore all configuration changes made by the Controller are passed via a Secure Shell (SSH) connection to and from Clients.

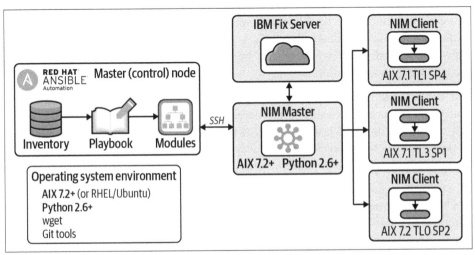

Figure 8-4. Ansible automates patching of an IBM AIX environment, ensuring the NIM Master is at least the same versioning level (or higher) as the cluster of NIM Clients

In this architecture, the NIM (Network Installation Manager) Master must have access to the public internet in order to download fixes and updates through HTTPs/FTP protocols from an IBM Fix Server. In terms of operating system (OS) version and patching level, the NIM Master must be at least the same versioning level (or higher) as the NIM Clients. The Clients themselves can each be running different release AIX OS versions. The NIM Master simultaneously monitors all of these Client nodes for updates (pending or already applied); logic conditions can be crafted to enforce versioning on all of these nodes, or likewise a Playbook could be authored to instruct the Controller node to coordinate consistent and uniform patching across all of the Client nodes via the NIM Master.

Automation Everywhere and for All

Innovative technologies, while powerful in their delivery and expansive in the scope of tasks they can accomplish, can often feel like they're getting in the way: they may initially feel too complex, too new, or too cumbersome to be worthy of the initial investment of time and resources needed to adapt to the new way of doing things. In time, of course, early adopters are able to move past those growing pains and realize the true value of these technologies—but along the way, many are too offput by the up-front discomfort to carry through the adoption to the end, or even to begin in the first place.

Automation holds immense potential for virtually every industry and business precisely because it reduces those complexities and erodes that sharp adoption cost curve into a gentle climb. Even the IT world's most complex administrative tasks—orchestration of multitier workloads that include infrastructure, networking, operating systems, applications, and services—can be transformed into consistent, repeatable patterns through automation.

Red Hat Ansible itself simplifies adoption of automation even further by enabling nearly every facet of the business, not merely those with deep technical skills, to build and execute automation tasks of their own. Lines of business, analysts, knowledge workers, and of course developers can each benefit (and amplify their output) by tapping into the capabilities that these automation engines provide.

All of this is enabled by a framework for automation that takes in the user's desired end state (reflecting how they want their IT estate to look), and then leaves the determination for how to get there up to Ansible itself—which draws upon the intelligence, best practices, and secure open source tooling built into the engine to automate the workflow. When automation is made available to everyone, it becomes possible to automate everything.

Speaking Kubernetes and Other Strange-Sounding Names

Open source software can be a fickle thing, with some projects blowing up like a viral TikTok trend, only to be forgotten a year later (OpenStack, we're looking at you). However, there are certain open source projects born to solve critical problems and combined with a strong community that go on to become indispensable—they live on to power the world's applications for decades to come. One of the first examples of this was Linux, which was born out of the need for a free operating system. Similarly, a number of projects revolutionized their respective areas—Jenkins for DevOps, NGINX for web servers, Eclipse for development environments...and the list goes on. Kubernetes revolutionized the container orchestration space and claimed its throne by defeating strong open source competitors, including Docker's own Swarm and Apache Mesos. So how did Kubernetes (K8s) stand so far ahead?

So far, we've kept our terminology very neutral and generic and consciously avoided the special language that has grown up around Kubernetes. In this appendix we wanted you to learn K8s in the same way you would prepare as a tourist if you were stopping at a Greek island for the day. While you may not learn how to say "I'd like the lamb rare please, on a bed of orzo in an avgolemono stock," you are certainly going to learn how to say "Efaresto" (Thanks), "Endaxi" (OK), "Kalosto" (Hello), or what to say when you take your first shot of Ouzo—"Stin ygeia sou" (To your health), which is ironic if you think about what you're doing.

We'll reiterate that the intention of this book is not to make you a Kubernetes practitioner. With that said, if you're a manager (or strategist) who runs an organization responsible for cloud deployments, you will need to be familiar with the basic terminology—not only does it keep your seat at the table, but it will empower your leadership of those that live for the nitty-gritty details of making this all work. Trust us on this: while being a guru is going to resonate with your technology teams, showing some level of knowledge (and effort to acquire it) is a different universe than being that leader we've all worked for or seen in action before—the ones that literally know nothing about the technology but will drop the word "transformation" at every opportunity.

Figure A-1 shows a Kubernetes cluster followed by some key definitions that will serve you well to remember. (Check out the Kubernetes Standardized Glossary (*https://oreil.ly/vMEiX*) for a comprehensive, standardized list of K8s terminology. This glossary includes technical terms that are specific to Kubernetes, as well as more general terms that provide useful context.)

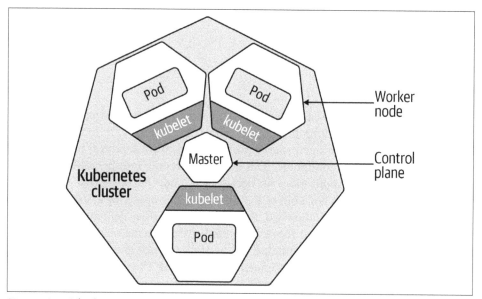

Figure A-1. The key components of a Kubernetes cluster

Node

A node is a worker machine. It might be a physical or virtual machine, it might be running in the cloud—wherever it is, for the purposes of understanding K8s, you shouldn't have to care. Each node has a Master Node that is responsible for scheduling pods in a cluster.

Cluster

A cluster is a collection of nodes running in a "datacenter" that runs container-ized applications. The datacenter could be anything from your laptop or some Raspberry Pi in your house to a cloud provider running "Kubernetes as a Ser-vice." If you're creating a hybrid cloud, you will also have hybrid clusters, in which a single Kubernetes control plane manages nodes in different physical datacenters, including on-premises nodes and nodes running in some public cloud—that's the whole cloud capability discussion we've been having throughout this book; when you think in this manner, your ability to modernize truly changes.

Pod

A pod is a group of one or more related containers running on a cluster—it's the smallest most basic deployable object in K8s. A pod is often a single container (like Docker, but it could be others), though it can be a group of containers that need to be run together. For example, a pod might be used to implement a single microservice.

Role-based access control (RBAC)

RBAC is a management framework that allows administrators to declare business-defined access policies and permissions for your application. Access policies define specific roles with certain permissions (abilities); role bindings associate those roles with specific users. This is imperative for distribution of duty; you're not just ensuring you are properly securing the administrative component of your Kubernetes cluster, but also being able to showcase these business rules, which goes a long way in pleasing auditors.

Control plane

The control plane manages the cluster—think of it as a Kubernetes cluster's nervous system. There are many components in the control plane; they're responsible for scheduling, integrating with cloud servers, accepting commands through the user interface, storing all the cluster declarations and states, and more.

kubectl

The open source command-line tool for submitting commands to the Kubernetes API Gateway, which routes commands to the control plane—this is a long way of saying it lets you run commands against the K8s cluster. You can use this tool to deploy apps, log diagnostic details for your cluster, manage the cluster, and more. Much like Terminal on macOS, you can do anything in the command line that you can in any management interface—and more.

The Perfect Open Source Project

In 2017, the Kubernetes project topped the GitHub charts for most-discussed repository, with the second highest project being OpenShift Origin, a distribution of Kubernetes by Red Hat often referred to as OKD. Kubernetes was and continues to be an exemplar of the perfect open source project, and it accomplished this in a few different ways.

In open source parlance, an *upstream* is the source repository and project where contributions happen and releases are made. (It might be easier to think of it like a river where the water flows downstream.) Contributions flow from upstream to downstream. In some cases, a project or product might have more than one upstream (like Hadoop relied on multiple upstream projects). OKD is the upstream Kubernetes distribution that is embedded in OpenShift. This distribution contains all the components within Red Hat OpenShift, which add developer- and operations-centric tooling on top of native K8s, and, like any other open source software, it can be used by anyone for free. A good analogy would be the Linux kernel. Kubernetes is like the Linux kernel in that the same Kubernetes can then run in a variety of distributions that support various developers' needs.

Kubernetes is not a traditional all-inclusive PaaS system. In fact, its own documentation makes this declaration. Kubernetes provides the building blocks to build developer platforms, while allowing organizations to take advantage of its pluggable architecture to customize where it makes sense. This is one of the main reasons (the other being vendor agnosticism) why those same organizations that shied away from first-generation PaaS technologies like Cloud Foundry, Heroku, or App Engine eventually flocked to Kubernetes. With the building blocks of a PaaS, cloud providers like Google, IBM, Red Hat, Amazon, and Microsoft started working to provide a PaaS powered by Kubernetes.

How exactly does Kubernetes tread this line of providing a platform without forcing an opinionated approach to extensions like observability, storage, CI/CD, all the other components of a full-blown PaaS? It does so by providing a pluggable architecture for everything a user might want to configure. In fact, the Kubernetes documentation has an entire section of what Kubernetes *is not*. This includes the fact that Kubernetes doesn't limit the type of supported applications, doesn't deploy source code or build your app, doesn't provide application services, doesn't dictate logging solutions, and a load of other things K8s simply *doesn't do*.

This list of what Kubernetes doesn't do (when compared to traditional PaaS) might just leave you wondering how K8s became a leading platform in the first place. Kubernetes is a masterpiece in that it does exactly what it is expected to do *really* well: things like service discovery, automatic self-healing, configuration management, and more—capabilities that the standard user doesn't want or even need to "shop around" for. For everything that a user might want to configure themselves, Kubernetes does not dictate the service to be used, but instead provides a pluggable architecture where services can insert themselves. For example, if you want to set up centralized logging for your Kubernetes clusters, you can use over 20 different tools, including Splunk, LogDNA, Fluentd, and Logstash. What if you don't want to set up any of these tools?

Well, Kubernetes conveniently has some barebones logging capabilities available out of the box as well! (Note that this is not always the case—Kubernetes doesn't provide a built-in way to enable CI/CD, for example.)

The growth of projects in the Kubernetes ecosystem can largely be accredited to the Cloud Native Computing Foundation (CNCF). The CNCF provides a sustainable ecosystem for open source projects in the Kubernetes space. In addition, the CNCF provides certification programs for Kubernetes, such as the well-respected CKA (Certified Kubernetes Administrator) and CKAD (Certified Kubernetes Application Developer) certifications. But here's a pro tip: if you're going to be successful with K8s, you don't just have to understand the technology, you have to also understand the ecosystem. We think it's nearly impossible to go into production using Kubernetes alone. In the next few sections, we'll cover some of the other open source projects in the Kubernetes ecosystem you need to know, most of which are part of the CNCF.

Day 1 on the Job: Helm Package Management

We've discussed application software as a series of components, implemented with containers, that provide services. So far, so good. But how does that all get installed? There are lots of components you'll need to stitch together in order to build your application: different kinds of databases, unique services for monitoring your application and building dashboards (which we'll discuss shortly), frameworks and platforms for web development, AI, and lots more. If you've ever managed an open source solution with lots of moving parts, the first thing you often ask is, "How do I get all the necessary components I need installed and running?" And if you've been through the ringer with some of these solutions like we have, you follow that question up with, "How do we automate the installation of our own software that relies on these components?"

The answer? *Helm*. Helm is Kubernetes's package manager. Package managers are responsible for installing software. They figure out what dependencies are needed to install any new package and activate those dependencies in the appropriate order. In the Helm world, you package your apps into *Helm Charts*. Helm Charts are package descriptions (written in YAML) that describe dependencies, configuration details, and other information needed to install the package (your app) properly.

Throughout this book we've boldly declared that Kubernetes is the operating system for distributed computing—so let's use that nuance to talk about Helm. Package managers are ubiquitous in programming languages and operating systems. If you're a Python programmer, you manage the installation of libraries for file management, computer vision, numerics, and more, using *pip*. On operating systems you use things like *yum* and *apt-get* (in the Linux world) or *homebrew* (if you're a Mac person). But it's not just operating systems that seek to simplify the up and running and maintenance experience of solutions with lots of independent components. What a package manager is to an operating system or programming language is what Helm is to Kubernetes.

In April 2020, Helm moved from "incubating" to "graduated status" within the CNCF, proving that Helm has thriving adoption and a strong open-governance community. Helm finds popularity among operations teams for Day 1 (initial deployment phase) DevOps processes, where it is able to significantly simplify the number of resources an application on Kubernetes might require. For example, to deploy a frontend service and a backend service, expose a route (giving a service an externally reachable hostname), and set up a custom domain, you'll need about four different Kubernetes resource configurations. These four configurations together create one application, so engineers can use Helm to consolidate them into a single "release."

However, Helm has not found popularity among services with hefty Day 2 operations, which involve management of stateful (or other complex) workloads such as Quay container registries and MongoDB databases.

Day 2 on the Job: Kubernetes Operators to Save the Day

Stateful or complex workloads like databases have other requirements. They need to be backed up. Schemas need to be updated. And now you know what *Operators* do. Operators are a way of packaging code that performs periodic, stateful maintenance operations that are often handled by human operators. Operators can be complex. Upgrading a database schema, for example, typically requires unloading and reloading the data, or perhaps a shadow copy of the table and a database quiesce. That's not necessarily simple work. And remember what we talked about earlier in this chapter —human error and complexity is a huge cause of downtime. There are many tasks that shouldn't be performed by hand because they are complex or dangerous, or perhaps so rote in nature that they handcuff knowledge workers from high-order tasks. Operators are no different. Each of us stand to gain more resiliency and efficiency through automation.

You might be wondering how Operators are allowed to behave as a literal human operations engineer configuring Kubernetes. This is in part due to two major concepts in Kubernetes: *control loop* and *Custom Resource Definitions (CRDs)*.

First, Kubernetes uses something called a *control loop* (see Figure A-2), which is the basis of self-healing Kubernetes resources. As we mentioned earlier, since Kubernetes is declarative (like a house thermostat), users can declare the state that they want with standard Kubernetes resources such as pods, deployments, and services (generally configured with YAML files). Kubernetes then applies the three simple phases of the control loop in Figure A-2 to make it all happen—*observe, diff*, and *act*.

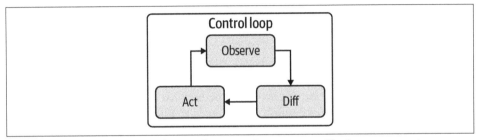

Figure A-2. The control loop: how Kubernetes Operators act like human operators

The first phase of the Kubernetes control loop is *observe*. This is where K8s is not just watching what's going on in the cluster, but it's making note of every single detail for any needed remediation to the declarative statements that serve as the "laws of intent" that govern the cluster. Next, K8s identifies what is different from the intended state of the ecosystem (what temperature and humidity did you want the house at)—this is referred to as the *diff*. Finally, if there's any *diff*erence, K8s will act to remediate any differences between the declared state and the actual state within the cluster. Kubernetes is forever running the loop in Figure A-2—like a hamster forever running in a hamster wheel.

Let's assume you created a deployment that demands three pods to be alive, but one of the pods eventually crashes? K8s to the rescue! You want three pods, and Kubernetes' control loop is always trying to maintain the environment you set (like that house thermostat) so it will continually restart that pod to resolve the "difference" between the current and intended state. This is in essence how "self-healing" works.

Things like pods, deployments, and services are default resources in the Kubernetes API—all Kubernetes clusters support these resources. They are the building blocks of deploying applications on Kubernetes.

Kubernetes also allows you to augment the default Kubernetes API by supplying CRDs to extend the standard resources found in Kubernetes (pods, services, deployments, and so on). In turn, Kubernetes provides a frontend API for the extended resources you've defined—and *these resources also follow the control loop*. The ability for Operators to utilize CRDs allows developers to create large-scale resources that may encompass many standard Kubernetes resources. For example, once you've installed a MongoDB operator, it will create a CRD for a MongoDB database. As a user, you can create a resource referencing that CRD and deploy it to Kubernetes, much like any other standard resource. The CRD (and hence the Operator) is responsible for creating the many underlying Kubernetes resources that make up the MongoDB instance. This means less work for you!

The key advantage to Operators is that they can effectively offload the responsibility of maintaining a particular service in your Kubernetes cluster and thereby significantly reduce Day 2 operations costs. Contrast this with Helm. Whereas Helm allows users to perform Day 1 operations that deal with deploying many resources together, Operators take it a step further and allow for the continued management and maintenance of complex services running on Kubernetes. This is why you'll find so many service providers beginning to develop Operators that Kubernetes administrators can implement to manage long-living services. This isn't to say that Operators are replacing Helm—Helm is still a critical part of simplifying standard deployments and plays an important role in CI/CD pipelines. Helm is great for when you don't need a sledgehammer to swat flies.

We've accomplished one of our major goals: *turn infrastructure, along with the processes for managing infrastructure, into code.* In a large, distributed system, that's the only way these maintenance tasks can be performed repeatably and reliably. Ensure you understand this last paragraph because this is what the whole Kubernetes ecosystem is about. It's the basis for modernization, agility, scalability, and more; it's what drives automation into our processes, which results in efficiencies and frees up resources to drive the business.

The Infrastructure...Of Course!

So far, our discussion has been very virtual: there's a cluster of machines (possibly virtualized) somewhere in the cloud (which could be public or on-premises) that do work for you. Kubernetes takes things like containers and runs them on those machines, all the while looking at what we declared the environment should look like, and it tries its hardest to make it that way. Great. But where do those machines come from? Cloud resources don't appear magically just because you want them; public cloud providers all offer similar, but not equal, services; and there is no end to the different kinds of machines you can use in cloud computing. Are you better off scaling a NoSQL data model with lots of small, distributed servers? Or do you use one more powerful server and scale up, which is less complicated? Do you load up your server with lots of memory? Do GPUs help? TPUs? How do you select all of this?

To help guide you, we're going to take advantage of the same ideas we've been using all along in this section and we mentioned in : infrastructure as code. That way, it's standardized and repeatable. You don't have to worry about the nightmare case where a system goes down and some person mistypes the number of virtual machine instances you need, where your app gets nicknamed molasses because the admin forgot a zero, or you get a giant bill because they typed too many of them.

Enter *Terraform*—an open source tool (developed by HashiCorp) for building, changing, and versioning infrastructure safely and efficiently. Think about the name: it's about shaping the earth and putting the material you're working with into a useful form. Or, if you're inclined to sci-fi, think about "terraforming Mars" (*https://oreil.ly/ sCfhx*): assembling all of Mars's resources to create a useable, livable environment. Terraform is *essential* to hybrid clouds because it really doesn't care what kind of "earth" it's forming. Yes, any cloud provider has their own way of specifying a configuration; but once you've told Terraform what resources you need, it takes over the process of figuring out how to acquire those resources. Describing what resources you need for AWS, Azure, GCP, IBM, and even your on-premises datacenter is a lot simpler than writing scripts (or tweaking dashboards) that do the work of acquiring those resources.

Terraform takes a page out of the Kubernetes book in its implementation—it's declarative. This has a fundamental advantage that you can simply tell it what you want, and it will handle the painstaking process of making the individual API calls to create the infrastructure. A simple analogy would be setting your car's GPS navigation to go to a destination versus simply calling a ride-sharing company. The prior requires that you control every turn, exit, and on-ramp, and even has the potential for error if you're not familiar with the roads (or if the maps are out of date). This is akin to developing manual scripts to handle your infrastructure automation, or even worse, trying to figure out the interface nuances of the CSP you've chosen to work with every time you need to deploy something (and remember, enterprises today are using multiple CSPs!). However, with ride sharing, you simply input your final destination, get in the car, and the driver takes care of the rest. That's why we like to think of Terraform as the Lyft/Uber of infrastructure automation.

It shouldn't surprise you that Terraform has a public registry service (*https://regis try.terraform.io*): that is, a repository for public configuration modules as well as Terraform providers to make it easier to work with major CSPs. You can find modules that implement many common forms of infrastructure: for example, implementing a Kubernetes cluster on different public cloud providers. Your teams will almost certainly need to customize the modules (for example, to specify the number of nodes the application needs, or which zones to use), but almost all of the work has already been done.

Making the Network Tractable: Service Meshes

You probably realize that the picture we've been painting might seem a little too rosy. We're talking about applications composed from many different services: frontends, databases, authentication, finance, shipping, manufacturing, and more. All of these services need to communicate with each other. They need the ability to find each other. And if you've thought about the implications of the cloud, you've realized that this is difficult. How can a service communicate with other services reliably if they're starting and stopping all the time? If, the day after Black Friday, you only need hundreds of nodes, rather than thousands?

The eight Fallacies of Distributed Computing (*https://oreil.ly/0mNID*) notes that the network is reliable, the network is secure, the network doesn't change, and so on. We know, we'd be skeptical too. But Kubernetes shows us that the only realistic way to escape these fallacies is to embrace them. Rather than pretend that networks are reliable or tie your code up in knots trying to handle outages, introduce another layer (yes, every problem in computing can be solved by adding another abstraction) designed to solve these problems. And that's why we need to start talking about service meshes.

It's certainly true that, in the cloud, networking is hard. Programmers just want to be able to open a connection to a service. They don't want to deal with services that appear and disappear almost at random, to find out what addresses those services live at, or to deal with issues like load balancing. (We're exhausted just thinking about it!) And dealing with the network becomes even more complex when you need to think about security, authorization, monitoring, and A/B testing. Early cloud applications forced that on them. They couldn't just call a network library; they suddenly had to understand how networks worked on a much deeper level.

This is where service meshes enter the picture. A service mesh is another set of services that takes the burden of networking away (abstracted) from your application code. Services no longer have to know the IP addresses of the services they need, open direct connections to those services, decide what to do when a service becomes unavailable, and so on. That is all managed by the service mesh. The services become "virtual services," and the mesh takes responsibility for routing requests (for knowing which services are available and where they are located, knowing which services are allowed to access other services, and even understanding service versioning; for example, a service mesh can make a new version of a service available to a group of users for testing). You might want to think of the mesh as a gigantic proxy layer that manages all of these issues and forwards requests to the actual services, which only have to concern themselves with the business logic required to respond to these requests.

So we're back where we want to be: the service doesn't need to know about the network, and the programmer doesn't need a deep understanding of network programming. All any service needs to know is the name of the other services it depends on. Services are exposed to each other through the service mesh, which understands resource discovery and routing, and keeps a close watch on where the actual services are, how many instances are running, the addresses of those instances, and so on.

But we get more in the bargain. Networking isn't the only thing we don't want our services to know about. Ideally, we'd rather not have them know about security (don't get confused here, this doesn't mean there isn't any): poor implementations of issues like identity and authorization are the cause of much misery. Better to leave identity and authorization to specialists. Security can be managed by the service mesh, which can use other services to determine which users, services, and roles are trusted. We absolutely don't want services to "know about" cryptography; no question about it, cryptography is important to security, but it is much easier to get cryptographic techniques wrong than to get them right, even if you're using a well-known and correctly implemented library. Why not hand this off to the service mesh (and cryptographic protocols and implementations that can be changed via configuration, rather than by modifying the services)?

If all a service needs to know about is its business logic, and nothing more, then we finally have, in the cloud, what software developers have been striving to achieve for years: component-based distributed software systems. A new kind of service can be added without touching the rest of the system. Clients using the service may need to be updated—or perhaps not. In many cases, all that's needed is a configuration change. Let's say you're an international business that's expanding into South Africa. You decide to add a service that converts between US Dollars and Rand. Existing services that need currency exchange are already accessing other exchange services, which makes adding this new feature at most a configuration change. Adding the ability to take payments in cryptocurrency will probably require a new service too, but the rest of the application can remain the same; it just needs to know that Dogecoin is a new payment option.

Step back for a moment because we went through a lot of stuff there. We want to pause so you fully appreciate that we've achieved a high degree of cohesion: the ability to compose complex applications from components, all with minimal coupling between those components. And once we can do that, with the components packaged in standardized containers, we can deploy them anywhere: literally. On those Raspberry Pis in the broom closet, in a giant datacenter, on a cloud provider—or any combination. We can tell Kubernetes how many instances of the *DogecoinExchangeService* we want, tell the service mesh how to route the requests, and we're up and running— without taking the application down for a second!

Again, we've been discussing service meshes in the abstract; we've talked about what a service mesh does rather than the specific software. While it's not the only service mesh implementation, the dominant implementation in the Kubernetes ecosystem is Istio (*https://istio.io*). Istio is an open source project started by IBM, Google, and Lyft; it incorporates Lyft's Envoy (*https://www.envoyproxy.io*) project, which still exists on its own.

Testing, Integration, and Deployment

The ability to run an application in the cloud, in a way that's independent of any cloud vendor—where your own datacenter or machine room can be one of those "vendors"—is a huge step forward. But there's more to the problem than running the application. You need the ability to deploy it, you need the ability to integrate components together, and you need the ability to test in a modern way. What's more, these capabilities all need to be automated—in part so they can be repeated reliably, but also so they can be performed repeatedly.

All of these capabilities come under the heading of CI/CD. The deployment scenarios of 20 or 30 years ago, when a "deployment" was very likely to be a break-the-world change, with the entire development and operations teams keeping their fingers crossed (probably with some of that vodka we talked about in the Preface to this book) and hoping nothing breaks, are a thing of the past for those that have embraced the very things we've been talking about all along in this book. We've discovered that the way to deploy software reliably is to deploy it frequently, where each deployment represents a minor change to a very small number of features. If each release represents a minor change, changes are easy to roll back; changes can be deployed to a small number of users for testing; and, most of all, short, reliable release cycles force you to commit your release process to software.

As we mentioned before, Kubernetes provides the building blocks of a PaaS—but it's not an all-inclusive PaaS. One of the things Kubernetes explicitly doesn't do is provide a native CI/CD process. In open source parlance, Kubernetes *doesn't have an opinion on CI/CD*—which is coder talk for they don't force you into a solution or template for this component; this can be good or bad. After all, developers definitely have formed their own opinions in this space, and DevOps processes tend to be custom fit to the team that implements them. This is one of the reasons that we think Kubernetes has become such an inflection point—K8s knows what it wants to do and it's extremely good at doing it. For everything else, the open source community always finds a way (and more often than not, multiple ways—but that's another story).

Tekton is an open source project that provides a strong framework to create cloud native CI/CD pipelines in a way that doesn't depend on a cloud provider. It is an extension that runs on your Kubernetes cluster. It also integrates with the widely used open source tools for CI/CD, such as Jenkins (a free and open source automation server that helps with some of the tasks in the CI/CD lifecycle: building, testing, deploying, and so on). Tekton structures the deployment process as a set of pipelines, which execute some larger goal (such as deploying a project). Pipelines are composed of tasks, which are specific actions (such as running a test suite or compiling an application). You can create Deployment pipelines that minimize the time to cut over from an old version to a new version; or to deploy a new version to some servers but not others, for A/B testing; or to do small canary deployments to test the system against the real world. And if you need to, Tekton can also be used to roll back to an earlier release.

In software engineering speak, a canary deployment is a process whereby you make a staged release to a subset of your user community first so they can test it out and tell you what they think. If they "vote your new feature off the island," you don't roll it out and save yourself from irritating your entire customer base. You see this all the time with apps on the iPhone where the update description tells you that you will see the feature over time or you've updated a new app and was told of a new feature in the update notes, but you don't see it.

But canary deployments are also used to understand how users will interact with potential changes like redesigning the interface and menu options. This affords an easy mechanism to "walk back" changes (it's risk-averse) as opposed to other strategies (like *Blue/ Green*), which make the changes in one step.

Monitoring and Observability

Whenever you deploy software, regardless of where it runs, you need to make sure that it runs reliably. You need to know that, at any time, the software is actually running, that it's handling requests, and that it's handling those requests in a reasonable amount of time. If the application is down, extremely slow, or malfunctioning in some other way, you need to know it. It doesn't matter if this is a huge public-facing ecommerce application or some internal management dashboards; your staff needs to get it back online and (even more importantly) prevent it from ever going offline.

One thing we've learned in the last decade of IT operations is the importance of monitoring. Monitoring is relatively simple: you develop specific metrics (or health tests) and watch your applications to ensure that everything is running normally. A health check could be a simple network ping, a measurement of a physical parameter (like CPU temperature), or something more complex and application-focused, such as the number of transactions per second or the time users wait to get a response. Monitoring includes alerting (for example, generating pager alarms) and providing data for debugging and trend analysis (for example, forecasting resource requirements or cloud expenses).

Monitoring is valuable, but it isn't the last word. The fundamental problem with monitoring is that you have to predict, in advance, what you will want to know. Sometimes, that's not enough to tell you that your system is (or about to go) down, and it's almost never enough to tell you what went wrong so you can bring the system back online. As modernized apps move to more and more distributed computing (the epochs we talked about in Chapter 3), and more and more components are part of an application's composition, figuring out a root cause to a problem can be like trying to unravel the Gordian knot of cable wiring to charge that thing you bought off Amazon five years ago. It's just not going to happen.

Observability could (perhaps should) be called the "next generation" of monitoring. It starts with a definition from control theory (*https://oreil.ly/KMEJm*): "In control theory, observability is a measure of how well internal states of a system can be inferred by knowledge of its external outputs." Observability means the ability to gather data about any aspect of your application when it's running, so that you can infer what's happening internally. That's the kind of information you need for debugging. It's all about the ability to find out what you need to know, because you can't guess with full certainty what you will need to know in advance.

We think observability is going to become even a bigger deal in the years to come as more and more apps are redesigned for the loosely coupled style of distributed cloud native applications. We'll use Figure A-3 to make our point.

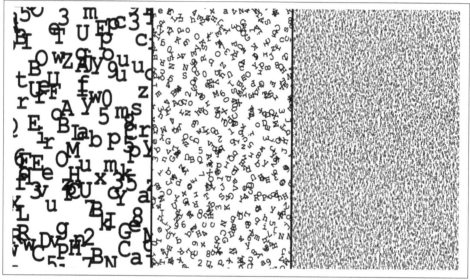

Figure A-3. Find the letter P: a depiction of the increasing complexity when moving from monoliths, to SOA, to microservices

Try to find the letter P (for problem). Easy on the left, harder in the middle, are you @$#~!$ kidding me on the right? That's akin to figuring out what's going on in your application stack from a monolith to service-oriented architecture (SOA) to microservices (cloud native). Think about it—if an app is composed of hundreds of microservices (some perhaps function as a service which run in under 10 seconds, if not milliseconds, then disappear because of their transient nature) how can you go from the mobile-native app sitting on your iPhone and trace that to the code running on the backend? Like we said, observability is a big deal that's going to get bigger, and it's why we're really impressed with software pushing this to the forefront today (like Instana).

Next, we're going to look briefly at some important tools for observability. We'll also look at some technologies for creating dashboards, which are an important asset to any operations team: what does "observability" mean if you can't actually observe what's happening? What's the point of having an observable system if you can't react intelligently and efficiently?

Prometheus

Prometheus (*https://prometheus.io*) is an application for collecting real-time time-series data for generating alerts and metrics. It can collect data for an arbitrary number of metrics; each metric is multidimensional, meaning that it can be composed of several data streams of its own.

It may help to think of Prometheus as a data collector that incorporates a time-series database, indexed by metric names and key-value pairs (for specific dimensions). It has short-term memory-based storage, with long-term storage on local disk drives. It can be sharded to distribute load and it has a sophisticated query language.

Prometheus works by scraping (or pulling) data from the systems that it is monitoring. Sending data to Prometheus when it comes to scraping is simple: developers need to add a small amount of code that calls a client library to their applications. To monitor third-party software packages, an *exporter* converts any logs the package generates to the Prometheus format, and sends the converted data to Prometheus on request. Exporters are available for many commonly used third-party software packages; developers rarely need to write custom exporters.

Grafana

Prometheus has an *expression browser* that lets you query its database. Grafana's expression browser is useful for taking a quick look at what's happening with your systems...but it's far from a final solution.

Grafana (*https://grafana.com*) is often used with Prometheus to build dashboards. Grafana is another open source project, independent of Prometheus, but Prometheus includes Grafana integration. It's simple to create a Prometheus data source for Grafana, and it's also simple to create a graph that plots the data from that source because that's the whole point of Grafana: to offer visualization and dashboarding services to a connected data source. Grafana also maintains a collection of freely reusable dashboards.

Alertmanager

Nobody appreciates waking up in the middle of the night because a system is down. But we all know it's necessary. Downtime is expensive. Any enterprise system needs the ability to alert operators when human intervention is needed.

Alertmanager (*https://oreil.ly/i5IKW*) is the part of the Prometheus project that is responsible for determining when a human needs to be notified, and sending that notification in an appropriate way. Alerts can be sent via a system like PagerDuty or, if they don't require immediate attention, via email or some other interface.

Alertmanager is responsible for minimizing alert duplication. Think about it…if your team is responsible for an application built on microservices, it's possible for a single failure of a key component to cascade into hundreds if not thousands of alerts. In addition to de-duping alerts, Alertmanager can be configured to inhibit or suppress alerts that are caused by failures elsewhere in the system. Alertmanager can also silence alerts, for example, to avoid distracting the response team once it has been activated.

The Paradox of Choice: Red Hat OpenShift

For many, less is more. In the past few sections, we've touted Kubernetes as a platform with boundless potential and seemingly endless choices for configuration and customization. This is not exactly an advantage for many consumers who may be paralyzed by choice. Seriously, does the world really need 21 Pop-Tart (a breakfast pastry) flavors?

In his book *The Paradox of Choice*, Barry Schwartz argues that the freedom of choice has made us not freer, but rather more paralyzed—not happier, but more dissatisfied. Applied to Kubernetes, we have seen first-hand how some clients got intimidated by choice. We've said it before and we'll say it again—the cloud is a capability, not a destination. The sooner we can dispel the notion that the cloud is a lofty, unattainable goal, the better.

But have no fear—there is a solution. Red Hat provides an open source distribution of Kubernetes called Origin Kubernetes Distribution (just pure K8s with none of the things that Red Hat does to make it more enterprise fulfilling and ready), but many people tend to gravitate to their flagship product—OpenShift Container Platform. Red Hat puts it succinctly: OpenShift is Kubernetes for the enterprise.

Red Hat is no newcomer to open source. It's quite literally paved the way for open source in the enterprise, and in 2012 became the first one-billion dollar open source company. Red Hat is one of the largest code contributors to the Kubernetes project, second only to Google.

Here's a simple example to show Red Hat's commitment to open source and Kubernetes. In the early days of Kubernetes, basic role-based access control (RBAC) was not a priority for the project, which was a dealbreaker for many enterprises. Red Hat started implementing RBAC directly within the Kubernetes project, instead of as an added-value feature of OpenShift. This is the type of thing that makes Red Hat…well, Red Hat. Quite simply, the Red Had OpenShift Container Platform comes with opinions, tools, and features that make it hardened for the enterprise. It's one of the special things that arise from IBM and Red Hat defining hybrid cloud.

Back to the matter at hand—how does Red Hat address this paradox of choice? As we've said before, Kubernetes provides the building blocks of an all-inclusive PaaS, without actually being one. Red Hat makes full use of these building blocks and has created a full-blown Kubernetes-powered PaaS. OpenShift is the best of Kubernetes with opinionated approaches for every capability we've talked about in the prior sections and more.

OpenShift comes embedded with Prometheus, Grafana, and Alertmanager for observability. It provides an embedded OperatorHub for installing additional services. It provides an enterprise-supported model for many open source capabilities such as Istio (OpenShift Service Mesh) and Tekton (OpenShift Pipelines). It embeds richer RBAC that goes above and beyond what is available in Kubernetes. The list goes on and on, and the support model that Red Hat provides on open source projects appeals to a number of enterprises that are faced with the paradox of choice.

 Red Hat OpenShift is different from the first generation of opinionated PaaS capabilities such as Heroku and Cloud Foundry for one major reason—although it provides recommended and supported extensions, it never dictates that you must use them. After all, OpenShift is Kubernetes underneath the covers and provides the same pluggable flexibility that Kubernetes offers.

No architect wants to be the one that decided to implement an open source project only for it to be eventually deprecated or unsupported. Although this is uncommon for mature projects (that became "CNCF graduated"), it does happen more than you might think. For example, Kubefed initially had large support as a multicluster tool for Kubernetes, but quickly lost traction and has remained in alpha for years.

Last but not least, one of the best perks of using OpenShift is the user interface. As practitioners will regularly say, learning to use Kubernetes can be extremely rewarding, but damn if it isn't difficult to learn. This is partly due to the amount of CLI commands you need to learn—Kubernetes is primarily CLI-driven (we're not casting shade on CLI or command-line tools; if you think vi is a productivity tool for word editing, have at it—but if you're a graphic interface kind of person, OpenShift will help you out). The process of going from source code on GitHub to a running application can take a Kubernetes newbie upwards of a full-day of documentation hunting, trial-and-error, and banging their head. With the OpenShift management tool, a developer can quite literally click three buttons (we counted) to deploy from source code to a running application with an accessible route. This particular flow we're referencing is called Source-to-Image (S2I), which OpenShift has open sourced by the way!

Index

About the Authors

Paul Zikopoulos is an award-winning professional writer and speaker who's been consulted on the topic of AI and big data by the popular TV show *60 Minutes*. At the time this book was written, Paul was IBM's VP of Skills Vitality and Enablement for its Technology Sales group, which encompasses its entire portfolio of software and hardware.

Paul's been named to dozens of global "Experts to Follow" and "Influencers" lists, including Analytics Insight's "Top 100 Global AI & Big Data Influencers." Paul's written 21 books (including *The AI Ladder* and three "For Dummies" titles) and over 360 articles during his accidental 26-year career as a data nerd. Paul leads from the front, owning accountability and strategic direction in a "tech years are like dog years" world for the entire IBM Technology Unit's (all IBM software and hardware) sales, tech sales, and partner ecosystem learning journeys and upskilling programs.

You'll find Paul taking a very active role around women in technology (he's a seated board member for Women 2.0, who he became involved with after his tweet was mentioned on the TV show, *The View*), general workplace inclusivity (completing an intensive D&I certificate at Cornell University), and a sponsor of Coding for Veterans Canada. In addition, Paul sits on the world recognized Masters of Management Analytics & AI program boards at Canada's prestigious Queen's University.

Paul's always keeping with his grass roots—a newbie with no computer courses before coming to IBM. He knows on his dumbest days he's never as dumb as he feels, and on his smartest days, he's never as smart as he feels either. Ultimately, Paul is trying to figure out the world according to Chloë—who competitively rides a horse he insisted be show-named "Better than a Boyfriend." Follow him on Twitter at @BigData_paulz.

Christopher Bienko is a data enthusiast, photographer, and outdoorsman. Raised in Halifax, Nova Scotia and now calling both San Francisco, CA and Jackson Hole, WY home, he's the author of several publications on modern database and analytics technologies, including *Big Data Beyond the Hype* (McGraw-Hill) and multiple IBM Red-Books. His specializations in database-as-a-service and distributed cloud computing have made him a trusted advisor to hundreds of global marketplace customers, as they look to transform legacy business services into cloud native and AI-ready applications. As a principal within IBM's Worldwide Technology Sales organization, he supports enterprises in their adoption of multicloud platforms and modernization strategies with Red Hat OpenShift, IBM Cloud Paks, and open source tools. When not in front of clients, you can always find him behind the lens of a camera.

Chris Backer is the Business Unit Executive (BUE) for IBM's Systems Software and Hybrid Cloud Platform where he leads global client adoption. He and his team of Solution Engineers are helping clients from all industries around the globe design and implement digital transformation strategies that incorporate secure hybrid multi-cloud capabilities. A 21-year veteran in the IT industry, Chris has spent his career focused on helping clients increase their competitive advantage through innovative use of automation, analytics, and cloud technology.

Chris was previously the BUE for the IBM Watson Customer Engagement team where he led Solution Engineering for its Marketing and Behavioral Analytics portfolio. He led the transition from delivering traditional on-premises capabilities to entirely SaaS-based offerings for IBM clients.

Chris has also led several Tiger Teams within IBM whose sole purpose was to bring new and emerging technology capabilities to market. His experience building and leading innovative first-of-a-kind technology projects spans across datacenter automation, mobile application development, IoT, connected vehicle, behavioral analytics, fraud analytics, and now hybrid cloud.

An avid outdoorsman, Chris enjoys spending his free time exploring all that nature has to offer and when he isn't immersed in technology you will find him in a Jeep traversing trail systems that offer breathtaking views and challenging obstacles along the route.

Chris Konarski is a thought leader with 20+ years in technology. He is known for his innovative approaches to technology sales and execution with an emphasis on helping customers unleash speed and innovation through digital transformation. He has worked throughout his career in the most challenging, high-profile sales and technical leadership roles in recognition of his innovation, culture building, and consistency of results. He has achieved outstanding success developing new business models leveraging technology, services, and solutions to help customers use technology as a competitive advantage.

Chris has repeatedly demonstrated the ability to develop and lead talented teams, accelerate go-to-market capabilities, and develop modern approaches—supporting rapid growth for world-class technology enterprise business units at IBM. His deep technical expertise and passionate leadership experience spans many areas: manufacturing, development, infrastructure, software, security, AI, and hybrid cloud.

Chris currently serves as Vice President of Technical Sales for IBM, where he has led the global technical sales for all business units. Chris has an MBA from Rensselaer Polytechnic Institute and a BSc in Chemical Engineering from New Jersey Institute of Technology. To balance his love for tech, he is an avid outdoorsman with a passion for nature, so if you can't reach him then he is likely off the grid chasing elk or 100 miles offshore catching tuna. Connect with Chris on LinkedIn to learn more.

Sai Vennam is a Solutions Architect at Amazon Web Services, but started his career at IBM as a developer, developer advocate, and product manager for nearly eight years. As an advocate of containers, Kubernetes, and everything under the sun cloud-native, he aims to grow adoption by creating digital content such as "lightboard" videos on YouTube. Chances are if you've looked into hybrid cloud or containers on YouTube, you've seen his face! In addition, he's developed free innovative lab experiences to teach Kubernetes and OpenShift.

His love for tech continues into his personal life, where he builds custom smart home automation with IoT devices. His metric of success is achieved when his wife learns and actually uses the home automation! In addition, he loves to cook Indian food and attend music shows and festivals.

Colophon

The animal on the cover of *Cloud Without Compromise* is a black swan *(Cygnus atratus)*. This large bird is native to Australia and Tasmania and can be found most often in the southern wetlands of those areas. They have been introduced as pets in New Zealand and North America, as well as in Europe, where they can now be found in the wild as well.

Black swans can live in fresh, salt, or brackish water, preferring habits with plenty of the aquatic foliage that makes up the majority of their diet, though they also eat insects on occasion. They use a variety of calls and visual signs to communicate, and have weak high-pitched voices. When threatened, these birds will raise their shoulders or loudly flap their wings to ward off or warn predators or other swans.

Black swans often have the same mate for life, engaging in what is known as the "triumph ceremony" during courtship. This ceremony, which also serves to strengthen bonds between parents and children or as a territorial display, involves a pattern of calls, neck choreography, and synchronized swimming patterns. Both parents will incubate eggs until hatching. The cygnets—baby swans—can feed and swim soon after hatching, although they will ride on their parents' backs when approaching deeper waters.

Despite the fact that their eggs and fledglings are preyed on by a variety of predators, populations of black swans are very healthy, with upwards of tens of thousands of birds in New South Wales. As such, their current conservation status is "Least Concern." Many of the animals on O'Reilly covers are endangered; all of them are important to the world.

The cover illustration is by Karen Montgomery, based on a black and white engraving from *British Birds*. The cover fonts are Gilroy Semibold and Guardian Sans. The text font is Adobe Minion Pro; the heading font is Adobe Myriad Condensed; and the code font is Dalton Maag's Ubuntu Mono.

O'REILLY®

There's much more
where this came from.

Experience books, videos, live online
training courses, and more from O'Reilly
and our 200+ partners—all in one place.

Learn more at oreilly.com/online-learning

Lightning Source UK Ltd.
Milton Keynes UK
UKHW030625100821
388578UK00005B/20